The Greatest Show in the Galaxy

The Greatest Show in the Galaxy

The Discerning Fan's Guide to Doctor Who

MARC SCHUSTER *and*
TOM POWERS

To Dan,
A fellow fan of
the good Doctor!
Cheers,

McFarland & Company, Inc., Publishers
Jefferson, North Carolina, and London

LIBRARY OF CONGRESS CATALOGUING-IN-PUBLICATION DATA

Schuster, Marc, 1973–
    The greatest show in the galaxy : the discerning fan's
guide to Doctor Who / Marc Schuster and Tom Powers.
        p.   cm.
    Includes bibliographical references and index.

    ISBN-13: 978-0-7864-3276-9
    softcover : 50# alkaline paper ∞

    1. Doctor Who (Television program : 1963–1989)
I. Powers, Tom, 1972–   II. Title.
PN1992.77.D6273S38   2007
791.45'72—dc22   2007026019

British Library cataloguing data are available

Cover images ©2007 Shutterstock

Manufactured in the United States of America

McFarland & Company, Inc., Publishers
  Box 611, Jefferson, North Carolina 28640
    www.mcfarlandpub.com

For Hugh Ormsby-Lennon (Time Lord Emeritus)
and Russell T. Davies (Reviver of Dreams)

Acknowledgments

We would like to give credit to previous works on *Doctor Who* that have influenced this book. David J. Howe and Stephen J. Walker's *The Television Companion: The Unofficial and Unauthorized Guide to Doctor Who* supplied us with plenty of pertinent trivia and criticism. An excellent comprehensive compilation of facts and details for every story also exists in the form of *Doctor Who: The Legend Continues* by Justin Richards, which was particularly helpful in our analysis of the Doctor's many idiosyncrasies. Additionally, we were often amused by the playful wit of *The Discontinuity Guide* by Paul Cornell, Martin Day, and Keith Topping, and the various volumes of the *About Time* series by Lawrence Miles and Tat Wood. To be quite honest, Miles and Tat's hilarious sidebars in those volumes set the tone for much of our own work. Last but surely not least, we acknowledge the countless great articles and overall joyful tenor established by the numerous editors and writers responsible for the always entertaining and insightful *Doctor Who Magazine*.

Contents

Preface

Why Who? (Marc Schuster)

Not too long ago, my wife asked me why I like *Doctor Who*, and I had to think about my answer for a moment. It was late at night, the television was tuned to a weak signal, the sound was terrible, the picture was fuzzy, and the players in the drama seemed hell-bent on running through corridors and trying to find their way back to a blue box that was larger on the inside than its outer shell might suggest. Needless to say, I was glued to the screen, and one of the reasons I took so long to respond to my wife's question was that it had to penetrate deep into my consciousness before I even heard it. After all, I was in Who-land, and nothing at that particular moment was more important than learning whether the Doctor and his companions could divine a way out of the labyrinthine corridors in which they'd found themselves trapped, and whether the TARDIS would be in working condition when they inevitably stumbled upon it.

I'm guessing the episode was "The Horns of Nimon."

Or maybe it was "The Ark in Space."

Then again, it could have been "Castrovalva."

Or possibly "Paradise Towers."

Or "Carnival of Monsters."

Or "Vengeance on Varos."

Or "Nightmare of Eden."

Or "The Greatest Show in the Galaxy."

Or "The Three Doctors" or "The Five Doctors" or "The Two Doctors," or any number of episodes in which the Doctor's fate hinges entirely on running through a series of identical corridors until he finds the TARDIS and makes a timely escape.

In any case, the Doctor was running for his life, and I was right there with him until my wife's voice brought me back to the real world. When her question finally registered, my instinct was to counter it with a question of my own—something along the lines of, "Well isn't it obvious?" A moment

1

of reflection, however, reminded me that *Doctor Who* is an acquired taste, and that, like fine wine, not everyone appreciates it as well as he or she might. Past the pasteboard sets, past the pseudo-science, past the flimsy monsters and equally flimsy plotlines of one or two of the Doctor's adventures, anyone who watches regularly enough and with an open enough mind will find that the program has not only heart and soul, but intelligence and a sense of social consciousness as well. Entertaining though it may be, *Doctor Who* isn't just mindless bubblegum for the masses. It's a show that, in its finer moments, aspires to greatness and proves that television still has the potential to broaden our perspectives and challenge our assumptions.

Before I could begin pontificating, however, my wife changed the question. Rather than wanting to know why I continued to like the show as an adult, she asked what attracted me to it as a child. Curiously, the answer was more or less the same: *Doctor Who* provided me with the only intelligent role model to be found on television—and, growing up in a part of Philadelphia where arson was considered a legitimate hobby and thuggery a promising career path, it was a role model I desperately needed. Unfortunately, however, it was also a role model that nobody seemed to share. When I was ten years old, my family moved to a new neighborhood, and in a misguided attempt to make friends, I tried to start a *Doctor Who* fan club at my new school. In many ways, this endeavor proved to be akin to starting an "I'm a Geek—Please Beat the Shit out of Me" club, because the end result was that for the remainder of my childhood, nearly everyone thought of me as "that *Doctor Who* fag" as they administered my daily allowances of bruises, lumps, concussions and contusions.

Undaunted, I soldiered on in my loyalty to the Doctor. I watched every episode. I spent every dollar I had on *Doctor Who* paraphernalia. When my grandmother knitted afghans for my sisters, I asked her to knit me a twenty-foot scarf instead. When birthdays rolled around, my mother sent away to England for exotic merchandise unavailable in the United States. And when conventions came to town, my father would take me into the city and stand among grown men and women dressed as aliens and robots as I stood in line after never-ending line for a chance to say hello to one of the Doctor's companions or, if I were especially lucky, to shake hands with the Doctor himself. Indeed, among my most exciting memories of childhood is having my grammar corrected by Colin Baker.

Had I my wits about me at the time, I might have invited the sixth Doctor out for a root beer and shown him photographs of the never-to-be-finished Dalek I was building in my basement. Or maybe I would have pitched my idea for a *Doctor Who*–themed restaurant. At the very least, I could have mentioned that he was—at that moment anyway—by far my favorite Doctor, but all I could do was thrust a photograph into his hand and stammer a nervous question: "Can you sign this?"

To which my idol replied, perhaps in character, perhaps simply tired after a long day of meeting with people who, like myself, refused to distinguish between the actor and the role he played on television: "Of course I *can*, as I have a pen in my hand and you've just handed me a photograph. The question is *will* I?"

No child has ever been more excited to be scolded for bad grammar.

In the years that followed, I lost touch with the world of *Doctor Who*. I went to high school. I discovered girls. I bought an electric guitar and started a string of terrible rock bands. Then came college and work and life, and the local stations stopped airing the program. Once in a blue moon, I'd catch the occasional ghost of an episode broadcast from a distant locale, as I did on the night my wife asked me to explain the roots of my wistful fascination. Every so often, I'd rent a *Doctor Who* DVD and bring it home discreetly, as if trying to conceal pornography. From time to time, I'd look up the Doctor online and reminisce over what the show once meant to me. Never in my wildest imagination, however, did I imagine that *Doctor Who* would return not only to the airwaves but to such a central position in my imagination as well.

As new incarnations of the Doctor resume their travels in time and space, I am reminded once again of the childhood "friend" I found in the renegade Time Lord. And as I become engrossed in the Doctor's latest adventures, I am constantly impressed with how revolutionary and vital the program continues to be. Like all of the best forms of art, *Doctor Who* doesn't simply hold a mirror up to society and its institutions. Rather, it challenges our assumptions about those institutions and forces us to look at the world in ways we might never have otherwise imagined. In many ways, I can honestly say that *Doctor Who* has made me who I am today. To put it bluntly, I love *Doctor Who*, and I don't care who knows it!

What's more, I'm more than certain that I'm not alone.

If you've ever daydreamed of taking off in the TARDIS . . .

If you've ever pretended a tire gauge was a sonic screwdriver . . .

If you've ever worn a scarf that was a little too long, or seriously considered pinning a stalk of celery to your lapel just to see how it would look, then this book is for you—because you know that *Doctor Who* matters and that a little bit of imagination can change the world.

We Murder to Dissect (*Tom Powers*)

> Sweet is the lore which Nature brings;
> Our meddling intellect
> Mis-shapes the beauteous form of things:
> We murder to dissect
> —William Wordsworth, "The Tables Turned"

I first met my co-author, Marc Schuster, nearly a decade ago while we were pursuing graduate degrees in English at Villanova University. At the time, I probably would have been incredulous at best if some incognito Time Lord possessing the requisite knowledge of future events told me that Marc and I would someday collaborate on a book about *Doctor Who*. Of course, I wouldn't have been surprised to learn that we would write together, since I already knew that Marc could spin words in wonderful ways. I would, however, have been shocked to learn that Marc was a die-hard *Doctor Who* fan— a *rarity* in the States. Luckily for Marc, this fact about himself remained hidden, and he only had to put up with me for a few semesters before we had our parting of the ways.

Seven years later, we met again as fellow English instructors at Montgomery County Community College, and we finally learned of our mutual love for *Doctor Who*. Marc, moreover, finally fulfilled his destiny of becoming the regular recipient of my long and winding three-hour phones calls that would begin innocuously enough with an "ood" comment on the show and then eventually degenerate into a tedious psychoanalysis of myself and why I still live at home with my parents despite the fact that I'm in my mid-thirties. Patiently enduring my tangential babbling, Marc kept collaborating with me, and we finished this book, which we have written (to some degree) as a tongue-in-cheek rage against traditional academic prose.

Our goal throughout this project has been to present scholarship on our favorite program in a fashion that would make the Doctor himself proud. To be sure, we've accomplished this goal by bringing *Doctor Who* into dialogue with a myriad of philosophers, psychologists, cultural critics and comic book writers in a way that casts new light on the program. Since we don't want to murder our subject for the sake of dry analysis, however, we try to maintain a sense of play throughout the proceedings. Imagine the Doctor fiddling with his yo-yo while developing the perfect strategy for defeating a megalomaniacal computer with access to nuclear weapons, and you'll get a sense of what we're up to.

Along these lines, another colleague of mine recently mentioned that he had always seen *Doctor Who* as a cross between Jules Verne and Salvador Dali—the perfect blend of philosophy, futurism and play. Although I immediately began to scrutinize my colleague's words, I stopped myself from over-analyzing and thereby—as William Wordsworth would describe it—"murdering" the moment. Instead, I tried to appreciate that moment for what it was: a rare opportunity to connect with a fellow Whovian. More importantly, I realized that my colleague's "beauteous" mixed simile was the poetic byproduct of his unique, personal response to the show, no less valid than the potentially controversial and occasionally off-the-wall readings that Marc and I will present to you.

In addition to program guides and other works that focus strictly on elements internal to the program itself, nonfiction books on *Doctor Who* have tended to fall under three categories: scientific, historical and critical. Michael White's *A Teaspoon and an Open Mind* and Paul Parsons' *The Science of Doctor Who* are fine examples of the first category. Writing from a historical perspective, former *Doctor Who* script editor Andrew Cartmel places the program in a cultural context in *Through Time*, while James Chapman's *Inside the TARDIS* examines the ways in which the program adapted to suit the changing needs of the BBC. Along similar lines, the *About Time* series by Lawrence Miles and Tat Wood does an unparalleled job of not only reading *Doctor Who* in a specific historical context but also offering entertaining and insightful commentary on almost all aspects of the program. In terms of purely critical works, John Tulloch and Manuel Alvarado's *The Unfolding Text* was among the first tomes to read *Doctor Who* seriously. More recently, *Doctor Who: A Critical Reading of the Series* by Kim Newman and *Back in Time* by Steve Couch, Tony Watkins and Peter S. Williams offer interpretations of the program in light of the newly revived version of the series. Our book, by way of contrast, is distinct from other visions of *Doctor Who* in that it uses psychology, literature, pop culture and the social sciences to frame its discussions. An intellectually stimulating yet highly readable take on *Doctor Who*, this volume provides timely, intelligent and sometimes humorous analysis of the program that we believe will appeal to fans of the show and intellectuals alike.

Introduction

To get the old time rotor moving, our first chapter, "One of Us: *Doctor Who* as Cosmic Spectacle," examines the Doctor's sense of showmanship. Traveling through time and space in an old British police box, our favorite Time Lord transports his traveling companions and the show's viewers alike to the far reaches of the universe on a regular basis. Yet while the Doctor frequently claims to be exploring the cosmos in the name of scientific inquiry or, on occasion, as a crusader for justice, his primary motive more often than not seems to be a desire to astound his audience with thrilling visions of future worlds and extraordinary specimens of alien exotica. Whether the Doctor is gallivanting off to Metebelis III in search of rare crystals or traveling in time to nineteenth-century England for a face-to-face encounter with a werewolf, the Doctor is, first and foremost, a showman. As this chapter demonstrates, it is the Doctor's very showmanship that has given the recently revived series the revered placed in the pantheon of science fiction it enjoys. Moreover, by constantly whisking viewers away to weird and wonderful realms of imagination, *Doctor Who* continues to serve as a complex forum for advancing revolutionary ideas about life, the universe and everything.

Being responsible for not only entertaining us but also expanding our minds must certainly take its toll on the Time Lord's psyche, so our second chapter, "I Am He, and He Is Me: Why *Doctor Who* Is Good for You," places the Doctor on the analyst's couch to determine whether he suffers from such conditions as multiple personality disorder, post-traumatic stress disorder, repressed memory and selective amnesia. As any fan of the program can tell you, throughout the long history of *Doctor Who*, behind-the-scenes personnel changes have caused the program's protagonist to be portrayed by many different actors. To explain this phenomenon within the context of the *Doctor Who* universe, the show's writers advanced the notion of regeneration, the process by which the Doctor literally becomes a new man. Although fans of the program like to think that the Doctor is always the same man regardless of appearances, the interests, words, and actions of one incarnation of the Doctor can easily be at odds with those of another.

In this regard, what makes the Doctor extraordinary is that he, unlike the rest of us, can meet past and future selves and acquire knowledge of his own future. One can only imagine the anxiety we humans might experience if we, too, could come into contact with our past and future selves. By traveling with the Doctor, we get a chance to ponder what this phenomenon might be like, and in so doing, we, like the Doctor, inch ever onward toward a greater understanding of ourselves and the roles we play in shaping our universe.

In addition to being shaped by the process of regeneration, the Doctor's sense of self also hinges on the personalities of his traveling companions. From a cultural perspective, moreover, the Doctor's personae are also signs of the times that reflect changes in entertainment standards and social norms. Consequently, we have a character who can be avuncular, bohemian, shy or flirtatious depending upon his circumstances and the program's social milieu. But we can also attach more controversial yet interesting terms to the Doctor in relation to his companions: messiah figure or cult leader, manipulator or trickster, lothario or player. As such, our third chapter, "Brave Hearts: The Identity Dance of Doctor and Companion," examines why the Doctor needs his companions, why they need him, and whether such issues as class, gender and sexual attraction factor into the relationships the Doctor and his companions share.

Of course, if his companions pull the Doctor in one direction, his Time Lord heritage is always there to pull him in the other, and our fourth chapter, "The Time Lord Manifesto: A Cautionary Guide to Gallifreyan Culture" focuses on the role of the Doctor's native culture in shaping his sense of identity. After all, as a Time Lord, the Doctor is beholden to many elements of this mysterious race's philosophical underpinnings. At the same time, however, the Doctor constantly rebels against the maddeningly *laissez-faire* attitude of his fellow Time Lords with regard to social injustice. In turn, the Time Lords take full advantage of the Doctor's rebellious nature and frequently use him as their pawn, disavowing any knowledge of his activities as they force him to police time and space. This chapter examines the political and philosophical notions that motivate the Doctor and his fellow Time Lords—as well as those of so-called "renegade" Time Lords like the Doctor's archnemeses the Master and Omega—to explain the Doctor's unconventional lifestyle. Applying a working model of French philosopher Michel Foucault's theories on the spirals of power and pleasure, this chapter also argues that the Doctor and the Master take great pleasure in their ongoing mutual attempts at defeating one another throughout their various encounters.

Our fifth chapter, "Cranky Cyborgs: Daleks, Cybermen and the Future of Humanity" puts the villains in the crosshairs for a change and attempts to find out what makes them so cranky all the time. Without a doubt, the Daleks are the Doctor's best-known antagonists, and the Cybermen are a close second. While these cybernetic races are indeed both terrifying and terrific, what makes them so popular among fans is not so much their alien nature but their similarity to humans. Focusing on the most prominent cyborgs in the *Doctor Who* universe, this chapter uses such phenomena as road rage, the rise of the twenty-four hour cable news television station and the proliferation of cosmetic surgery to argue that humans and the technologies we employ have become so intertwined as to render the boundary between the individual and the machine virtually nonexistent. As we grow increasingly dependent upon such technological marvels as iPods, television and computers to serve not only as purveyors of entertainment but also as conduits of information—or, more to the point, as our virtual eyes and ears—we become all the more cybernetic with each passing day. In this context, *Doctor Who* proves particularly prophetic, and adventures featuring the Daleks and Cybermen serve as telling reminders of the fragile nature of the human spirit.

As well as battling Daleks, Cybermen, Omega and the Master, the Doctor has frequently been known to take on corporate juggernauts as well, and our sixth chapter "Intergalactic Culture Jam: The Doctor vs. the Mega-Corporation" examines the Time Lord's ongoing war against corporate greed and corruption. By drawing attention to the potential hazards of bowing unquestioningly to the wisdom of massive corporations, *Doctor Who* provides viewers with both the ability to recognize the insidious sway corporations hold over the mass consciousness of the "civilized" world and the tools for resisting this influence. In other words, the Doctor's longtime career as an iconoclast amounts to what many cultural and media critics might refer to as an extended culture jam—the practice of reclaiming the public sphere by turning the overblown ethos of mass consumption and corporate culture on its head. This chapter examines the ways in which the Doctor's ceaseless suspicion of corporate leviathans challenges us all to probe beneath the surface of the candy-coated messages that saturate our cultural landscape and to become socially responsible citizens of the world (if not the universe).

Beyond its ability to strengthen our collective sense of social responsibility, *Doctor Who* also encourages us to question the very nature of our universe. In "Red Kangs Are Best: Language Games in the Whoniverse," we discuss the ways in which our sense of language shapes our sense of reality. Among other things, this examination investigates the power of myth and fiction to influence our lives (as in the second-Doctor serial "The Mind Robber") as well as the power of rhetoric to divide cultures (as in the fourth-Doctor serial "The Face of Evil") and the potential for the spoken word to shape reality (as in the fourth-Doctor serial "Logopolis"). And as the title of this chapter might suggest, we also attempt to determine once and for all whether Red Kangs are indeed the best as suggested by those self-same Kangs in the seventh-Doctor serial "Paradise Towers," or, assuming this question is ultimately nonsensical, why it and meaningless questions like it still carry so much weight in cultures everywhere.

Our final chapter, "Wrinkles in Time: Life, Death and Everything in Between," turns to what might be described as more existential matters. On one hand, we begin with ninth-Doctor Christopher Eccleston's assertion that what makes *Doctor Who* stand out among all other science fiction dramas is that the show serves as a celebration of life. On the other hand, even casual viewers of *Doctor Who* know that this celebration usually takes place against a backdrop of death and destruction. To make sense of this apparent conundrum, we return to some of the themes discussed throughout this volume and examine the Doctor's long-term relationship with his companion Sarah Jane Smith, his ability to regenerate and his distaste for vampires (among other things). What emerges from this discussion in particular and from this book as a whole is one (but certainly not the only) explanation for the longstanding popularity of the program: always challenging us to examine our assumptions and to look upon all of creation with a sense of wonder, *Doctor Who* demonstrates time and again that the human spirit is capable of nearly anything.

In a touching moment of candor, the Doctor exclaims in the 2006 Christmas special "The Runaway Bride" that one of the things he loves most about humans is our dedication to making sense out of chaos. In many ways, this is what we have attempted to do throughout this project. Any TV show with a history as long and complex as that of *Doctor Who* is bound to generate some degree of chaos, and any attempt to make sense of that chaos is bound to be imperfect. In our excitement and fervor over this project, we imagine ourselves to be walking in the Doctor's shoes to some degree as we jump back and forth in time, touching on elements seen in the more recent tenth-Doctor adventures one minute, jumping back to the early days of the program the next, and then landing somewhere in the middle with the fourth Doctor, for example, as we bring any given discussion to a conclusion.

By the very nature of such an undertaking, we're bound to miss the occasional fan-favorite episode, moment, quotation or confrontation. Our goal however, has not been to create a comprehensive and final reading of *Doctor Who*. Indeed, with a show as complex as *Doctor Who*, there can never be a *final* reading or interpretation; there can only be eternal discussion and debate. As a result, our goal has been to scratch the surface of a massive body of work in an effort to perpetuate ongoing, intelligent conversation about our favorite science fiction series. To this end, we welcome criticism and disagreement with the ideas we advance in the following chapters. In fact, we encourage it. So sit back, put on your floppy hat and long scarf, break out your sonic screwdriver and join in our ongoing discussion of cranky cyborgs, Mafioso Time Lords, and the sundry self-loathing alien freaks who populate the mad yet marvelous world of *Doctor Who*.

1

One of Us: Doctor Who
as Cosmic Spectacle

On the xenophobic world of Inter Minor, ashen-faced laborers grunt and squeal as they process the planet's imports and their blue-skinned superiors quibble endlessly over petty matters of politics and public policy. Against this backdrop, a mustachioed showman named Vorg and his voluptuous assistant Shirna tumble out of a space cruiser's cargo hold and get right to work in their efforts at attracting a crowd.

"Roll up, roll up!" Vorg shouts like a carnival barker, drawing attention to a device he's likely been toting across the galaxy for ages as Shirna stands by and tries her best to look pretty. "Roll up and see the monster show! A carnival of monsters living in their natural habitat—wild in this little box of mine! A miracle of intergalactic technology!"

Given that Inter Minor is just one of the many fantastic worlds in the ever-expanding universe of *Doctor Who*, it comes as no surprise when this so-called miracle of intergalactic technology malfunctions and a tiny man in a velvet smoking jacket stumbles out of a crack in the machine's façade. What may come as a surprise, however, is that while this swiftly growing man is immediately recognizable as the Doctor, the intergalactic carnival barker identifies him not as a Time Lord but as a fellow showman: "I do believe he's one of us!" the barker explains to his perplexed assistant. "He's in the carnival business, I'm sure. I mean, look at his manner, and look at his clothes!"

While this remark may well be interpreted as a mere gag at the expense of the velvet Doctor's fashion sense, it carries more than a grain of truth. More than anything, *Doctor Who* is a *show* and, as such, depends not merely upon a small army of writers, producers, actors, script editors and other professionals to stay afloat, but upon sheer numbers as well. As was clearly demonstrated when the initial run of *Doctor Who* drew its final breath at the conclusion of the ironically titled "Survival" in 1989, if we fans don't turn out en masse and plunk down our metaphorical tuppence, our favorite Time Lord will surely die.

Like Vorg, the Doctor must frequently employ the tools of the circus barker in order to make a living. Traveling through time and space in his trusty TARDIS, the Doctor implicitly promises his fans and traveling companions alike that each trip will be greater than the last and that each new world will hold wonders heretofore unseen by the average human. Indeed, while the Doctor frequently claims to be exploring the cosmos in the name of scientific inquiry or, on occasion, as a crusader for justice, his primary motive more often than not seems to be a desire to astound us with thrilling visions of future worlds and extraordinary specimens of alien exotica.

Whether the Doctor is gallivanting off to the year five billion to witness the destruction of Earth (as in the ninth-Doctor adventure "The End of the World") or traveling backwards in time to nineteenth-century England for a face-to-face encounter with a werewolf (as in the tenth-Doctor adventure "Tooth and Claw"), the Time Lord is, among other things, a showman. Yet while the sense of showmanship that drives *Doctor Who* certainly proves entertaining and, at times, thought-provoking, some of the Doctor's methods hearken back to those of nineteenth and early twentieth-century freak show proprietors and, as such, raise significant questions with regard to the objectification of anyone deemed different from the majority of people in mainstream society. What, for example, makes the Doctor different from the various stripes of carnie folk he has, on occasion, stumbled upon in his travels? What is the place of "the other" in his universe? And, perhaps most importantly, what can we learn about ourselves as the Doctor brings us into contact with increasingly unusual life forms throughout the universe?

For a tentative answer to these questions, we can turn to "The Leisure Hive," a fourth-Doctor serial in which the natives of a war-ravaged planet explain that part of their business as proprietors of an intergalactic holiday destination is to "promote understanding between life forms of all cultures and genetic type" so that each race might learn to understand "what it is like to be the foreigner." Which is to say that the purpose of the Leisure Hive is not merely to entertain, but to provide a forum for cross-cultural dialogue. In many ways, this is also the purpose of *Doctor Who*, and while the Doctor's innate sense of showmanship has certainly given the program the revered place in the pantheon of science fiction that it enjoys, that same sense of spectacle has also allowed the much-loved series to serve as a complex medium for advancing revolutionary ideas about life, the universe and our relationships with everything contained therein.

Nothing Serious?

As Vorg and his lovely assistant Shirna begin to attract a crowd at the Inter Minor spaceport in the third-Doctor serial "Carnival of Monsters," they also attract the attention of the local authorities. Upon being accosted by a tribunal of three blue bureaucrats showing signs of advanced male-pattern baldness (and, curiously enough, predating the formation of the Blue Man Group by several decades), Vorg insists that his show poses no danger and that his purpose is "to amuse, simply amuse—nothing serious, nothing political." Belying this argument, however, is the fact that the members of the tribunal immediately recognize the political edge they stand to gain by allowing Vorg to carry on with his business: the mode of entertainment Vorg offers distracts the lower-class, gray-skinned "functionaries" of Inter Minor from the drudgery of their work and therefore renders them less likely to contemplate revolution. At the very least, then, the Miniscope at the center of Vorg's show serves, much like television, as a diversion for the masses, if not as an outright opiate. Thus, despite the showman's claims to the contrary—and even despite the allegedly apolitical content of his act—Vorg's Miniscope demonstrations hold distinctly political overtones that call attention to the potentially political nature of all forms of entertainment. To wit, anything that occurs in the public sphere is bound to influence the public.

What "Carnival of Monsters" demonstrates, then, is that regardless of the quality of the content it provides, the entertainment industry can have a profound effect on the masses—even if that effect is to render the masses as mindless as the programs they are watching. This argument, of course, is nothing new; the poet Juvenal lamented the use of "bread and circuses" to pacify the poor in ancient Rome, and critics since the dawn of television have been using the same phrase, along with a host of overworked others, to decry the role of electronic media in the modern world. What's interesting in the case of "Carnival of Monsters," however, is the framing of the argument. By *overtly* telling us within the context of a public spectacle that the spectacle itself is in no way political while at the same time *covertly* showing us that it truly *is* political, this *Doctor Who* adventure practically begs us to examine the political content of the entire series in greater depth even as the program purports, like all of television, to be "nothing serious, nothing political." So while many fans might prefer to view the program as nothing more than (admittedly highly entertaining) escapist fare, the opening scenes of "Carnival of Monsters" all but demand that we watch *Doctor Who* with an eye for what the series might tell us about the world at large.

That "Carnival of Monsters" uses the language of the circus sideshow or dime-museum freak-show as its dominant idiom casts further doubt on Vorg's assertion that his act is "nothing serious, nothing political." As Leslie

Fiedler notes in her landmark study of freak theory, *Freaks: Myths and Images of the Secret Self*, the "normal" world's relationship with so-called freaks of nature speaks volumes with regard to our own cultural attitudes toward "the other" (or, in the parlance of the 1982 *Doctor Who* serial "Kinda," the "Not-We"). The freak, Fiedler notes, "stirs both supernatural terror and natural sympathy, since, unlike fabulous monsters, he is one of us, the human child of human parents, however altered by forces we do not quite understand into something mythic and mysterious, as no mere cripple ever is."[1] As a result, the freak also "challenges the conventional boundaries between male and female, sexed and sexless, animal and human, large and small, self and other, and consequently between reality and illusion, experience and fantasy, fact and myth."[2] This observation proves particularly valid in "Carnival of Monsters" in that the entire adventure amounts to a veritable parade of the kinds of dichotomies Fiedler lists. In point of fact, the title of the adventure works on many levels, and the scope of the "Carnival of Monsters" is not restricted to the contents of Vorg's miracle of intergalactic technology. Rather, the carnival's boundaries extend beyond the purview of the Miniscope to entangle Vorg, Shirna and the residents of Inter Minor, and beyond the barrier of the television screen to implicate the denizens of TV-land as well—all the while forcing us to wonder who the true monsters really are.

The big joke in "Carnival of Monsters" is that the freaks are running the show. The blue-skinned members of Inter Minor's "official species" consider all other forms of life absolutely repulsive and, as such, discuss Vorg and Shirna's visit to their planet in hushed tones of horror and dread. "One was afraid they might have four heads," one member of the tribunal opines while another laments that members of alien races tend to have "ridiculous names." That their own names—Pletrac, Kalik and Orum—may themselves seem ridiculous from a human perspective never occurs to the members of the tribunal and therefore underscores the subjective nature of normalcy. Similarly, their observation that Tellurians (*i.e.*, Earthlings) "all look alike" sounds very much like the kind of observation that the racist Archie Bunker of *All in the Family* fame might make about any race other than his own.

Driving this point home, the racist attitudes of the members of Inter Minor's ruling class are shared by the Tellurian specimens held captive in Vorg's Miniscope: one human complains that Indian servants tend to be "a bit idle" and are therefore not suited for work on his plantation, and another refers to an individual of Eastern extraction as "Johnny Chinaman." Clearly, then, the members of the ruling classes on Earth and Inter Minor agree that difference and inferiority walk hand in hand. Paradoxically, however, their shared ideology dictates that each regard the other as alien and therefore inferior, and the very worldview that would otherwise render them intergalactic soul-mates is what ultimately ensures that the upper class citizens of Earth and Inter Minor will never intermix in polite company.

For the Doctor and Jo, everything hinges on perspective as well. Trapped in the Miniscope, the Doctor's young companion quickly realizes that she has become a minor attraction in "a sort of peep show" and that somewhere past the boundaries of her miniaturized world "there are people and creatures just looking at [her] for kicks." While the prospect of such voyeurism didn't stop Katy Manning from posing in the nude with a Dalek in 1978, her onscreen alter-ego is clearly vexed by the situation. Yet when Jo insists that she and the Doctor don't belong in the Miniscope because they're "not animals," the Doctor is quick to point out that they are, from another perspective, mere specimens to the beings who are observing them from above. Predictably, this fact doesn't make their predicament any more palatable, and the Doctor soon confesses that the sense of objectification Jo correctly associates with the use of the Miniscope is what moved the High Council of Time Lords to rule the machine "an offense against the dignity of sentient life forms" and to subsequently ban its use. As if to prove the High Council's point regarding the dignity of sentient life, the Doctor continues to be regarded as a specimen even after he escapes the Miniscope's miniaturization field, and it isn't until he demands that everyone kindly stop referring to him as "the creature" that he begins to gain a modicum of dignity from those who might otherwise see him as inferior.

Even as he accepts the Doctor as a potential equal, however, Vorg persists in describing the prisoners of his Miniscope as "livestock," and even the Time Lord's vehement assertion that "the collection of civilized, intelligent beings is a positive crime" is not enough to make the showman reconsider his position. While Vorg does allow the Doctor to re-enter the Miniscope in order to return its sentient specimens to their points of origin, he still has every intention of continuing to feature the machine in his act. Meanwhile, the blue-skinned members of the tribunal are hatching yet another scheme for using the Miniscope to further their political aims: by clandestinely allowing the deadliest of Vorg's specimens to escape from the confines of the Miniscope, one member of the tribunal hopes to cause enough damage to the spaceport to convince the masses that stricter border policies are in Inter Minor's best interest. Here, the program's critique of television and freak shows as politically charged media gains another layer in that the numbing of the masses and the objectification of "the other" are no longer the only issues at stake. Rather, the first two phenomena engendered by the Miniscope pave the way for a third: propaganda. Once critical thought has been eliminated and all foreign entities have been painted as savages, it doesn't take much effort to convince the public that said foreign entities are not only primitive but threatening as well.

While the Doctor does make a number of brief speeches decrying the use of the Miniscope throughout "Carnival of Monsters," the formal dictates of television require the resolution of the plot to arrive not through eloquence but through action. In other words, the adventure can't end with the Doctor sitting down with Vorg, Shirna and the Inter Minorians and launching into a lengthy explanation as to why everything they've been up to over the past hour and a half is morally reprehensible. In order to satisfy the needs of the medium, the show needs to end with a bang, which it literally does when the Miniscope is destroyed amidst a violent fracas. Given the machine's destruction, discussion of the ethical implications of its use becomes moot, and the Doctor leaves Inter Minor without so much as a goodbye. As a result of this abrupt departure, however, the Doctor never learns of the harsh conditions under which the planet's lower-class functionaries live, and he therefore misses the opportunity to launch into further speeches about the evils of exploiting intelligent beings. Nonetheless, the conclusion of "Carnival of Monsters" suggests that the gray-skinned laborers may well find a place in the upper levels of their own planet's society; as the TARDIS dematerializes, Vorg is being touted as both a hero and a contender for the office of president. Heretofore unimaginable on the xenophobic planet, this proposition eases the imaginary line between "official" and "unauthorized" species upon which the parochial ideology of Inter Minor rests and also blurs the boundary between self and other that frequently yet erroneously justifies the exploitation of all sentient life throughout the universe.

Something Novel by Way of Spectacle

Predating Arnold Schwarzenegger's bid for the governorship of California by decades, Vorg's almost seamless transition from show business to politics in "Carnival of Monsters" serves as a telling commentary on the relationship between two (preferably) disparate modes of public discourse. Along with Schwarzenegger, pro-wrestler Jesse "The Body" Ventura, Ronald Reagan and countless other entertainers who have acceded to public office, Vorg demonstrates that putting on a good show is by and large the bread and butter of a life in politics—a premise upon which the sixth-Doctor serial "Vengeance on Varos" expounds in chilling detail. In this adventure, the Doctor and his American-born companion Peri land on the mining world of Varos only to discover that the planet's chief export is not the highly valuable mineral Zeiton 7, which the Time Lord needs to repair his TARDIS, but the spectacle of torture in the form of mass-market snuff-films. Because the governing bodies of Varos have little to offer by way of tangible public services, they must, to borrow a phrase from the Doctor, offer their constituents "something novel by way of spectacle" on a regular basis in order to prevent revolution. To this end, the government of Varos has created a world in which political prisoners are tortured and sometimes executed on live television, the lives of government officials depend entirely upon the results of televised referenda, and beautiful young women are literally turned into animals just for the fun of it. And so it is that with "Vengeance on Varos" *Doctor Who* returns once again to the idiom of the freak show in order to highlight not only the political nature of entertainment but the vacuously entertaining nature of politics as well.

What immediately distinguishes "Vengeance on Varos" from many *Doctor Who* adventures that have gone before it is the presence of Arak and Etta, a Varosian couple who only tangentially take part in the action of the serial as they are too busy watching television to do anything more than argue with each other and vote when necessary. Although some commentators have justifiably likened these characters to a "sort of Greek chorus," their purpose in the adventure involves more than merely "offering comment on the action as it unfolds."[3] Rather, Arak and Etta frame the adventure in a self-referential postmodern context. That is, the presence of these characters demonstrates that *Doctor Who* recognizes itself as a television program and is therefore capable of critiquing not only itself but its viewers as well. *The Simpsons* notwithstanding, television audiences are rarely treated to the sight of people watching television because, to put it bluntly, watching people watch television is boring. What this observation implies, moreover, is that watching television is itself a boring activity and that people who do little more with their free time than watch television are boring people. What television normally does, then, is dole out violence, melodrama and slapstick to distract the dull, entertainment-addled masses from their day-to-day drudgery and ennui. Yet when a show like *Doctor Who* takes the *verboten* step of giving us characters like Arak and Etta, it essentially holds a mirror up to our unfulfilling and uneventful lives and challenges us to prove ourselves better than the sad, bickering, TV-swilling people we're watching.

Needless to say, the complex framing of "Vengeance on Varos" effectively turns the tables on the viewer insofar as the true spectacle is no longer the freak of nature inside the "little box" (to borrow a term from "Carnival of Monsters") but the couch potato sitting comfortably outside the box and looking in. This reversal gains particular relevance in the character of Sil, the slug-like representative of the Galatron Mining Corporation who spends the majority of his time gorging on marsh minnows and flicking his tongue in nearly orgasmic anticipation of whatever violence he may be about to witness. Referring to televised execution as "most wonderful entertainment," Sil is the ultimate couch potato, and the fact that the trailer for episode two of "Vengeance on Varos" uses a shot of the Doctor in a hangman's noose in order to draw in the maximum number of viewers suggests that our own collective appetite for blood and gore can't be all that different from the alien's. Like Sil, we crave the spectacle of a good, old-fashioned (if ersatz) lynching—even if it *is* our hero's neck in the noose.

And what the audience wants, the audience gets. Among the more controversial scenes in "Vengeance on Varos" is one in which a pair of mortuary attendants fall to their deaths in a vat of acid. All but turning to face the camera directly, the Doctor jokes to no one in particular that he hopes the victims will forgive him if he doesn't join them in their acid bath, and the incidental calliope music of Jonathan Gibbs gives the scene a musical stinger, the equivalent of a vaudeville rim-shot. While many critics complained at the time of the serial's original broadcast that the Doctor's callous disregard for life in this instance signaled that the program had sunken to a new low, a more generous reading suggests quite the opposite. Since the acid-bath victims are either already dead or too panic-stricken to hear what the Doctor has to say, he has no real audience for his joke. And while the sixth Doctor proves to be somewhat of an egomaniac over the course of his travels, he isn't generally prone to making private asides. Actually, what drives this Doctor most is the opportunity to impress an audience, and since there's no audience to be had in the acid-bath mortuary on Varos, the only audience remaining for the Doctor to address is the one sitting at home on the sofa. Violating the so-called "fourth wall" of television, the Doctor is practically turning to the audience and chastising our bloodlust as if to remind us all that we're no better than the slimy, disturbing Sil himself.[4]

In fact, one can almost hear the famous chant of the circus freaks in Todd Browning's *Freaks* or Jack Cardiff's *The Mutations* (curiously starring fourth Doctor Tom Baker as a deformed circus performer) as Sil continues to revel in the violence going on all around him: *One of us! One of us! One of us!* To drive this point home, Sil demands that Peri be placed in a "reshapement chamber" so he can "watch her change into beast or bird." That she turns into the latter is reminiscent of the conclusion of the Browning film, which sees a scheming trapeze artist transformed into a freakish bird woman by way of a punishment for, among other things, sneering at the circus freaks with whom she performs. From Sil's perspective, Peri's crime may be of a similar nature since she reacts with disgust when she first lays eyes on the alien and refers to him as a "thing." Again, we can almost hear the chant— *One of us! One of us! One of us!*—as we are informed that the process of transmutation "focuses on the seeds of fear" in the victim's mind and makes those seeds grow until her "entire being" takes on the physical form of what she fears most. Since it's unlikely that Peri has a particularly strong fear of peacocks, it's quite probable that what she truly fears most is being rendered a "freak" like Sil, regardless of the form her freakery takes—bird, beast or otherwise. And since the Doctor's companion can generally be regarded as a surrogate for the viewer, Peri's transformation is very much our own, and it doesn't take long to realize that we have so much more in common with Sil than with any of the "normal" inhabitants of Varos.

None of this is to say that the seemingly normal Varosians aren't victims of their own sense of spectacle in one way or another as well. The Governor of Varos, who looks vaguely like Robert Redford, amounts to little more than a game-show host in that his tenure in office hinges not on the strength of the planet's economy or any legislation he might sponsor but on the quality of the entertainment he provides to his constituents. In the words of the rebel Ereta, the descendants of the colony's original officers "still rule by fear," using "the spectacle of death" as a means of both subjugation and entertainment. As a result of this state of affairs, civic life suffers on Varos, and democracy amounts to nothing more than yet another form of entertainment. While the people of Varos can vote on whether their governor remains in office or is killed by a torrent of death rays, they have no real voice in the (admittedly feeble) political processes that govern their world—hence the television-addicted Etta's remark to her husband that while everyone on Varos has the right to a vote, nobody has the right to an opinion. That is, the voting process merely proffers the illusion of democracy, but because the people of Varos are so distracted by their appetite for violence, they never get around to voting on anything that matters.

Sound familiar?

In our own world, we have the obvious plethora of shows that resonate with the kind of programming that holds the masses in check in "Vengeance on Varos." For lack of a better term, these so-called "reality TV" programs include such artless tripe as *Big Brother, American Idol* and somewhere in the neighborhood of a million variations on *Survivor*. So similar, in fact, are these shows to the programming on Varos—which depicts (among other things) two men in diapers fighting over what appears to be a chicken leg, as well as the Doctor fighting for his life within the labyrinthine corridors of the planet's Punishment Dome—that it's hard to fathom how *Doctor Who* predicted the coming of such shows nearly a decade before they hit the airwaves.

Superficially, one element that the programs on Varos have in common with many of our own "reality-based" TV shows is that both call upon viewers to cast votes from home. And while no one to date has ever been killed via this voting process here on Earth, one might judge by the reactions of contestants who get "voted off" their respective programs that sudden death awaits them just off camera—as is actually the case in the ninth-Doctor adventure, "Bad Wolf." What truly *does* suffer in our current relationship with mass-media, however, is the individual's sense of having a meaningful voice within the realm of public discourse. If shows like *American Idol* teach us anything, it's that the only avenue open to the average citizen with regard to "being heard" in this media-saturated world of ours involves humiliating oneself on national television. Hence the long lines of potential contestants featured at the start of each season of *American Idol*; people are so desperate to be seen on television—to be granted the illusion that the world at large might, however momentarily, love them and that they might, for the briefest of moments, *matter* to anyone other than themselves—that they'll do anything for a shot at getting inside the "little box" that, as "Vengeance on Varos" demonstrates, will ultimately only amount to a prison. And for those of us at home, there's always the consolation prize of being allowed to vote. Sure, we don't get to see ourselves in the spotlight as the finalists on these programs might, but we convince ourselves that phoning in our votes makes us part of the action and somehow assures us of our place, however small, in history. To paraphrase Etta's formula, none of us is entitled to voice a complex opinion, but at least we're all entitled to a vote.

Where "Vengeance on Varos" and the likes of *Survivor*, *American Idol* and other shows like them diverge, however, is that while *Survivor* claims to proffer "reality," "Vengeance on Varos" goes to great lengths to remind viewers that what they're watching is anything but. This distinction is important in that by denying its own status as an orchestrated phenomenon, "reality television" attempts to alter our common-sense definition of reality in much the same way the hallucinatory effects of the Punishment Dome nearly convince the Doctor that he's dying of thirst in some far-off desert when really he's safe and sound in yet another hallway. Yet by giving us Arak and Etta, "Vengeance on Varos" effectively turns television inside out to reveal the truly freakish nature of everyone and everything involved in the television viewing experience, including the "stars," the audience and the trappings of the medium itself. While so-called reality television provides a mind-numbing experience that ultimately robs us of a sense of meaningful participation in the truly real world at large, self-consciously artificial television along the lines of "Vengeance on Varos" tears away the beguiling veil of the medium to reveal the disturbing spectacle that lies underneath: under television's thrall, we all become freaks in one way or another.

Monsters or Beasts?

The word *monster* is easily bandied about by both the show's creators and fans to refer to any life form—organic, robotic or cybernetic—that is not overtly human in appearance. But in the case of many alien races presented on the show, *monster* is a misnomer since many of these races, unlike the Daleks or Sontarans, are not driven by a single-minded need to kill and conquer. On the contrary, *Doctor Who* frequently presents its audience with aliens that anthropomorphically correspond with Earthly animals, and as Peri's near-transformation into a bird-woman in "Vengeance on Varos" aptly demonstrates, these zoomorphic aliens speak volumes about the fine line that separates us from our own animal tendencies.

In "Unpicking the Seam: Talking Animals and Reader Pleasure in Early Modern Satire," Kathryn Perry comments upon the role of the animal in Early Modern English Culture:

> In the fantasy world of the talking animal text, humans are not automatically the most excellent of creatures, nor are they the only ones capable of organizing civil societies... By appropriating the power of speech, talking animals undermine convictions of human superiority and uniqueness and, by extension, hierarchical structures and discourses in general, such as the language of chivalry.[5]

Applying Perry's flattering vision of fantasy animals to the various alien races in *Doctor Who* is by no means a difficult task, as becomes apparent when we examine the messages offered by just a handful of these zoomorphic beings:

- The Cheetah People: A once fun-loving and peaceful feline species, the Cheetah People savagely hunt human prey in "Survival," the final serial of the original *Doctor Who* series. Since the Cheetah People must seek fleshly sustenance for their very survival, it is difficult to label their actions as "evil" even as their natural instincts lead them to "play" with their prey. More importantly, the fact that the Doctor's companion, Ace, begins to mutate into a Cheetah Person herself as she gives in to her baser instincts further blurs the line between human and beast.

- Empress of the Racnoss: As her name implies, the Empress of the Racnoss has the lower body of an arachnid and the upper body of a human. The last of her kind, the Empress arrives on Earth in the tenth-Doctor adventure "The Runaway Bride" to awaken the pod of ancient Racnoss hatchlings that are hibernating in the planet's core. Taking a cue from the itsy-bitsy spider, the Doctor washes the Empress out by draining the Thames and sending her offspring down a four-thousand mile shaft that leads to the center of the Earth. And if the tale of the itsy-bitsy spider is any indication of what's to come, then the only question that remains is not whether but *when* the children of the Empress will climb up the shaft again.

- The Giant Spiders of Metebelis III: Evolved from everyday Earth spiders (which may themselves be evolved from the children of the Empress of the Racnoss), the Giant Spiders of Metebelis III have gained advanced intelligence and extrasensory perception after being exposed to the planet's blue crystals. With their newfound powers, the spiders enslave the human colonists of Metebelis III and plot to take over the universe, only to have their plans foiled by the third Doctor. In the end, however, the collective greed of the spiders is what leads to their undoing, for the Doctor defeats them, quite ironically, by giving them what they want: a crystal that should, by all accounts, give the spiders unlimited power. But as no lesser authority than Spider-Man himself well knows, with great power comes great responsibility, and because these spiders can handle neither, they collapse under the pressure.

- The Garm: The living embodiment of the long-held belief that a dog is a man's best friend, the canine Garm dutifully oversees the cure for Lazar's Disease in the fifth-Doctor serial "Terminus." While the corrupt Vanir—essentially a band of drug-dependent rent-a-cops in golden armor—believe that their enslavement of the Garm is the sole means of ensuring that the old dog will carry out his duties, the fifth Doctor quickly disproves their theory when he destroys the electronic device that controls the animal. Heroically, the Garm continues to assist in caring for infected humans even after the Doctor sets him free and, in so doing, demonstrates that he truly is man's best friend.

- The Silurians and Sea Devils: Resembling giant bipedal turtles, the Sea Devils and their Silurian cousins band together in the fifth-Doctor serial "Warriors of the Deep" to regain control of Earth after a prolonged hibernation. Like the third-Doctor serials "Doctor Who and the Silurians" and "The Sea Devils," "Warriors of the Deep" suggests that humanity need not look to the stars for alien invaders since we already have them here on our home planet. Of course, to the Silurians and Sea Devils, we are the true alien invaders, since their species ruled the Earth long before humanity had so much as uttered its first word. What's more, the Sea Devils and Silurians also offer an implicit warning: just as they have been displaced by a species that seems to them like a gaggle of talking monkeys, so might we, the talking monkeys, one day be displaced by yet another species that is better adapted to survival in our rapidly changing environment.

- The Sisters of Plentitude: Unlike the Cheetah People, the feline Sisters of Plentitude are fully cognizant of their cunning ways as they take extreme measures to achieve miracle cures for humanity in their hospital right outside of New New York in "New Earth." The price for these cures, unfortunately, is paid by the humanoid stock being bred in disease vats to be used as human lab rats. Luckily, in an act that reverses his image as the "Oncoming Storm" or avatar of death, the tenth Doctor, soaked in various miracle cures, manages to treat the contaminated "disease rats," thereby freeing them from bondage and establishing them as a new species of humanity. In the end, it is the Doctor's humane act that serves as a counterweight to the cold-hearted, calculating sense of morality that the Sisters practice, offering biting commentary on contemporary attitudes toward healthcare worldwide.

- The Terileptils: Generally speaking, these erect reptiles aren't so bad, but when the fifth Doctor encounters a trio of criminal Terileptils in "The Visitation," they destroy his sonic screwdriver. To add insult to injury, they also attempt to spread a genetically enhanced version of bubonic plague throughout seventeenth-century England with an eye toward eradicating humanity altogether. Fortunately for the Doctor, the Soliton gas which the Terileptils breathe becomes highly flammable when combined with oxygen, and the alien invaders go out in a blaze of agony at the conclusion of the serial. In some ways, however, their destruction is quite tragic insofar as the Terileptils might have gotten along quite well with the Silurians when the latter cold-blooded species eventually emerged from their underground caves in the twentieth century.

- The Tetraps: Last seen in the seventh-Doctor serial "Time and the Rani," these bat-like henchmen of the Rani hail from the planet Tetrapyriarbus and, despite their poor character judgment, aren't as bad as one might guess. In fact, upon realizing that the evil Time Lady is using them with little if any regard for their own well-being, they turn on her in a heartbeat. Lesson learned? Never turn your back on a bat with eyes in the back of its head.

- The Tharils: Once rulers of an empire, the leonine Tharils of the fourth-Doctor serial "Warrior's Gate" have learned humility as a result of their more recent reversals of fortune. Throughout children's literature, particularly stories of African origin, the lion is typically presented as the king of the jungle. Ruling over their empire from a castle known as the Gateway, the time-sensitive Tharils were likewise once able to access the entire universe. Since no other species had the ability to ride the time winds, the Tharils were able to misuse their power in order to build an empire. Consequently, if one were to view the story of their downfall and subsequent enslavement as a fable, the moral of the Tharils' tragic story is that those who abuse power are destined to be enslaved by others who covet that very power. The Tharils, fortunately, have gained wisdom as a result of their experiences, granting them the chance for a better future as neither slavers nor the enslaved.

- The Mara: Drawing upon classical Biblical allusions to the serpent representing evil, the Mara resides within the "dark places of the inside" with the hopes of possessing human minds in order to gain control of corresponding bodies. Those of us who are fond of snakes may be upset by this not-so-complimentary yet archetypal view of them as represented by the unapologetically evil Maras found in both "Kinda" and "Snakedance," whose bad behavior perpetuates the anti-snake theme found in such movies as SSSSSSS, *Raiders of the Lost Ark* and *Snakes on a Plane*. Yet as the Dukkha Mara is thwarted by a circle of mirrors in "Kinda," the serial's climactic message emerges as a laudatory one, for it reminds us that evil cannot gaze upon its own reflection—and, by extension, that honest reflection is the first step in conquering all of our demons, both internal and external.

• The Werewolf: When the tenth Doctor and Rose stumble upon a genuine werewolf in "Tooth and Claw," they don't know whether to run for their lives or howl with glee, but since they're already running, they don't have much choice in the matter. Worshipped by a band of monks as a creature of divine origin, the werewolf is actually a human-alien hybrid stemming from the curious mingling of alien cellular matter with human tissue. Accordingly, this creature challenges not only the conventional boundaries between animal and human but between terrestrial and extraterrestrial life as well. Sadly, this particular werewolf threatens to kill Queen Victoria in a bid to take over the Earth, so the Doctor is forced to dispose of it.

This, of course, is only a partial list of the many zoomorphic creatures found throughout the world of *Doctor Who*. What's more, as the Time Lord's adventures continue and beasts who inhabit his universe proliferate, the Doctor emerges not simply as a guide through the wilds of the cosmos but as a savvy showman as well.

The Greatest Showman in the Galaxy

As Vorg intimates in "Carnival of Monsters," the Time Lord's clothing and demeanor certainly match those of an old-time carnival barker, as does the name he commonly goes by. When he first hears the Doctor's moniker, the showman assumes that it's merely a stage name and remarks that it's a "great title," the likes of which will always serve to attract suckers and, in all likelihood, separate them from their money. And to be fair, Vorg is more or less right about the Doctor's name. In the fourth-Doctor serial, "The Armageddon Factor," a fellow Time Lord refers to the Doctor as Theta Sigma and reveals that he went by the name "Thete" as a student on Gallifrey. "The Doctor," then, is a title our hero picked up along the way and for reasons unknown. What is known, however, is that from a marketing perspective, "the Doctor" makes for a much better name than "Theta Sigma," given that a show with a title along the lines of *The Continuing Adventures of*

Theta Sigma or even *Sigma Who* probably wouldn't have lasted nearly as long as the original twenty-six year run of *Doctor Who*. As a name, moreover, "the Doctor" carries with it an air of mystery that practically begs the obvious question: Doctor *Who?* Add to that the ubiquitous question marks that started punctuating the Doctor's outfits in the "The Leisure Hive" and the fact that, like Vorg, the Time Lord uses his own "little box" to dazzle the young men and women he meets in his travels, and the notion that the Doctor is himself a deliberately mysterious cosmic showman doesn't sound all that far-fetched.

In terms of both form and function, the Doctor fills the role of the circus barker almost perfectly. Describing this role in "The Social Construction of Freaks," Robert Bogdan notes that although pamphlets and signs were frequently used to generate interest in traveling circuses and freak shows in the nineteenth and early twentieth centuries, "the person who stood outside the entrance spieling to the crowd about the attractions inside was the key to the promotion" and that the job of the so-called "talker" or "outside lecturer" was to influence people to "step right up" and buy tickets.[6] While the Doctor doesn't, strictly speaking, stand to gain financially from attracting a crowd, he does, on occasion, go above and beyond the call of duty in his efforts to entice attractive young women to join him on his travels.

As with the talkers and outside lecturers Bogdan associates with circuses, the Doctor's standard *modus operandi* is to charm potential companions with his wit and intelligence before moving on to promises of adventure and intrigue. For example, after a long day of helping the ninth Doctor battle Autons and the Nestene Consciousness in "Rose," the Time Lord's latest prospective companion needs a slight nudge before deciding to join him on his travels. Sensing that this is the case, the Doctor notes that in addition to being larger inside than out, the TARDIS can travel in time as well as space. When even this point fails to seal the deal, the Doctor finally makes it known that their journeys together will involve a good deal of danger, at which point Rose finally (and quite enthusiastically) gives in and decides to run off with the mysterious man from another world.

In this particular instance, the notion of the Doctor's companion serving as a surrogate for the viewer once again proves instructive in interpreting the Time Lord's behavior. Considering that "Rose" is the first of the Doctor's regularly televised adventures since seeing his show axed in 1989, he needs not only to convince the shapely nineteen-year-old that casting her lot with him is a good idea but also to convince the (more-than-likely) less shapely among us who are watching at home to tune in regularly. In other words, as the Doctor makes his final plea to Rose, he's also making a promise to his viewers. To wit: *If you thought this adventure was good, keep watching!* To sweeten the deal, moreover, he gives us Rose to look at as well, for in addition to serving as our surrogate, the Doctor's companion frequently serves to draw in certain viewers—yet another factor that links the Doctor to the world of spectacle.

In "The Social Construction of Freaks," Bogdan asserts that in order to attract a crowd, "the talker often had a 'bally'—one of the exhibits out front as a lure to move the customers closer. A scantily clad woman with a python around her neck or a colorfully dressed person with a blatant physical deformity would serve the purpose."[7] For the Doctor, this phenomenon is distilled most purely in the form of Leela, the scantily clad "savage" whose presence in the TARDIS allegedly gave the Doctor's ratings a decent jolt among football fans in the 1970s. Though dressed a little bit more conservatively than Leela, Rose has a degree of streetwise charm and sex-appeal that suits the role of bally quite nicely and, in any case, won't likely turn viewers away.

Is all of this to say that the Doctor's companions are little more than arm candy for the old space dog? Do Rose, Leela, Jo and all of the other fellow travelers he's picked up over the years serve no other purpose than to attract a crowd? Are they, like the creatures trapped in Vorg's Miniscope, nothing more than interesting specimens whom the Doctor totes around through time and space solely for his viewers' (and perhaps his own) pleasure and amusement?

Though it may be tempting to critique the Doctor in this light, a brief exchange in the seventh-Doctor serial "The Greatest Show in the Galaxy" reveals the true nature of the Doctor's relationship with his companions: when an apparently famous intergalactic explorer named Captain Cook refers to his own companion as a "specimen," the Doctor pauses for a moment and replies that he's never thought of his current companion, Ace, in such terms. That Cook's specimen, Mags, is ultimately revealed to be a werewolf further cements their respective roles as talker and bally, and the fact that Cook is so willing to sacrifice Mags in order to save his own skin demonstrates the vast difference between the Captain and the Doctor. Where the Captain is self-centered, coldhearted and prone to viewing all manner of phenomena in the universe as objects, the Doctor takes a genuine interest in such phenomena as subjects or self-actualizing individuals. In this respect, the Doctor's self-sacrificing nature is manifest in the fact that he's willing to give of himself so that others—his traveling companions included—might reach their full potential.

Despite his apparent altruism, however, the Doctor is never one to shy away from the spotlight, and, as the remainder of "The Greatest Show in the Galaxy" demonstrates, the role of the showman is central to his sense of identity—and to the survival of his television program. As the serial opens, the Doctor is practicing his juggling act, and it isn't long before a piece of cosmic junk-mail in the form of a robot appears in the TARDIS control room bearing an ad for a so-called Psychic Circus. In addition to prophesying the coming of the ubiquitous and infinitely aggravating pop-up ad in the age of the internet, the sudden and inexplicable appearance of this robot within the TARDIS also signals the encroachment of commercial concerns upon the show itself. Having peaked in ratings with a regular viewership of somewhere between ten and twelve-million households weekly in the mid 1970s, the program's audience had dwindled to less than half that number by the time "The Greatest Show in the Galaxy" hit the airwaves in the late 1980s. Concurrently, as is widely known among many hardcore *Doctor Who* fans, former Controller of BBC1 Michael Grade was not a fan of the series at all and had already gone so far as to cancel the show once, reinstate it with a reduced episode count and eventually demand that Colin Baker be removed from the role of the Doctor. Given these circumstances, it's no wonder that we see the seventh Doctor brushing up on his juggling at the start of "The Greatest Show in the Galaxy." In effect, the character is singing for his supper and doing all he can to please his own masters in order to stay alive.

Given its focus on public spectacle, "The Greatest Show in the Galaxy" represents a retelling of "Vengeance on Varos" except that in this case, it's the Doctor's own head on the chopping block rather than that of a politician. Metaphorically speaking, then, the entire episode is about the Doctor's relationship with his audience—defined either as viewers watching at home or executives monitoring the program's numbers in BBC boardrooms. This explains the prevalence of eye imagery throughout the adventure: kites emblazoned with eyes fly high above the surface of the planet where the Psychic Circus is based, a giant eye appears to be regarding the Doctor from the bottom of a well and a similar eye appears in a fortuneteller's crystal ball. Then, of course, there are the spectators in the stands at the circus who serve as more sinister versions of Arak and Etta from "Vengeance on Varos." Continually expressing their boredom over the acts that parade beneath the big top, a family of three, representing a stereotypical middle-class unit of father, mother and child, literally hold the power of life and death over those who pass before them. That the members of this family are eventually revealed to be the Gods of Ragnarok only serves to draw attention to the degree of power inherent in the role of spectator in that, from the point of view of a character on a television program, the folks at home who determine a show's ratings and the TV executives who control its budget must appear to be gods.

Further commenting on the relationship between the Doctor and his audience is the presence of Whizzkid, a bespectacled fan of both Captain Cook and the Psychic Circus who somehow manages to traverse the galaxy and arrive at the big top on a bicycle. Although the boy knows plenty of trivia regarding Cook and the circus and yearns to be a part of the show, it isn't long before the audience grows tired of his shtick and kills him. While this turn of events may suggest that the average television viewer has little patience for the die-hard *Doctor Who* fan, the fact that nobody lifts a finger to save the boy also suggests that the Doctor himself refuses to cater to the kind of fan Whizzkid represents.

The point of *Doctor Who* is not to generate volumes and volumes of trivia for fans to consume and spit back and forth to each other as they pur-chase armloads of the latest *Who*-related memorabilia at conventions. Rather, the point of the program is to open people's minds and challenge them to look at the world from new, frequently more critical, perspectives. As a matter of fact, what separates the Doctor from nearly every other char-acter in "The Greatest Show in the Galaxy" is that while everyone else is distracted by the spectacle of the circus itself, the Doctor is more interested in peeking behind the curtain, as it were, to discover the secret behind the show. To put it more plainly, when *Doctor Who* is at its best, the Doctor is much less interested in the *what* of strange phenomena throughout the uni-verse but in the *how* and *why*.

From a marketing standpoint, however, the trouble with focusing on the how and why of strange phenomena is that doing so makes for a more complex and therefore potentially less saleable commodity. If, for example, *Doctor Who* were reduced to the simple brutality depicted in "Vengeance on Varos" or merely provided viewers with the kind of violence implied by the offerings of the Miniscope in "Carnival of Monsters," then the program would always be as popular and marketable as pro wrestling. Yet because *Doctor Who* advances ethereal theoretical concepts and frequently attempts to untangle thorny philosophical issues, the show tends to appeal to a more select group of followers. Sure, the Daleks and Cybermen show up from time to time to blow things up and inspire a few pieces of merchandise, but by and large, even the most commercial elements of the program materialize in the service of more subtle and nuanced concepts. "The Greatest Show in the Galaxy," then, also reads as an allegory for a struggle over the very soul of *Doctor Who* in that the Psychic Circus itself represents that which the show might have become if it went down the dark path of playing to humanity's basest yet most profitable instincts.

The circus performers, the Doctor learns, long ago made a Faustian deal in which they sacrificed their own freedom for power, and the "friendly hippie circus was turned into a trap for killing people." Significantly, the former leader of the circus has been reduced to a mindless groundskeeper as a result of the deal he's struck with the Gods of Ragnarok, and his intel-ligence is locked away in a small box throughout much of the serial. What this scenario implies is that the cost of stardom is eternal idiocy and that only the simplest of shows will ever have a shot at success in the cutthroat world of television programming. Given these parameters, a complex show like *Doctor Who* could never survive, hence the Doctor's interest in restoring the circus to its former idealistic glory. After all, if he can wrest the reins of the Psychic Circus away from the Gods of Ragnarok, then there's always the potential for rescuing *Doctor Who* from those in the BBC who would reduce the show to mindless, violent sci-fi swill.

Since this is *Doctor Who*, the serial ends on a positive note: the former ringmaster gets his mind back and is restored to his proper place as leader of the circus, the Gods of Ragnarok are defeated, and the Doctor suggests that the surviving members of the original Psychic Circus go back on the road to further their efforts at bringing magic to the far corners of the universe. And although the members of the Psychic Circus ask him to join their motley crew, the Doctor declines. Never one to play second-fiddle to anybody, he knows that he has his own magic to spread through time, space and, more importantly, through the speculative worlds of imagination and potential in which all of his fans dwell at one time or another. As "The Greatest Show in the Galaxy" and other *Doctor Who* adventures like it demonstrate, what makes the Doctor a great showman is not simply his capacity to amuse or distract, but his ability to open our minds to the vast potential for awe and wonder inherent in the worlds we inhabit.

2

I Am He, and He Is Me: Why Doctor Who Is Good for You

To celebrate the program's tenth year on television in 1973, the producers of *Doctor Who* concocted a script that brought together all three actors who had assumed the lead role to date, so when "The Three Doctors" opened the show's tenth season, viewers were exposed for the first time ever to the phenomenon of the Time Lord meeting himself. To make sense of this event for the show's younger fans (who were likely of the opinion that the third Doctor—that is to say, *their* Doctor, or the one they'd grown up watching, anyway—was the *only* Doctor), the lovely Jo Grant asks *her* Doctor to explain his relationship with the funny man in the baggy trousers who has just materialized in the TARDIS control room with nothing more than the sudden appearance of a small woodwind instrument to herald his coming.

"It's all quite simple," the third Doctor says in an attempt to explain the Time Lord equivalent of coming to terms with one's past. "I am he, and he is me."

Yet even as this exchange between the Doctor and Jo evokes overtones of the Beatles' "I Am the Walrus" and its underlying vibe of peace, love and understanding, what immediately becomes clear is that the various incarnations of the Doctor are going to need a lot more than love in order to get past their differences. Rather, they're going to need counseling and a great deal of it, for far from being groovy soul brothers, the second Doctor, with his Beatles mop-top, and the third Doctor, with his Kinks and Jimi Hendrix-style sense of panache, are at loggerheads from the word *go*. In psychological terms, the two bickering personas could even be described as literal representations of dissociative identity disorder (DID) or multiple personality disorder, a condition in which two or more distinct personalities occur in the same person—but more on this later! For the time being, suffice to say that we in the audience find the Doctor's identity crisis both amusing

32

and enlightening precisely because it's all so human. Or, to put it another way, we are he, and he is us.

Not to belabor debate over the Doctor's humanity, but it's worth noting that the Doctor is himself half-human, as revealed in the ill-fated yet canonical 1996 made-for TV movie, *Doctor Who*. As such, he is perhaps more susceptible to human personality flaws than are the majority of his Time Lord brethren. Moreover, unlike his half-human, half-alien TV-land cousin, Mr. Spock of *Star Trek* fame, the Doctor doesn't repress his emotions to the point where just the hint of a smile becomes a major revelation. Sure, he may be subject to the occasional "I'm a Time Lord—I walk in eternity" fit of melancholy, and the odd anti-human oath may occasionally cross his lips, but all of those negative exclamations can be read as a form of self-loathing, which, in the final analysis, is itself a very *human* trait. And if the confessional nature of such programs as *The Jerry Springer Show* and *Dr. Phil* is any indication, then one thing we humans love to do is talk *ad nauseam* about our troubles in public, so it makes perfect sense for the Doctor to use television as the medium through which he works out many of his own issues.

One of the reasons shows like *Springer* and *Dr. Phil* are so popular is that they offer the audience at home a regular (if primitive) dose of catharsis—or, at the very least, allow us to find comfort in the fact that we're not as screwed up as the sexually insatiable nymphomaniacs, hapless cuckolds and other grossly pathetic individuals who grace those programs on a regular basis. Oddly enough, the Doctor's adventures provide a similar (albeit infinitely more nuanced) form of release: we like watching *Doctor Who* because the Doctor is as screwed up as any of us, if not more so, and watching the Time Lord work through his issues provides us with the opportunity to resonate with a like-minded soul and to gain perspective on the nagging issues that loom over our lives. The Doctor, then, serves as both scapegoat and sacrificial lamb as he accepts burdens and confronts demons that the rest of us might rather avoid altogether.

Chronic Hysterisis and the *Doctor Who* Pleasure Pattern

As a collective audience, we've been enthralled by the Doctor's adventures in various media for over four decades. On a simple level, and in a manner that can best be applied to the "classic" series, we are entertained by men in rubber suits and actors in Dalek casings chasing the Doctor through generic, polystyrene corridors. We need—nay, *demand!*—our wobbly spaceships, puppet dinosaurs, clunky giant robots, tin-foil-covered Cybermen, inflatable Maras, and loose-necked Sontarans precisely because they offer us comfort. As a result, many of us spend not just money but Herculean amounts of time and effort to keep the Doctor alive in the public consciousness. Yet just as the second and third incarnations of the Doctor never seem to get along, we fans seem to be experts at bickering as well. Whether we're arguing over which Doctor is the best, which producer left the strongest mark on the show or which villain is the most threatening, we manage to find areas of disagreement with regard to every aspect of the program. What's even more astounding, however, is that our ceaseless debates over *Doctor Who* reveal that many of us also manage to foster a love-hate relationship with the show itself.

Case in point: many of us have noted that the Doctor seems to be trapped in a state of chronic hysterisis—the condition in which his fourth incarnation, Romana and K-9 find themselves at the start of the season-eighteen serial "Meglos" when time begins to fold back on itself for no apparent reason. Also known as a time-loop, chronic hysterisis is, the Doctor informs his companions, a state in which history repeats itself *ad infinitum*—something the Doctor's adventures themselves tend to do on occasion. As most *Doctor Who* fans probably know, the formula for the majority of his adventures works like this: the TARDIS materializes, the Doctor and his companion(s) get separated, intergalactic hijinks ensue, the Doctor and his companion(s) are reunited just in time to face imminent doom, imminent doom is averted, and the Doctor and companion(s) pile back into the TARDIS to move on to their next adventure. Generally speaking, there's plenty of running through corridors thrown in for good measure as well.

Conceivably, the episode of chronic hysterisis depicted in "Meglos" may serve as wry commentary upon the show itself. After eighteen seasons, *Doctor Who* was certainly starting to show its age—hence the introduction of newly reworked theme music and opening titles at the start of the previous serial, "The Leisure Hive"—and the repetitive nature of the Doctor's adventures was very likely growing apparent. Repetition, however, is not necessarily a bad thing, as evidenced by our continuing desire to see the Doctor defeat his foes again and again in order to reassure us that he is a timeless hero. Like children who need the same story told repeatedly in order to reinforce memory pathways, we adults are also comforted by regularly hearing the same tale, spanning time and space, of one good Time Lord triumphing over evil.

Discussing why children, which the majority of us were when we started watching *Doctor Who*, enjoy oft-repeated tales, humorist Laura Lee explains that "Favorite stories evoke strong emotions, joy, excitement, and catharsis. Children want to feel those emotions again, and they know they can do so by hearing the same story."[1] Likewise, as children, we were endlessly intrigued by the Doctor and company being chased around all of creation by both ridiculous and horrifying foes. In our later and less magical years as adults, we enjoy the repeated narratives that *Doctor Who* offers us because we not only like experiencing variations on a theme but because the show takes us back to a childlike state.

Maybe, then, *Doctor Who* works as a sort of comfort food, or the audio-visual equivalent of a McDonald's Happy Meal. Oblivious to adult concerns over fat, sugar and cholesterol content, kids tend to eat fast food with reckless abandon and are rewarded for their efforts with a chintzy plastic toy that brings unparalleled joy to the little buggers for a good ten seconds of post-gorging bliss in the wake of said "meal" (using the term loosely). To recapture this joy, many adults also make the occasional late-night trip to the McDonald's drive-thru in order to buy *just one more* Happy Meal in a desperate but understandable attempt to reconnect, however briefly, with a fleeting reminder of their lost childhood.

Watching *Doctor Who* from the vantage point of adulthood is in many ways similar to consuming fast food—and is also, needless to say, much easier on the arteries. After our early years, when everyone in the neighborhood was watching whatever dross was being aired on TV at the time, being a *Doctor Who* fan was actually counter-productive to our assimilation into mainstream society. The cool in-crowd, unless we honestly considered this crowd to consist of the nearest *Doctor Who* fan club, would never acknowledge or accept our love and devotion to the show as a path to becoming one of their select number. Moreover, no potential love interest would be impressed or seduced by our knowledge of arcane *Who* lore or the exact number of times K-9 said *affirmative* over the course of his tenure as the Doctor's loyal if sometimes aggravating robot dog. Nonetheless, whether we've been consistent in our devotion to the show or—like prodigal fans—have strayed into big-budget Hollywood territory only to return, emotionally destitute, begging for reliable and satisfying storytelling in the House of Who, we find solace and continuity in the television adventures of the mysterious man from Gallifrey.

Some of us, of course, rationalize our viewing of *Doctor Who* by claiming that we do so for the sometimes high-caliber British acting, which has its pedigree in a nation of theater, but all of the program's fabulous regulars and guest stars would probably be the first to say that although they enjoyed working on the show, none of them would consider their performances therein the finest of their careers. Others of us, additionally, may swear that we love *Doctor Who* because it is knowingly campy and kitsch, that its stories are clever nudge-nudge, wink-wink pastiches of literary and television conventions from horror, romance and adventure genres. But the fact remains that we always need new *Who* coming down the pipeline in one form or another (but preferably through the medium of television) because it is, in fact, repetitive.

To explain why we need the kind of repetition that *Doctor Who* provides, literary critic J. Hillis Miller notes, "If we need stories to make sense of our experience, we need the same stories over and over to reinforce that sense making. Such repetition perhaps reassures by the reencounter with the form the narrative gives to life. Or perhaps the repetition of a rhythmic pattern is intrinsically pleasurable, whatever that pattern is. The repetitions within the pattern are pleasurable in themselves, and they give pleasure when they are repeated."[2] And, indeed, we do receive pleasure from the repeated experience of the Doctor's adventures and from the fantasy world to which they offer us access. In other words, we can call the Doctor's adventures fictions, but something about them strikes us as not only inherently true but as intrinsically good as well.

But we can only sit on the sidelines and watch the new series in the hope that he'll encounter old foes so that we can receive a nostalgic thrill that will allow us to connect, however briefly, with our childhood selves. Even if this devotion to the show offers only diminishing returns, we keep watching—but not just for the thrill of returning to a childlike state. In fact, half the pleasure of watching the Doctor repeat himself derives from watching him change ever so slightly from one iteration of his story to the next.

Remixing the Formula

Like the techno DJ who spins old digital beats into a seemingly new harmonic convergence for hard-core, pacifier-sucking ravers and experimenting poseurs, the producers of the new series may be just remixing old Who story tropes to please rabid long-term fans and to ensure high ratings from the greater secular viewing audience (*i.e.*, non-devotees of the Church of Who). For an example of recycled story beats that yield repeated pleasure in the act of their "retelling," we can dissect the 2006 series two-part finale: "Army of Ghosts" and "Doomsday." This successful storyline features two cybernetic races (the Daleks and Cybermen) battling head to head for total control of the universe. It also introduces the mysterious Genesis Ark, depicts the Doctor committing necessary genocide upon both species of cyborg by sucking them into a void, and ends with a tear-filled goodbye that demonstrates the Doctor's more-than-platonic affection for his companion, Rose. Yet despite offering TV audiences their first-ever glimpse of the long-awaited battle between Daleks and Cybermen, this climactic pair of episodes matches the seventh-Doctor serial "Remembrance of the Daleks" beat-for-beat.

Where the Daleks battle the Cybermen in the more recent epic couplet, so-called Imperial Daleks battle Rebel Daleks in "Remembrance of the Daleks." Similarly, the Genesis Ark, a piece of mysterious Gallifreyan technology upon which the fate of the universe hinges in "Army of Ghosts" and "Doomsday," is preceded by the Hand of Omega, yet another piece of mysterious Gallifreyan technology upon which the fate of the universe hinges in "Remembrance of the Daleks." The British Army of "Remembrance" finds its analogue in Torchwood in "Army of Ghosts" and "Doomsday," and just as the Doctor uses the Hand of Omega to destroy the Daleks' home planet Skaro in the former story, he defeats the Daleks and Cybermen in the latter using the Genesis Ark. What's more, where Davros appears to be the sole survivor of the Dalek massacre in "Remembrance of the Daleks," the Supreme Dalek manages to escape the void at the conclusion of "Doomsday."

More than likely, these comparisons are fairly obvious to anyone who's seen both adventures, and many fans can probably point out that "Remembrance of the Daleks" echoes the classic third Doctor-UNIT-alien threat formula in which a mysterious force threatens Earth only to be defeated by the Doctor and the boys from the United Nations Intelligence Taskforce. At the same time, however, we would be remiss if we failed to point out one other replicated trope: the tenth Doctor's emotional reaction to losing Rose's companionship at the conclusion of "Doomsday" is also reminiscent of the third Doctor's reaction to Jo leaving him for a man she deems to be a younger version of him, Professor Cliff Jones, at the end of "The Green Death." In the story perhaps unfairly referred to as "the one with the maggots," the third Doctor, obviously disturbed by Jo's departure from his life, appears before the camera with a please-feel-sorry-for-me look and then drives off in Bessie. But, even if he's crying on the inside as many of us have theorized over the years, we don't see one lachrymose emission (i.e., tear). Of course, coming from an era built upon the traditions of James Bond and the cinematic tough guy, the third Doctor knows that a hero never cries or shows emotional weakness for too long. By the time of "Doomsday," however, the heroic paradigm has shifted to something more feminine, something more emotionally healthy.

In early interviews upon first landing the role of the Doctor, Christopher Eccleston remarked that since the Doctor has two hearts, he risks the chance of having them broken twice as hard. While Eccleston never had the chance to demonstrate the full effects of a twice-destroyed Time Lord heart since he only served one brief but memorable season in the role, it would be David Tennant who had the honor of showing us the full emotional gravitas of the Doctor's grief when the tenth Doctor sheds two long-trailing tears at end of the story which may someday be referred to as "the one with Cybermen and Daleks." Left with the tragic realization that he will forever be separated from Rose, the woman to whom (we guess and hope) he was about to profess his feelings of true love, the Doctor finally lets us see some emotion.

Since we are now accustomed to seeing people break down on both reality TV programs and scripted dramas, it's now okay for us to see our hero (in this case, a centuries-old emotionally repressed Time Lord) break down and shed a tear or two. As those of us inclined to retain a smidgen of the essential intellectual nuggets that are afforded us according to a traditional liberal-arts education can attest, the role of tragedy, best realized by the Greeks with their tragic heavy-hitter Oedipus Rex, is to offer up a hero's worst-case scenario, one we recognize or have experienced to some extent, so we can achieve a vicarious emotional release in the form of the catharsis. Thus, the Doctor's apparent irreversible separation from the woman he loves may mirror the very heartbreak or emotional pain of our own lives. As the Doctor moves on with his life, we too are given instruction and guidance for moving past our own heartbreak, and so the show, regardless of its formulaic traditions, still manages to touch us.

Consequently, we must ask ourselves: *Is formula so bad?*

If something ain't broke, should we try to fix it with so-called modern TV-storytelling techniques? The new series may be more psychologically driven in terms of character development and more soap-operatic as a whole, but it still delivers spine-tingling thrills for both a new generation of children and the inner child in each of us. More importantly, as the Doctor continues to retread seemingly old ground, he also manages to change with the times and thereby grow as an individual—which goes a long way toward explaining why successive Doctors can't seem to agree on much of anything whenever they bump into each other.

Contact!—Multi-Doctor Reintegration

Unlike those of us who live in an unbroken linear manner, the Doctor has encountered alternate versions of himself on several occasions, and because the personality of each incarnation is in many ways formed by the values and attitudes of his day, he tends not to get along with himself when such meetings occur. From a purely nostalgic perspective, most fans agree that all three stories where the Doctor encounters his past selves are classics (due, no doubt, to the bickering that such encounters engender), but the general consensus among fans seems to be that the stories themselves contain simplistic, contrived plots that work solely as vehicles to bring the Doctors together. This being the case, characterization is of primary importance in these tales, and an analysis of the Doctor's (or Doctors') character in these apparently unsophisticated multi-Doctor stories reveals that due to the ever-changing nature of his personality, his most significant journeys may well be those in which he seeks himself.

The so-called First Law of Time decrees that a Time Lord should never encounter oneself while exploring time and space. Rather than viewing this supreme Time Lord law as crucial for the protection of the fabric of all reality, we should begin by thinking of it as a guarantor of guilt-free travel across time and space. Consider, for example, a curious, time-and-dimension-gallivanting Time Lord taking a trip through the galaxy in order to lose himself in the universe. For the sake of argument, let's say he's in one of his later regenerations and quite content with his present self. If, however, this otherwise happy Time Lord stumbles upon a past or future self, his blissful state will deteriorate faster than you can say *The Terrible Zodin* because A) the other self's presence shows the Time Lord that he once did, or will, possess traits that are rude and annoying, or B) the current Time Lord sees, but most likely denies, that the other self is a more refined, dynamic version of himself.

The Time Lords have therefore wisely erected a law that generally obviates any single Time Lord's potentially embarrassing or upsetting encounters with alternate incarnations. While none of us who live in a linear fashion have to deal with the anxiety that would result from literally encountering our past selves, we occasionally, according to some psychologists, tend to repress our own memories and deny other people's recollections of our past behavior. Like the newly regenerated fifth Doctor unraveling his predecessor's long burgundy scarf, we humans have been known to rip up old photos, throw away old clothing and possessions, and construct rose-tinted, revisionist models of who we used to be in order to fool the rest of humanity into believing that we're happy, well-adjusted individuals. When we are reminded of our ungainly past selves, moreover, we sometimes react with denial and anger. This is not to say that we fail to mourn or appreciate kinder, gentler, and more innocent incarnations of ourselves, but that, for the most part, regret and a sense of loss always coexist with our more positive emotions.[3]

Earlier in this chapter, we mentioned that the multi-Doctor stories suggest that the Doctor may, in some ways, suffer from DID or, as it is more popularly called, multiple personality disorder. The application of this theory, of course, does not say that the Doctor is always experiencing this disorder; with the exception of post-regenerative trauma (which we'll tackle in a moment), the Doctor is generally a stable individual who can keep his head centered while dealing with even the most mind-bending hallucinations and vicious attacks upon his psyche. What this theory does intimate, however, is that the enemy who most unsettles the Time Lord is *himself*, which goes a long way toward explaining why an identity crisis ensues when the first three Doctors meet in the generically titled "The Three Doctors."

According to the American Psychological Association, DID is at work when "two or more distinct, unique personalities exist in the same individual, and there is severe memory disruption concerning personal information about the other personalities."[4] The symptom of "severe memory disruption" immediately explains why the third Doctor is genuinely surprised to see his second incarnation appear before him in the TARDIS console room during episode one of the serial. After all, if he does possess all of his second incarnation's memories, wouldn't the third Doctor nonchalantly accept the former persona's materialization in the TARDIS as if he were an expected dinner guest? The apparent solution to this quandary is that he has (temporarily, at least) forgotten the self-reunion he's experiencing as events in the serial unfold.

While this solution preserves the agency of each Doctor in terms of the overall timeline, it also creates anxiety, tension and disagreement between the second and third Doctors. To be perfectly accurate, however, the third Doctor elsewhere proves uncomfortable with encountering even other iterations of his current persona. In the "Day of the Daleks," the third Doctor and Jo, while doing work on the TARDIS console in his lab, are suddenly faced with their future selves. Instead of politely greeting his near-future self, the Doctor asks, "Oh no, what are you doing here?" He then proceeds to gripe to his future self: "This won't do at all; we can't have two of us running about." Consequently, if the third Doctor cannot abide the presence of his current self (with whom he obviously has so much in common), then he must definitely loath any former persona, such as his second incarnation, whose personality and interests differ greatly from his own.

As a result of the second and third Doctors' escalating belligerence toward each other, the Time Lords pull the first Doctor from his time stream. Unfortunately, the first incarnation cannot physically interact with the others, as he's caught in a time eddy (which may be to their advantage since he's later just as argumentative with them both when they all meet again in "The Five Doctors"), but both of his future selves respect him, and he can advise them via the TARDIS monitor. Borrowing psychological terminology once more, we can say that the essentially disembodied first Doctor then operates as a *host personality*, who, as is usually the case in instances of DID, sits in the metaphorical driver's seat for the largest percentage of time.

The first Doctor, as the host personality-cum-mediator, reminds his future selves that they have to work together as one if they are going to succeed in their mission to solve the mystery of the black hole that's threatening their universe. Additionally, it is he who encourages his second incarnation to follow the third Doctor into the black hole at the heart of the adventure. The second Doctor, while imprisoned with his successor in the megalomaniacal Omega's fortress in the anti-matter universe, is then given the opportunity to make nice with his future self as the two combine their mental might to will into existence the small door through which they escape. The third Doctor's congratulatory reply of "Well done!" to his for-mer(ly) loathed self, reciprocated by the second Doctor's "I couldn't possi-bly have done it without you!" shows that there is hope for all of us self-haters.

The verbal medium for this emotional breakthrough is the word *Con-tact!* With this simple word, the two Doctors are able to set aside their differences and find common ground by succeeding together in an impor-tant task. A single, fully integrated third Doctor, not divided in three, may have been able to singularly will a door into existence, yet he grows as an individual by learning to work with himself. Later, the third Doctor gains a total immersion into himself, as *Contact!* is the spoken catalyst for all three of his incarnations as they mentally reintegrate their respective selves in a telepathic conference that grants them the power to defeat Omega and to return to the positive-matter universe.

Most importantly, we the viewers can personally identify with this moment of *Contact!* since there's so much in our own lives that we tend to forget—until, that is, third parties remind us of that which has slipped our minds or we catch up with our old selves by paging through journals and photo albums. As with the Doctor, such "reunions" can be traumatic, but at the same time, they can also be informative and, if "The Three Doctors" is any indication, liberating as well. By the story's end, while he still agues with his second incarnation, the third Doctor has nonetheless learned to respect his former self and has therefore validated a part of his past for which he may have once felt emotions of shame and embarrassment. Along similar lines, we, too, can follow the Doctor's lead by coming to peace with our own pasts and acknowledging that our "former" selves, regardless of their flaws, have shaped us into the people we are today.

Into the Labyrinth

Multiple Doctors next come together in "The Five Doctors," which, like "The Three Doctors," is a story concocted to mark a major milestone for the program: this time around, twenty years on television. As the tale com-mences, the Doctor and his companions are visiting the Eye of Orion for some well-earned peace and tranquility. Ironically, however, it is in the hal-cyon atmosphere of the Eye that the Doctor starts feeling "great chunks of

[his] past detaching themselves like melting icebergs" from his psyche. As his former incarnations continue to be snatched from his life, the Doctor laments, "I am being diminished, whittled away piece by piece. A man is the sum of his memories ... a Time Lord even more so."

The Doctor's comments in this instance offer some degree of insight into what happens to any given incarnation of the Time Lord when a fragmentation of his past occurs: rather than simply losing his memory, he has it forcibly removed from his person. As a result, each incarnation of the Doctor can encounter his other selves "for the first time" without the cumbersome presence of layered and competing memories presenting the same details from different vantage points. Otherwise (that is, if the Doctor were to retain all of his memories), each incarnation's vision of events might work in a manner akin to multi-angle camera shots and therefore prove terribly confusing. As it stands, however, the Doctor can approach the predicament of a multi-persona reunion in a way that is unfettered by too many memories and eliminates the potential for feeling trapped by his obligation to maintain his predestined role in events that have yet to unfold. More to the point, having his memories ripped away gives the Doctor yet one more opportunity to get to know himself.

In "The Five Doctors," Doctors one, two, three, and five enter a labyrinth of sorts—the Death Zone on Gallifrey, whose physical terrain offers the Doctor's various incarnations one more opportunity to come together for the purpose of reaffirming the Time Lord's mental cohesion and moral clarity. While mazes have certainly played a major role in other *Doctor Who* adventures—most notably in the form of the Exxilon city in "Death to the Daleks," the path leading to Sutekh's tomb in "Pyramids of Mars," and the Nimon's base in "The Horns of Nimon"—the labyrinth that is Gallifrey's Death Zone is slightly different.

Historically, the maze has been viewed as a literal and figurative representation of the human mind, and one entering or thrown into a maze must physically explore the environment, usually running into one dead-end or trap after another before either failing to find the egress or making a successful escape. Yet where a maze includes dead-ends, a labyrinth serves as an intricate path through which one walks in order to reach an inevitable center. Thus, in "The Five Doctors," the term *labyrinth* is an apt term for describing the landscape of the Death Zone insofar as the Doctor overcomes all obstacles in order for all of his personas to reach their (pre-ordained?) destination in the chamber of Rassilon's tomb.

To further complicate this analysis, we can say that the labyrinth of the Death Zone is a physical analogue for the labyrinth that is the fragmented Doctor's brain, and that by walking the twisting path that is the labyrinth, the Doctor works toward becoming whole again—a phenomenon we can read in light of the "New-Age" trend of building backyard labyrinths. Having constructed such a structure, a person wishing to meditate enters the path and ponders the situation that requires thought and a possible solution. As one gradually approaches the center, one should also come closer to the heart of one's problem. Likewise, as the Doctors come closer to their goal of entering Rassilon's tomb, they are both unraveling the mystery of why they've been placed in the Death Zone and working towards reuniting their splintered selves.

Significantly, the first, second, and third Doctors all choose separate paths to enter the tomb. Following the dictates of an old Gallifreyan nursery rhyme—*Who unto Rassilon's Tower would go, must choose: above, between, below*—the first Doctor chooses to pursue the most direct entrance to the Dark Tower; the second, the caves beneath the tower; and the third, the tower's roof. One explanation for this three-pronged approach to the Dark Tower could be that on a subconscious or telepathic level, these Doctors are able to communicate with one another. Alternately, Doctors two and three may also possess a rudimentary, buried version of the first Doctor's memories of his adventure in the Death Zone, and this memory tells them to choose the "below" and "above" options since their first and weaker self is gently strolling through the tower's front door.

Within the Dark Tower, Doctors two and three continue to demonstrate that they somehow know they've been there before. When Tegan is afraid to proceed through the Tower's corridors, the first Doctor tells her to just ignore her fears since, "Fear itself is largely an illusion, and at [his] age, there's little left to fear." At the same time, in different parts of the Tower, the third Doctor is able to dispel the illusions of Liz Shaw and Mike Yates, and the second Doctor realizes that the appearance of Jamie and Zoe is a mental deception. In the case of these two companions, the second Doctor declares, "It's a matter of memory," before concluding that they couldn't be real since most of Jamie and Zoe's memories of their travels with him were erased by the Time Lords at the conclusion of "The War Games."

In the end, the reprisal of the *Contact!* telepathic communion at the conclusion of this anniversary tale helps the Doctors reassemble their mental might in order to fight President Borusa's mindblock over the fifth Doctor and, by extension, free themselves as well. Listening to the first Doctor's command, "Concentrate: we must be one!" the Doctors proceed to successfully free their newest self from the grip of the power-mad Lord President and stand united as a reintegrated whole against Borusa, who goes on to receive Rassilon's nightmarish "gift" of immortality. On one hand, Rassilon declares that "he who wins shall lose," and Borusa falls neatly into this category when his soul, to all appearances, becomes trapped in stone. On the other hand, meanwhile, the Doctor receives the flipside of this decree, as he who loses wins insofar as the errant Time Lord manages to maintain his renegade lifestyle.

If we can manage to squeeze any life lessons out of this anniversary tale, we can recognize that our own family and school reunions are quite similar to the Doctor's reunion with his past selves in that such reunions, despite reminding us of how great or foolish we once were, work as reminders of how much we have grown and evolved since we last saw our old friends or relatives. More importantly, the Doctor can, by the conclusion of "The Five Doctors," sweep away any self-doubt he may have harbored concerning his current incarnation's worthiness, as evidenced when he announces, "I'm definitely not the man I was—thank goodness!"

Ultimately, then, we can say that, aside from the groups of bullying Cybermen, a murderous Raston Warrior Robot, electrified checkerboard floors, phantom illusions of the mind, a Dalek, a Yeti, a morally confused Master, and one megalomaniacal Lord President, the Death Zone is actually quite therapeutic for the Doctor, ironically functioning as a psychological Gallifreyan Club Med.

Snap!

The most recent multi-Doctor story to date, the "The Two Doctors," presents Doctors two and six encountering one another simply because they have, by chance, crossed each other's paths. On this occasion, the Time Lords haven't directly plucked the second Doctor out of his time stream, but they are still manipulating the Doctor(s) and events to influence the outcome of the time-travel experiments of a pair of scientists named Kartz and Reimer. Because the Time Lords are acting more subtly than usual in this adventure, previously established explanations for the Doctor's amnesia do not apply. Instead, we learn that the sixth Doctor doesn't remember the time he spent on space station Camera or in Spain during his second incarnation because the villainous Joinson Dastari has used the drug Siralanomode, one of "the Anomode group," to render that earlier incarnation unconscious. Because one of the side effects of the fictitious Siralanomode is that it affects memory, the second Doctor's recollection of this episode of his life is wiped clean as a result of being given the drug. Freed from the shackles of memory, the sixth Doctor can enjoy this adventure with his past persona. At the same time, however, he is literally coming to realize the truth of philosopher George Santayana's wise words: "Those who cannot remember the past are condemned to repeat it."

Upon running into each other, the two Doctors simultaneously speak a single word—Snap!—to indicate that they share the same mind. Though not as elegant as *Contact!* this exclamation serves a similar function in that it cements the relationship between Doctors two and six, demonstrating that they are indeed a single being. When the two Doctors find themselves locked up in a wine cellar, they simultaneously speak the same line to Peri: "Can you reach that wheelchair?" While two characters speaking the same line at once is a commonplace tradition in the sphere of slapstick comedy, well-informed *Doctor Who* fans enjoy the joke on a deeper level: not only is the Doctor repeating his own past, but he's repeating it as it's occurring right in front of him! In many ways, however, this repetition of the past is reassuring, for even though the Doctor has forgotten his past, he repeats it with relish. In other words, what "The Two Doctors" demonstrates is that given a pair of identical situations, Doctors two and six would respond not merely in similar ways, but in *exactly the same way.* Which is to say that despite their apparent differences—fashion sense being the most obvious among them—the Doctors are indeed parts of a largely consistent whole, and that after changes upon changes, the good Doctor remains more or less the same.

Or does he?

Although the multi-Doctor adventures generally suggest that the Doctor is consistently heroic and noble, many elements of *Doctor Who* lore cast doubt upon our hero's inherent goodness. As early as "The Brain of Morbius," we are given hints that the televised progression of the Doctor from his first incarnation to his fourth may not represent all of the mysterious Time Lord's lives. In this story's depiction of the Doctor engaging in a mental wrestling match with the evil Morbius, each combatant calls upon memories of past selves in order to destroy the opponent's mind. As the contest rages on, the visual representations of their conflict show the Doctor and Morbius reaching further and further back toward previous selves for strength, but if we evenly distribute the memories we are given, then the Doctor is not in his fourth incarnation at this point (as is generally accepted) but is instead in his twelfth.

The Doctor's other faces were in reality provided by the show's production staff—the result of a little in-joke at the time of filming. Basically, producer Philip Hinchcliffe and company joyfully experienced the luxury of not having to take the show's continuity as seriously as they would if they were still producing the show a mere five or so years later, which was around the time when the fans started to emerge from behind their couches and permanently sit down upon their cushions in their full, pimply faced critical modes. So, as a direct result of Hinchcliffe's playfulness, a throwaway scene has become a source of ceaseless debate among the program's continuity cops.

A psychological reading of "The Brain of Morbius" may suggest that the Doctor is suffering from amnesia or repressed memories, but examining the conundrum presented in this serial is probably more interesting if we attempt to solve the issue using the "Other," a character obliquely mentioned in "Silver Nemesis." If what is known as the "Cartmel Master Plan," a term attributed to script editor Andrew Cartmel's ultimate but unrealized vision for the show during the McCoy era, had been completed, we may have eventually learned that the Doctor, through the Gallifreyan birthing technology of "the Looms," is a reincarnation of the "Other," as revealed in the final New Adventure novel, *Lungbarrow*, written by Marc Platt. This novel is non-canonical and apocryphal since it argues that the Doctor was born from the Looms, while the story set directly after it—the 1996 TV Movie—reveals the Doctor's mother to be a human. Platt's novel can also be viewed as a misplaced attempt to restore a sense of mystery to a character who had perhaps become too human and predictable over the years, but its commentary on the Other is nonetheless interesting and applicable to our theory.

According to the novel, the Other, one of the three most significant figures in Time Lord history, along with Rasillon and Omega, helped transform Gallifrey into a time-travel empire. To protect their new empire, the triumvirate invented such mass weapons of vast universal destruction as the Hand of Omega and the Nemesis Statue. The fact then, that the Doctor has access to these ancient weapons in "Remembrance of the Daleks" and "Silver Nemesis," somewhat links him to the Other. Dialogue alluding to the Other in the television show proper, however—one instance, a filmed scene in "Remembrance of the Daleks" hinting that the Doctor is "more than just a Time Lord," and the second, a scripted scene at the end of "Survival," where the Master realizes that the Doctor is not the man he thought he knew—were deleted or excised from their respective episodes. Only one piece of dialogue, which could be regarded as circumstantial evidence of the Doctor also being the Other, remains in "Silver Nemesis." This telling revelation occurs when Lady Peinforte threatens to reveal the Doctor's secrets to Ace, secrets given to her by the Nemesis statue, by asking, "Doctor who? Have you never wondered where he came from? Who he is? ... I shall tell them of Gallifrey—tell them of the Old Time, the time of chaos."

If indeed the Doctor was present at the Old Time in the form of the Other, then we can link the Other's many incarnations to him. Therefore, returning to the fourth Doctor's various pre-first-incarnation faces we see being displayed during his mind-bending contest with Morbius, we can argue that when Morbius taunts the Doctor by asking how far back he can go in their contest, how many lives he has lived, the answer may rest in the visual proof of the Doctor's past life as the Other.

But the figure of the Other is not the only dilemma the show presents to continuity-minded viewers. One can also present the case of the Valeyard.

Eventually revealed by the Master to be an amalgamation of the Doctor's darker natures, somewhere between his twelfth and final incarnations, the Valeyard spends the majority of the sixth-Doctor serial "The Trial of a Time Lord" attempting to prove that the Doctor is himself quite villainous. On one hand, much of the evidence the Valeyard produces in his efforts at sidelining the Doctor is false, but on a more disturbing level, the mere presence of the Valeyard suggests that the Doctor does indeed have a dark side.

In the final episode of "The Trial of a Time Lord," our hero follows his foe into the Matrix and asks the Valeyard why he has gone to such extraordinary lengths in his efforts to kill him. To this query, the Valeyard proudly replies, "Come now, Doctor, how else can I obtain my freedom, operate as a complete entity, unfettered by your side of my existence? Only by ridding myself of you and your misplaced morality, your constant crusading.... Only by releasing myself from the misguided maxims you nurture can I be free."

Could we find a better case of self hatred?

Not only does the Valeyard loath his past as a goody two-shoes, but he also wants to obliterate all memories of his altruistic self for regenerations seven through twelve! In this respect, the Valeyard serves as a literal representation of Carl Jung's theory of the Shadow, which postulates that all of us have a dual, darker nature that we repress (most of the time, anyway) from ourselves and society. By the climax of "The Trial of a Time Lord," however, the Valeyard is letting his wicked, shadowy self run wild, and, since he's already dressed in black for the part and eager to wreak havoc upon his brighter half, we can also conclude that the Valeyard is the living embodiment of the Doctor's own self-hatred. Just imagine a scenario in which a violent schizophrenic's selves could be divided and placed in a locked room together, and you can probably begin to understand both the sixth Doctor's and the Valeyard's plight when facing one another.

Fortunately, however, not all of the Doctor's potential selves foreshadow the evil of the Valeyard. For example, we learn in the seventh-Doctor serial "Battlefield" that a future incarnation of the Doctor adopts the guise of Merlin the Magician on a parallel Earth as he fights on the side of Arthur and the Britons against the armies of Morgaine. Applying T.H. White's vision of Merlyn from *The Once and Future King*, a modern reworking of Sir Thomas Mallory's *Le Morte d'Arthur*, to this mysterious Doctor, we can say that the Doctor, like White's Merlyn, is virtually living his life backwards. This comparison, however tenuous, may work, since we know that the Doctor, particularly his seventh persona, sometimes has the benefit of knowing his future actions before he commits them. Thus, for the Doctor, possessing knowledge of events that are destined to come to pass is the same as actually living those events. If this knowledge of future behavior is applicable to all Doctors, then we have been watching a show whose main character's actions have been "fixed" since the first episode aired.

Nonetheless, we're still stuck with the problem of the Valeyard. Where does he come from? What brings him about? What allows him to emerge from the Doctor's otherwise good-natured psyche? What, to put it bluntly, causes the Doctor to *snap*?

Although he generally appears to be well-adjusted, consider the fact that the Doctor is the same man whose personality print causes the super-computer Xoanon go insane in "The Face of Evil" and whose mind causes the Rani's composite brain to suffer from acute schizophrenia in "Time and the Rani." Moreover, the regeneration process also tends to become more difficult as Time Lords age. The Doctor, for example, claims that he and the Master were once friends, yet the disparity between their dispositions suggests that neither Time Lord would ever get along with the other. One explanation for this apparent incongruity is that while the Master may once have been as noble as the Doctor, he grew corrupt over the course of his regenerations. The same theory, in fact, could hold true for Lord President Borusa, who quickly goes from being the Doctor's esteemed mentor in "The Deadly Assassin" to a power-crazed despot in "The Five Doctors." The accumulated trauma of frequent regeneration may account for the eventual unhinging of the minds of both the Master and Borusa, and may also explain how the shadowy Valeyard emerges from the Doctor's psyche in "The Trial of a Time Lord."

Reviewing the Doctor's regenerations, we can easily see that the first occurs in order to renew a tired body. The second regeneration is forced upon the Doctor by the Time Lords, and the third is the price the Doctor pays for defeating the Great One in "Planet of the Spiders." As the Doctor convalesces after each of these regenerations, a normal period of mental upheaval follows while the Doctor's mind adjusts to the physiological and psychological rhythms of his new form. Following his fourth regeneration, a stressful one foreshadowed by the appearance of the mysterious Watcher, however, the recovery process becomes more difficult for the Doctor, and his newly born fifth incarnation requires assistance from both the TARDIS and his companions in his struggle to establish a sense of identity in "Castrovalva."

Furthermore, in "The Twin Dilemma," the newly regenerated sixth Doctor attempts to strangle Peri. The Doctor's actions in this shocking sequence perhaps can be better understood if we theorize that he's still recovering from the traumatic experience of "giving birth" to himself, and that he's suffering from something akin to post-partum depression. We can also speculate that the Doctor's seemingly erratic behavior makes a great deal of sense insofar as the reason he seems so paranoid with regard to his companion, Peri, may be that he has just sacrificed one of his lives to save her. At some level, he may even be resentful of Peri and perceive her as a continual threat to his latest chance at life, a possibility that would go a long way toward explaining his defensive, child-like manner.

The Doctor's next regeneration, apparently triggered by a blow to the head, goes rather smoothly, but we are left shaking our continuity-addled heads by the time his seventh incarnation reaches the end of its run. If the seventh Doctor is so all-knowing—indeed, the ultimate grandmaster of cosmic machinations, as he proves himself to be throughout much of his tenure—then why does he foolishly allow himself to be gunned down by San Francisco gang members outside of his own TARDIS at the beginning of the 1996 TV movie? We're talking about the same Time Lord who, in his ninth regeneration, steps out of his TARDIS to confront the Daleks and their God-Emperor in "The Parting of the Ways" without suffering so much as a scratch—yet he can't even stop Dr. Grace Holloway, who is obviously not versed in the intricacies of Gallifreyan physiology, from operating upon his two hearts and causing his temporary death!

Was the seventh Doctor's demise all part of his mysterious and murky master plan, assuming there ever was one? Like a middle-aged man who trades in his old, reliable Honda for a flashy new Porsche, does the Doctor allow his aging seventh self to die in order for a younger and better-looking self to take the reins and seduce the ladies? Or, like the weakened first Doctor we see at the end of "The Tenth Planet," is he merely old and tired? All of these questions can be thrown in the pile dealing with the notion that at times in his life, the Doctor may indeed loath himself. As for the eighth Doctor's regeneration into his ninth self, our various media spin-offs and pieces of speculative fan fiction will have to pick up on that story point. By the time the ninth Doctor regenerates into the tenth, however, he has the stabilizing presence of Rose Tyler to help him remember his own truly heroic nature.

The Saga Begins Anew

In 1989, the final year of the original series of Doctor Who, BBC executives dismissed the show as being outdated, cheap, and childish. What these executives didn't take into consideration, however, was that devout fans had come to expect great things of the program's ever-developing storyline and that the cancellation of Doctor Who would do little to crush these expectations. This, of course, was neither the first nor the last time television executives would dash the hopes of sci-fi fans worldwide, and the cancellation of Doctor Who only set in motion an almost inevitable (if slow-moving) set of events that was mirrored many years earlier upon the cancellation of *Star Trek*.

When NBC cancelled *Star Trek* in 1969, the crew of the Enterprise had only completed three-fifths of its five year mission. If the show had always begun with Captain Kirk telling the audience that the Enterprise would boldly go where no man had gone before as part of a mere *three*-year mission, then there wouldn't have been a problem. The fans would have belly-ached a bit and then moved on to obsess over other realms of science fiction and fantasy. However, NBC, without foreknowledge of syndication ratings and DVD sales, pulled the plug on the show. Consequently, the fans, who felt cheated out of two years of a show whose third-season scripts largely presented a case study in diminishing returns, began organizing conventions and writing a plethora of zines. From these humble, grass-roots efforts, *Star Trek* resurrected itself more powerfully than ever with the premiere of *Star Trek: The Motion Picture*. But a continuing movie series was not enough, so *Star Trek: The Next Generation* premiered in 1987, spawning seven seasons, four films, and three more spin-off shows.

Another example of a resilient sci-fi series, albeit one that endured a longer gestation period before its revival, is found in *Battlestar Galactica*. After this show's first iteration was dropped by ABC in 1979 and its dismal, short-lived spin-off, *Galactica 1980*, was put out of its trite misery, it seemed as if Apollo and Starbuck would never fly their Vipers again. Many years later, however, the Sci-Fi channel miraculously ran a four-hour mini-series that "reimagined" the saga, resulting in Starbuck undergoing a sex change and the crew of the Galactica once more beginning their search for Earth and incessantly inserting variations of *Frak!* into their speech patterns to the point where the fans themselves now use the word in their everyday conversations. The following year, a new version of *Doctor Who* emerged as well, and a leather-jacketed ninth Doctor and his sexy companion Rose began operating in a universe brought to life by superior special effects, a spacious TARDIS set, and mature scripts that reflected the fears and dreams of our increasingly complex world. What's more, when *Doctor Who* triumphantly returned to TV screens in the spring of 2005, we were presented with a Doctor who was more of a mystery than ever.

While it is uncertain whether or not the Doctor has recently regenerated at the start of "Rose," we do catch a glimpse of him looking into a mirror in the Tylers' home and playing with his ears in a style reminiscent of the newly regenerated fourth Doctor in "Robot." He also behaves in a more manic fashion in "Rose" than in later stories, and we see him shuffling cards, speed-reading books and generally behaving like someone with Attention Deficit Disorder throughout his struggle against the Autons. Yet while this behavior may well be attributed to a recent regeneration, it could also suggest that without the steadying hand of a companion at his side, the old Time Lord tends to get a little loopy.

Let's face it: the Doctor is in top form when he's part of a double, triple, or quadruple act—a state he achieves through the presence of the inquisitive companions who accompany him on most of his journeys. Throughout the first season of the new series, the Doctor especially needs a companion in order to begin the process of coming to terms with the traumatic events of the Time War. After all, if the Doctor had continued his adventures *sans* a shoulder to cry on (as it were) after his encounter with the Nestene Consciousness in "Rose," the Time War would likely have remained an unspoken tragedy. Rose, however, is our witness and serves as our eyes and ears for the Doctor's narrative confession. Significantly, this confession establishes him as a "posttraumatic victim and storyteller," who, to borrow a phrase from psychologist Wendy Williams, has a "story to tell that oscillates between 'the unbearable nature of an event and the unbearable nature of its survival.'"[5]

Essentially, Rose serves as a worthy recipient to hear the narrative of the Doctor's pain, lending credence to theory that, in the words of Williams, "the trauma victim surrenders his or her story to the right audience."[6] Accordingly, over the course of the 2005 series, we learn through Rose that the Doctor was the only member of his race to survive the Time War, and that he was also responsible for the apparent destruction of both the Daleks and his own people. By the end of the first season, however, the Doctor has worked through many of his lingering demons, and even the surprise return of his longtime foes the Daleks is not enough to get him down.

Although the Doctor is certainly willing to sacrifice himself—to enact the ultimate gesture of heroism—in order to finally destroy the last of the Daleks at the end of "The Parting of the Ways," it is Rose who ultimately puts an end to the intergalactic menace by harnessing the power of Time Vortex to disintegrate the Dalek army. This move, however, proves nearly fatal to Rose, and the Doctor returns the favor by kissing her on the lips and absorbing the power of the Vortex into his own body. Symbolically, this gesture suggests that the Doctor has finally—after a season of extreme emotional caution—let his guard down completely and allowed himself to connect with another individual. Simultaneously, the metaphoric act of sucking the Time Vortex into himself through the act of a kiss that is more life-giving and indicative of agape or selfless love than any erotic or romantic meaning reaffirms the Doctor's life mission to be a protector of all life throughout time and space. Dying with a selfless smile on his face, the ninth Doctor sets the stage for his next incarnation, one who is largely free from the emotional baggage and trauma of his predecessor.

This instance of emotional cleansing and rebirth does not mean that the tenth Doctor has nothing to learn, but that the issues he must address are substantially less traumatic than those addressed by his previous incarnation. Nonetheless, he still must deal with his growing feelings for Rose and the constant, nagging knowledge that he is virtually immortal compared to her. And so it is that by the climax of "Doomsday," when Rose admits that she loves the Doctor and we finally see a Time Lord cry, we begin to recognize that he is finally growing up—and perhaps that we in the audience are growing up as well.

3

Brave Hearts: The Identity Dance of Doctor and Companion

The dramatic pairing of the Doctor and his companions is as important to the show as the concept of regeneration.[1] On average, every season or so, a naive young woman (or man, on occasion), wanders into the Doctor's blue box to offer us a fresh perspective on the wonders of traveling through time and space. Identifying with the Doctor's companions in many ways, we view these novice time travelers as our avatars or representatives in the fictional world of *Doctor Who*—hence the propensity for characters ranging from Ian Chesterton to Rose Tyler to force the Doctor to explain himself or to work through the often mind-bending logic of the Doctor on their own. Yet even as these companions serve a practical dramatic purpose, they tend to get in the Doctor's way and frequently turn out to be more trouble than they're worth—which begs the question of whether the Doctor truly needs his companions, and if so, why?

If we disregard any of the non-televised spin-off adventures produced between 1989 and 2005, we can argue that the Doctor has been flying solo for quite some time. At the conclusion of the 1996 television movie, the Doctor dematerializes without picking up any new companions, and at the start of "Rose," he's still doing his best to avoid any personal entanglements. Furthermore, judging by the way he almost single-handedly saves Gallifrey in "The Deadly Assassin," we can also surmise that he has the capacity to save the entire universe on his own under any circumstances if he were so inclined.

Apparently, however, he is *not* so inclined.

The Doctor, it seems, is a co-dependent person at the core of his two hearts and secretly needs his companions to need him. To better understand why the Doctor pathologically requires the company of others, we can look at the character of Victor Mancini in Chuck Palahniuk's *Choke*. Victor, who has been raised entirely by his single mother, feels obligated to pay her $3,000-a-month hospital bills. Consequently, he has dropped out of medical school and earns the money he needs to support his mom by pretending that he's choking on food in swanky upscale restaurants. His wealthy rescuers, in turn, not only "save" his life but continue their relationship with him afterwards by sending him birthday cards and cash gifts. During one such choking-scam episode, Victor rationalizes his behavior thusly: "Why I do this is to put adventure back into people's lives.... Why I do this is to make money.... You gain power by pretending to be weak. By contrast, you make people feel strong. You save people by letting them save you."[3]

With the exception of the need for money, Victor's words could easily be attributed to the Doctor, since our favorite Time Lord allows people who have no prior experience with time and space adventuring to travel with him. We must remember, more importantly, that the Doctor is over nine-centuries old and that his average companion has been alive for less than a quarter-of-a-century. Regardless of this centuries-wide gulf in age and experience, however, the unspoken contract between Doctor and companion is that the arrangement should be mutually beneficial. The Doctor can help his companions learn about themselves and gain a sense of empowerment as a result of their contributions to his adventures, and, in a reciprocal fashion, the companions make the Doctor feel good about himself because they can easily be (or at least pretend to be) impressed by his vast store of knowledge and his boundless courage. In the various permutations of our relationships with friends, families and lovers, are the rest of us any different?

The Doctor's Many Hats

Over the span of his various lives, the Doctor assumes roles that are shaped by his personality and the personalities of his companions. In sociological terms, people frequently hold more than one role at once; we can be both children and parents, lovers and enemies, protégés and mentors at the same time. From a cultural perspective, we can also say that the writers of each Doctor's era inject personality traits into the titular character that reflect the respective mores and trends of their times. As a result, an examination of the numerous roles the Doctor adopts and assumes in relation to his companions can show us how he evolves from being inspiringly avuncular to a skillful player:

- Favorite Uncle: The Doctor often assumes the duties of an uncle or mentor as he protects his younger companions and allows them to expand their horizons by traveling with him. The first Doctor's relationship with Vicki, the second Doctor's warm connection with Victoria and Zoe, the third Doctor's protective attitude towards Jo and Sarah Jane, and the seventh Doctor's tutelage of Ace all serve as fine examples of the Doctor's avuncular attitude. Likewise, the familiar mentor-protégé dynamic of the Doctor-companion construct can also be found in the manner in which he treats Leela and Nyssa. Ultimately, it is the Doctor's role as mentor or beloved uncle figure that many fans believe to be an expression of the Time Lord at his best.

- Teacher: The Doctor can also be considered a teacher, particularly with regard to the vagaries of time travel. The first step to becoming fluent in a Time Lord's lifestyle is for one to be invited into, wander innocuously aboard or stow away in the TARDIS. The second step involves having the TARDIS's telepathic field, to paraphrase Rose Tyler, muck about one's brain in order to grant the ability to understand and speak alien tongues. From here, all that's left is to find a room in the TARDIS and assiduously apply oneself to becoming acclimated to a life of fighting the various and sundry forces of evil infesting all sectors of the universe while simultaneously learning when to reverse the polarity of the neutron flow and how quickly to run when the Doctor says to do so.

- Metrosexual: The pop-culture neologism *metrosexual* is often bandied about in the media to describe city-dwelling, male professionals with an eye for fine clothing, cutting-edge entertainment, and alternative lifestyles, but who, while possessing many qualities that are traditionally ascribed to women and gay men, are (surprise!) redecorating the gender closet without actually coming out of it. Since the Doctor has declared that he is a "citizen of the universe and a gentleman to boot," we can easily define him as being the definitive metrosexual. The clearest expression of this idea may well be the image of the third Doctor wearing his ubiquitous frilly shirt and velvet smoking jacket as he enjoys the wine and cheese of Sir Reginald Styles in "Day of the Daleks." Then there are the examples of the fifth Doctor in his neatly pressed Edwardian cricketer's uniform or the eighth in his totally foppish-but-remember-you-saw-him-kiss-a girl-twice fancy dress. Despite the brief period of the crew-cut, minimalist anti-fashion statement put forth by the ninth Doctor, his natural metrosexual ways are indubitably restored with his tenth incarnation's stylish and, in the words of the tenth Doctor himself, "geek chic" pin-striped suits and brown overcoat that make him look ubiquitously fashionable in any cultural or life-threatening situation.

- Cult Leader: In most religions, the spiritual leader performs rituals in front of an altar. The altar serves as both a visible link to the traditions of the faith and a reminder that the leader holds a position of power and respect. If we're going to consider the Doctor as a cult leader, then the TARDIS console makes a fine altar. Consider for a moment that the Doctor and his companions are frequently seen standing around the TARDIS console as the time rotor rhythmically rises and falls, and you'll begin to get a sense of the totemistic relationship among the Doctor, his companions and the TARDIS itself. And, even though companions may fall into skepticism or doubt when they complain that the Doctor cannot properly steer his ship, they frequently return to their "religion" after such lapses in faith, reaffirming their belief in the Doctor as they gather around his six-sided altar to bear witness as he pushes his buttons and pulls his levers in the ritualistic performance that, to the Time Lord, is the simple act of time travel.

- Mid-Lifer: No one is saying that the third Doctor, who would have fit in well with the cast of *Manchild* if the series were produced in the 1970s, is an aging loser who would disrespect his companions by hitting on them. At the same time, however, he must be aware that he's experiencing some sort of Time Lord mid-life crisis as he dresses like a younger Londoner and tears up the streets in the sporty yellow roadster he affectionately calls Bessie or in the ultra-cool Whomobile. To the average Londoner, the sight of the Doctor whizzing by in the Whomobile probably evokes nothing but pity for the old coot—until, that is, he guns the engine and makes that baby fly! Additionally, his ninth incarnation deals with his own midlife crisis by donning a weathered leather jacket in a manner that would even embarrass the most clueless dad who dreams of recapturing some modicum of coolness in the eyes of his cynical teenage children.

- Player: Thanks to series lead writer Russell T. Davies' playful reimagining of the Doctor's long-dormant libido, we can now truly enjoy the romantic machinations of a Time Lord trying to figure out if he wants to be naughty or nice. Just watch how the ninth Doctor flirts with Lynda-with-a-y in order to make Rose jealous in "The Parting of the Ways," or how the tenth Doctor ignorantly rubs his obvious affair with Madame De Pompadour in Rose's face in "The Girl in the Fireplace." And to think the Doctor behaves in this deplorable way after he's stolen her away from poor old Mickey! If Rose weren't so bedazzled by the TARDIS and the extraordinary places the Doctor takes her, she probably would have slapped his smug, polyamorous face quite early on and in a manner that would certainly have made her mother Jackie proud.

Sex and the Single Time Lord

While describing the Doctor as an interstellar player may strike some in the Cult of *Doctor Who* as a distinctly blasphemous move, doing so is not without precedent or reason. Since the first Doctor serial "The Aztecs," in which the Time Lord unwittingly proposes marriage to the aging beauty

Cameca via the Aztec courting ritual of cocoa-making, many fans have been preoccupied with the mystery of whether or not the Doctor is a sexual being. Apparently a parent at some point in his life (given the presence of his alleged granddaughter, Susan, in the original lineup of the TARDIS crew), the Doctor has clearly "known" women in the biblical sense, but children's television programs generally avoid the topic of physical relationships. Along these lines, original series producer Verity Lambert and her production team were mainly concerned with creating a show that was both entertaining and educational for children, and romance barely registered with regard to either of these prerequisites. More importantly, to apply the ick-factor, it's also conceivable that Lambert recognized the plain fact that none of us, regardless of age, really wants to see a libidinous old fart chasing all types of younger alien tail through the temporal and dimensional nooks and crannies of the universe. As a result, the Doctor's sexual leanings remain veiled throughout much of his journeys.

As the Doctor regenerates into progressively younger incarnations, the emotional inclinations of his two hearts become ever-so-slightly exposed, but any sexual tension that may exist between the Doctor and his companions remains strikingly subtle, if not sublime. When the third Doctor bids a reluctant farewell to Jo Grant at the conclusion of "The Green Death," for example, his otherwise platonic feelings for the (much) younger woman give way to what many fans rightly interpret as a broken heart. Similarly, while the sight of the fourth Doctor and Romana frolicking hand-in-hand through Paris in "City of Death" doesn't exactly ooze with sexuality, there is an undeniable sense of chemistry between the two travelers. At the same time, however, this same Doctor, in spite of being more or less viewed as an ex-boyfriend by Sarah Jane Smith in "School Reunion," also comes off as a free-spirited Bohemian too breezily preoccupied with his travels to be distracted by the scantily clad Leela after unceremoniously leaving Sarah Jane behind in "The Hand of Fear." And if Leela can't turn the Doctor's head, then what woman can?

Of course, if we analyze the Doctor's indifference to the physical temptations that Jo, Sarah Jane and Leela represent in the context of class relations, we see that these companions stand well below the Doctor on the intergalactic social scale. As a result, it's conceivable that he prevents Sarah Jane from accompanying him to Gallifrey not because of some outmoded rule stating that outsiders aren't allowed to visit but because he's simply embarrassed to be seen with her by his peers. And when he does bend the rules by allowing Leela to join him on a return visit to Gallifrey the following season, the reason he's more than happy to leave her there may well be that he expects the Time Lords to refine and shape her in their own image, thereby making her "acceptable" for entry into their class structure. As for the Doctor's latter-day romance with Rose, class has been rendered a non-issue in the newer series insofar as the destruction of his home planet means that the Doctor no longer has to fear the disapproval of his fellow Time Lords regarding passionate dalliances with alien species.[2]

Next!

Once the fourth Doctor is joined by his intellectual equal—or perhaps superior—in the form of the female Time Lord Romana, he gains increasing opportunities to follow the dictum he gives to Sarah Jane at the conclusion of "Robot": "There's no point in being grown up if you can't be childish sometimes." At the same time, however, his reactions to the potential selves Romana test-drives at the start of "Destiny of the Daleks" reveal the Doctor's libidinous side, and the scene serves as an uncanny model for the contemporary MTV dating show Next, an amped-up version of The Dating Game in which contestants reject potential mates with an indifferent Next! before moving on to subsequent suitors.

To set the scene, the fourth Doctor is conducting repairs upon K-9 when he's greeted by a regenerating Romana who has appropriated the appearance of Princess Astra, whom they met in the final story of the sixteenth season, "The Armageddon Factor." Appalled by this corporeal version of copyright infringement, the Doctor tells her to "try" another body, so she exits and quickly returns as a cute and diminutive blue female. The Doctor, however, agrees with Romana that the second body is too short and that she should lengthen it. For her third attempt at choosing a body that pleases the Doctor, Romana enters looking like an outer-space prostitute, complete with excessive make-up, gaudy jewelry, a fuzzy-collared semi-translucent robe and, to absolutely top off the tawdry look, a gold-tasseled brassiere.

"No thank you," the Doctor gasps in the dramatic whisper he reserves for both somber and semi-serious occasions. "Not today."

At this point, the audience can reasonably guess that Romana's main goal is to please the Doctor, and that the Doctor's main goal is to be pleased by Romana. But this seemingly reciprocal arrangement is decidedly lopsided, since he keeps grimacing at all of her potential bodies and rejecting them as if he were sending back an undercooked meal at the Olive Garden. This is not exactly a union of equals—but unlike his nefarious foe the Master, the Doctor doesn't have to resort to hypnotism to get someone to bend to his will. He simply uses his charisma to ensure that he gets whatever he desires from his companions, especially Romana.

But what precisely does Romana want from the Doctor? That is, why is she trying so hard to please him? Is she looking for respect? Affection?

Love? Although the Doctor certainly respected Romana's first incarnation, his affection for her over their quest for the Key to Time in season sixteen was lukewarm at best. Perhaps sensing this herself, Romana has decided by the beginning of "Destiny of the Daleks" that the Doctor will never love her the way she may love him.

Farfetched? Maybe. But why else would Romana choose to regenerate? Despite being nearly 140 years old, her first incarnation is practically a teen in Time Lord years, and she hasn't suffered a single life-threatening trauma prior to her regeneration. Perhaps, then, she regenerates out of a need for the Doctor's love—or possibly his approval. Or, at the very least, maybe she simply wants the Doctor to stop playing with his robotic dog and take notice of her for a change.

And notice her he does.

After the Doctor rejects Romana's courtesan look, she challenges his notions of beauty by appearing as a statuesque Greek beauty, toga and all.

"Too tall," the Doctor responds. "Take it away."

The it in this predictable response is quite telling since the neuter pronoun suggests that the Doctor sees Romana's body as an object or commodity that can (and should) be easily exchanged for another, more pleasing one. This utterance of it, more importantly, is given ironic significance when juxtaposed with what the Doctor tells K-9 only seconds before the statuesque version of Romana appears: "It's what's on the inside that matters. That's what's important."

Describing what Romana should be looking for in the ideal body, the Doctor opines that his fellow Gallifreyan needs "something warm and sensible, something with a bit of style and, well—style!"

And what does the Doctor's advice get him? A small, perky, feminine mirror-image of himself. Or, more accurately, a replica of Princess Astra's body concealed beneath layers of the Doctor's own bohemian attire. Sensibly recognizing at last that he can't "next" his stubborn companion yet again, the Doctor accepts Romana's new form, but her veiled attempt at turning her fellow Time Lord's head never pays off completely. Sure, there's the aforementioned hand-holding of "City of Death," and Romana does slip into a schoolgirl's uniform in the aborted "Shada," but something—perhaps a sense of cultural propriety similar to that depicted in the long-running stage play No Sex Please, We're British—always keeps the Doctor from following his instincts (for lack of a better phrase).

Then again, the Doctor's libido is subtly resurrected several seasons later when the fifth Doctor innocently flirts with the scientist Todd at the end of "Kinda." Moreover, Peter Davison was a national British heartthrob as a result of his sensitive performance as young veterinarian Tristan Farnon in All Creatures Great and Small, so his portrayal of the Doctor gave the character the appearance of an attractive and eminently available young man. It is then not accidental that producer John Nathan-Turner gave this Doctor not one, but two beautiful young female companions, and that the somewhat less eye-catching male companion, Adric, was fairly quickly killed off.

Over the course of the fifth Doctor's era, the Doctor's relationship with Nyssa naturally develops into one of common scientific interests and mutual respect, a relationship that was reinforced by both the scripts and the performances of Davison and Sarah Sutton. The chemistry between the Doctor and Tegan Jovanka, however, is another matter. Many fans theorize that the Doctor and Tegan's constant arguments belie a degree of sexual tension or the hidden fact that the two are secret lovers. To support this possibility, we have the facts that A) the Eternal Mariner in "Enlightenment" remarks that Tegan holds a special image of the Doctor in her mind, and B) Tegan gives a farewell to the Doctor in "Resurrection of the Daleks" that is more suited to a lover who wants to be with her mate but simultaneously cannot stand to be around him than to a companion who's had her fill of time travel. Given this interpretation, it's quite possible that the Doctor's oft-quoted advice to his companion in "Earthshock," "Brave heart, Tegan," refers not only to Tegan's need to stand firm against the ultimately fleeting threat of the Cybermen, but also to her need to protect herself from the potential heartbreak that could result from his unrequited feelings for her. In fact, that Tegan repeats this advice to herself after the Doctor dematerializes without her at the end of "Time-Flight" supports the notion that the phrase contains a more romantic connotation than a heroic one.

And who knows—maybe in an untelevised adventure, the Doctor and Tegan traveled to the year 2004, where Tegan picked up a copy of the popular dating tome *He's Just Not That Into You* and finally came to the realization that the Doctor was completely oblivious of her attraction to him. Thus, the departing Tegan's tears at the end of "Resurrection of the Daleks," while ostensibly falling for the carnage she's witnessed and for her sadness at leaving the Doctor, may also be an overt manifestation of her emotional and *sexual* frustration at being, time and again, passively rejected by him. What's worse for Tegan may also be the implicit knowledge that she's neither the first nor the last woman to attempt to catch the Doctor's eye.

As with the case of Philip Hinchcliffe's choice to provocatively costume Leela in animal furs, Nathan-Turner thought that dressing his companions in sexy outfits would be a guarantor for higher ratings, a strategy that culminated in the gaudy yet eye-pleasing outfits slapped upon Nicola Bryant for her role as Perpugilliam Brown. If the sixth Doctor had been more sensibly dressed, he may have looked the part of a potential romantic partner for his companion. Instead, his appearance only served to visibly exacerbate the tension between Peri and himself. This tension, moreover, gave the Doctor and Peri the appearance of an old married couple rather than a potentially (though admittedly mismatched) romantic pairing. Again, the ick-factor applies as few of us could imagine the Doctor and Peri knocking time-traveling boots (as it were) in the TARDIS. As a result, the closing scene from "The Mark of the Rani" best summarizes the nature of their relationship. When Lord Ravensworth asks the Doctor what, precisely, the Doctor and Peri do in their mysterious blue box, the Doctor replies, almost with a sigh of resignation, "Argue mainly."

Placing the utter lack of any sexual chemistry between the sixth Doctor and Peri aside, we can begin to understand Nathan-Turner's sensible decree that there should be no hanky-panky in the TARDIS, since the man was rightfully attuned to a 1980s audience's expectations for sci-fi television. This cautionary decree also tells us why Peri wears more conservative clothing for her final season, and why Mel and Ace never wear outfits that would make any of our younger, pimply selves frantically reach for the trusty pause button on our VCRs. We must also acknowledge that the thought of Mel snogging the sixth Doctor, or either Mel or Ace passionately embracing the seventh, are images our fertile imaginations should best avoid. But if companions such as Mel and Ace have no obvious physical attraction to the Doctor, then why do they travel through time and space with the mysterious and sometimes crotchety alien?

Due to sketchy scripting in "The Trial of a Time Lord" series, we will never know the exact circumstance or reasoning for why Mel joined the Doctor, but we can likely conclude that, in all probability, it was an impulsive one. Through her brief tenure with the sixth and seventh Doctors, Mel constantly reveals herself to be a screaming, giddy, hyperactive mess of a companion. More significantly, she leaves the Doctor in order to run off and explore the galaxy with Sabalom Glitz, a most untrustworthy and unscrupulous con-man if ever one existed. Ace, likewise, is equally impulsive when it comes to deciding to join the Doctor in his adventures in "Dragonfire." After helping the Doctor defeat the mad intergalactic criminal Kane in this serial, she immediately and without question accepts the Doctor's offer of a "quick spin around the twelve galaxies." This immediate acceptance of the Doctor's proposal is understandable since Ace is only sixteen and has already experienced the absolute weirdness of being plucked from her own proper time and place by a time storm and being deposited on the mysterious Iceworld depicted in "Dragonfire." The appearance of a time-traveling alien who dresses liked a fashionably hopeless middle-aged man and a prime candidate for a makeover on *Queer Eye for the Straight Guy*, then, is par for her extraordinary course. And even though Ace is young and relatively naive, she's certainly no fool since she recognizes earlier in the serial that accepting Kane's offer of a golden sovereign is, to say the least, a bad idea.

Candy from strangers, indeed!

On an obvious level, Kane's cold and intense demeanor doesn't compare with the Doctor's open and friendly one when it comes to Ace making a choice between potential mentors. But for all Ace may know, the Doctor could actually be a molester, con man, or murderer. Yet somehow Ace *knows* that she can trust the Doctor. Perhaps writer Malcolm Gladwell's theory of thin-slicing sheds light on Ace's sense of the Doctor's inherent goodness. In his best-selling book *Blink*, Gladwell explains that thin-slicing "refers to the ability of our unconscious to find patterns in situations and behavior based on very narrow slices of experience."[4] Ace, then, essentially performs the unconscious act of rapid cognition that is thin-slicing when she agrees to travel in the TARDIS, which represents a doorway to an extremely hazardous lifestyle. In other words, while she's basing her snap decision upon the brief time she's spent witnessing the Doctor serve as a heroic and wise leader during their adventure together on Iceworld, Ace's positive assessment of the Doctor is also likely influenced by past situations in which people demonstrated positive traits similar to the Time Lord's.

In the end, Ace's intuition is undoubtedly correct, for her subsequent escapades with the Doctor allow her to mature as she proves her bravery by fighting alien menaces and through facing her inner demons in serials such as "Ghost Light" and "The Curse of Fenric." The seventh Doctor, with his restless energy, also benefits from Ace's presence, because, like him, she is a rebel at heart, a trait she demonstrates as she detonates nearly everything in her path with an apparently endless supply of Nitro 9. There is a true kinship between this Doctor-companion team, and, while it exists on a kinesthetic, emotional level, it is not sexual by any means. Though constant danger is one of its prerequisites, their relationship is pure in its sincerity and contagious exuberance. It's a shame, then, that the program's premature cancellation meant that we never got to see the televised conclusion of this always dynamic and successful partnership.

Two Hearts, One Kissing Fool

By the time the 1996 television movie premiered on both British and American screens, the existence of the Doctor's sexuality could no longer be ignored. Philip Segal, the producer of the ambitious but ultimately failed attempt to resurrect the show, knew that he had to add a romantic element to the eighth Doctor's narrative—perhaps simply to establish that the Doctor was not asexual, but more likely to make the adventures of the enigmatic alien more palatable to American tastes. Yet while the dramatic convention of the hero's female love interest may allow some of us to accept the image of the Doctor kissing Grace Holloway on the lips, watching this kiss for the first time was, for many longtime fans, akin to watching a 950-year-old teenager take his first awkward steps into the confusing world of sexuality.

Fans who prefer to discard the TV movie as non-canonical disapprove of the adventure for a variety of reasons, including the likelihood that they, up until the Doctor's first kiss, could readily identify with a hero who never got it on with the ladies because they themselves had never scored. Within the gay community, moreover, fans of the show objected to the movie's obliteration of the image of the Doctor as a gay icon. To them—like a generation of gloriously gay glam rockers who felt betrayed when David Bowie famously, or infamously, admitted that he (*gasp!*) was actually attracted to women in the May 12, 1983, issue of *Rolling Stone*, which contained three simple but sobering words in large bold print letters: David Bowie Straight—the party was over and the demands of the so-called heterosexual majority were firmly if perhaps unfairly applied to the status-quo-enforcing eighth Doctor. Ultimately, however, it may have been the sudden nature of the Doctor's first kiss that rubbed viewers the wrong way. Due to the constraints of one-off movie production as opposed to multi-episode serial production, the Doctor's kiss could neither be foreshadowed nor predicted. As a result, when the program finally returned nine years later, the Doctor was once again a member of the intergalactic lonely hearts club, and his first kiss of the new series would not occur until an entire season had passed.

But talk about a May-December romance! In reality, Christopher Eccleston was forty when he assumed the mantle of the ninth Doctor, and Billie Piper was eighteen years his junior, but if we look at the characters' ages according to the show's continuity, the Doctor was well over nine-hundred years old while Rose was a mere nineteen. Metaphorically speaking, then, this isn't just a May-December romance we're talking about, but a May-December-ten-years-down-the-road romance. Sure, if this were a run-of-the-mill TV fantasy in which the Doctor were simply *a* doctor and Rose the average department store clerk she appears to be at the start of "Rose," then we might expect the older male to tear off his aging-rocker leather jacket and throw his young lover on a big bouncy bed during sweeps-week, but this is still *Doctor Who*, and certain rules necessarily apply.

Judging by the wide variety of toys up for grabs in the merchandising blitz that has accompanied the return of the classic sci-fi series to the airwaves, *Doctor Who* still appeals to a young audience. At the same time, however, the show's longtime devotees also constitute a major *Doctor Who* constituency, so Russell T. Davies was wise to add at least a modicum of both romance and sexuality to the show. Davies, who is openly gay, first flirts with the idea of the Doctor's sexuality when Rose refers to her first trip in the TARDIS as a "date" in "The End of the World." Subsequently, in the same adventure, the Doctor offers Jabe of the tree-people the fairly sensual gift of his own breath in exchange for a cutting from one of her relatives. More noticeably, the Doctor is frequently jealous of Mickey, Adam, and Captain Jack throughout the series before taking part in the cruel romance game himself in "The Parting of the Ways" by openly flirting with former *Big Brother* contestant Lynda, to Rose's visible ire. And when Rose provokes the Doctor with the sexual innuendo of her double-entendre-laden "Do you dance?" line of questioning in "The Doctor Dances," he reacts in a mildly offended manner, declaring that he too has *danced*.

We are now, therefore, not just dealing, as in the case of his last incarnation, with a newly regenerated and arguably mentally unstable Doctor, but a man with at least a passing interest in both the fairer sex and his own— as evidenced by the fact that he experiences a number of kisses over the course of his first two seasons onscreen. In "The Parting of the Ways," Jack's memorable farewell "you-made-me-a-hero-Doctor" kiss, which exemplifies Jack's progressive fifty-first century, heteronormative-ideal-challenging approach to sexuality, is gladly reciprocated by the Doctor. And while we can legitimately write off the life-saving kiss between the Doctor and Rose that caps off that adventure as something more akin to mouth-to-mouth resuscitation than an act of passion, his third kiss in "New Earth" elicits a reaction that paints the Doctor as a man who has experienced at least a degree of physical intimacy in his life. To wit: "Yup ... Still got it!"

As a follow-up to the ongoing sub-plot of the Doctor as a lover, "School Reunion" depicts the Doctor once more flirting, to Rose's dismay, with another woman—this time his former companion, Sarah Jane Smith. The story, through Sarah Jane's subtle yet suggestive dialogue with Rose, hints that Sarah's relationship with the fourth Doctor may have been more than a platonic one in that her three-decade wait for the Time Lord's return suggests the long-burning feelings of a jilted lover. Similarly, the subsequent adventure, "The Girl in the Fireplace," offers a touching delineation of the Doctor's decades-long intermittent dalliance with the striking Madame De Pompadour courtesy of the Star Ship Madame De Pompadour's time windows. After a passionate lip-locking encounter with Reinette, the Doctor immediately learns her name from a manservant who reveals the woman's true historical importance as the mistress of French King Louis XV. The manservant, perplexed by the Doctor's giddy outburst, exclaims, "Who the hell are you?" to which the Doctor responds in a manner both egotistical and immature: "I'm the Doctor, and I've just *snogged* Madame De Pompadour!"

Surprisingly, after all of the incidents of physicality between them in three of the tenth Doctor's first four adventures, subsequent episodes quietly veer away from the subject and return the Doctor and Rose to less intimate footing. There is, of course, a discussion of the pair needing to buy a house with a mortgage in "The Impossible Planet," and their tear-soaked farewell to one another at the conclusion of "Doomsday" is rife with tension, but the complications of the flesh never really intrude—which isn't necessarily a bad thing insofar as most healthy couples will admit that sex, while a major part of the equation, isn't the only ingredient in a loving relationship. Perhaps, then, the Doctor's advice to Rose in "Fear Her" is one any of us who are helpless romantics can heed: "There's a lot of things you need to get across the universe—warp drive, wormhole refractors, and you know the thing you need the most of all? A hand to hold."

A question, however, remains as to why Davies has chosen to shake up long-standing fan assumptions that the Doctor is above the base concerns of sex. While we won't know what the present generation of kids watching the show, many of whom still have yet to experience a first kiss, think about the Doctor being an overtly sexual character until they have grown into corrupt adults such as ourselves, for us "mature" fans, the answer is obvious: in addition to the thrills and violence presented on the show—elements we have enjoyed since our pre-pubescent states—we now have the allure of sex and romance to hold our collective interest.

For a better understanding as to why our contemporary Doctor is more "adult" in character, we can also look to the comic book medium. Spider-Man, a fictional character whose regular adventures began only a year before the Doctor's, has also evolved more or less synchronically with his audience. Over the course of his first twenty-five years, Peter Parker, Spider-Man's civilian self, only aged at roughly one third the normal human rate—graduating high school as a teen, completing an undergraduate degree in his early twenties, and beginning graduate school sometime in his mid-twenties. Furthermore, during the sixties, seventies, and eighties, Parker epitomized a New York bachelor as he dated a series of women, including the ill-fated Gwen Stacy. But, as with Gwen, who was engaged to Parker and died at the hands of the fiendish Green Goblin, writers always chose to end the hero's relationships whenever they became too serious or the potential for marriage came too close to becoming a reality.

To return to *Doctor Who* for a moment, at the beginning of "Army of Ghosts," the Doctor seems content with the possibility of Rose spending the rest of her life with him when she informs the Time Lord that she plans on staying with him "forever." But Davies, in this instance, is only playing a game with us: as much as we know that the Doctor, a lucrative BBC character, will never be killed off, we also know that he will never settle down with one companion or—heaven forbid—get married. In Parker's case, however, the opposite came true in 1987 when Annual 21 of *The Amazing Spider-Man* depicted his marriage to on-again, off-again love interest Mary Jane

Watson. At the time, the wedding served as a great media event for Marvel Comics, and it presented a textbook example of successful media synergy since the Parker of the syndicated newspaper strip also got hitched with the corresponding Mary Jane. For several years thereafter, the depiction of the Parkers as frisky newlyweds was entertaining for the majority of fans, but reality loomed its all-too serious head when Mary Jane became pregnant. and the strip's storytellers advanced the possibility of a "Spider-Baby." Of course, just as Rose had to leave the Doctor's side eventually, Mary Jane miscarried the baby, and the status quo was maintained.

As with Spider-Man, the messy prospect of fatherhood goes largely unexplored in *Doctor Who*, but questions regarding the Doctor's status as a family man certainly invite analysis. We know from the continuity established in "An Unearthly Child" that Susan is the Doctor's granddaughter. At no time in those early tales is it stated that the connection is a biological one, but the notion that the Doctor is Susan's grandfather remains undisputed twenty years later in "The Five Doctors." Beyond this, we are given only a few other hints about the Doctor's family. In response to a companion's disbelief over his inability remember his own kin in "The Tomb of the Cybermen," the second Doctor famously and soulfully replies, "Oh yes, I can when I *want* to ... bring them back in front of my eyes. The rest of the time they sleep in my mind, and I forget." And sleep they apparently do, for five incarnations later, in "The Curse of Fenric," the seventh Doctor, when asked by Kathleen Dudman about whether or not he has any family, darkly replies that he doesn't know. Both quotes can be reconciled if one believes that the Doctor's family is either dead or missing, but a darker explanation would be to say that the Doctor, by the time of his seventh incarnation, has either consciously or subconsciously chosen to forget about their whereabouts.

Maybe the hope that the Doctor has come to terms with his family memories can be realized in the new series, as the tenth Doctor displays good feeling towards being a parent in "Fear Her." In that story, the Doctor and Rose are arguing over how best to deal with children, when the Doctor asks, "What about trying to understand them?"

"Easy for you to say," Rose replies. "You don't have kids."

And then we are reminded, for the first time in over twenty-two years, that the Doctor may have reproduced when he shockingly retorts, "I was a dad once."

The significance of this? Who knows. Maybe Davies is simply sticking with tradition and reminding fans of the Doctor's origins. Alternately, he may be dropping hints for adventures to come. After all, first Doctor William Hartnell did suggest years ago that a son of the Doctor might make a wonderful enemy for the Time Lord. And Davies does allow the tenth Doctor to coin the term "textbook enigmatic" in "New Earth." Could it be that the Doctor's son suffers from a "textbook oedipal complex"? Perhaps, like a textbook author who slowly and painfully offers solutions to a problem, Davies is sowing the seeds for a bigger revelation in the seasons to come. Whatever the case, speculation regarding the Doctor's family (or lack thereof) serves largely to remind us that although some of us would love to see the Doctor stay with one of his companions forever, the long-term detrimental ramifications upon the show's marketability to new generations of fans would become very apparent several seasons down the road.

Ward Cleaver as the Doctor?

We think not.

The Doctor's Problem with Men

Having established that the Doctor isn't one to settle down and start a family with any of the women in his lives, let's turn our attention to the men with whom the Doctor has shared the TARDIS over the years, beginning with old Ian Chesterfield.

Or was it Chesterson?

In any event, the Doctor's inability to remember his first male companion's surname underlines the Time Lord's disdain for his (alleged) granddaughter's math and science teacher. To be honest, the Doctor isn't a huge fan of Barbara Wright, Ian's fellow teacher, either—this despite (or perhaps because of) the fact that both are highly educated individuals. As evidenced by his relationships with future companions, the Doctor loves to impress his fellow travelers with feats of intellect and his familiarity with the different species that populate the universe. While Ian definitely enjoys visiting distant planets and witnessing key events in Earth's history, he is never quite as awe-struck by the Doctor as he should be. Which isn't to say that the Doctor *hates* the younger Chesterton. In fact, he's probably glad to have an ablebodied younger man around to serve as a protector and bodyguard, which would explain why the first Doctor more or less readily accepts the company of spaceship pilot Steven Taylor and sailor Ben Jackson once Chesterton bids the TARDIS adieu. Both men are undeniably intelligent and clever, but their youth and physical vigor are their most noticeable characteristics.

Once the Doctor regenerates into his second and more agile incarnation, however, his need for a male protector is reduced. Still, the presence of Highlander Jamie McCrimmon throughout the second Doctor's life does help the Time Lord survive many adventures. Moreover, the relationship between the two men is mostly healthy and harmonious as they display a sincere sense of affection for one another, albeit one that is masked by the gruff and mutually mocking façade most male friendships traditionally evince. The Doctor, more importantly, can accept Jamie as a true friend, since there is much he can teach his younger, ill-educated and naive hairy-legged-Highlander companion. Additionally, the second Doctor's friendship with the Brigadier is also a strong one, since their personalities complement each other well. While the Brigadier may not technically be a "companion" to this Doctor in the strictest sense of the word, it is a touching testament to the Time Lord's respect for his friend that he "bends the laws of time a little" in "The Five Doctors" to visit the future Brig at a UNIT reunion.

When the Doctor is forced to regenerate and exiled to earth, his relationship with the Brigadier sours slightly, an attitude that culminates in the Doctor mirthfully reducing the head of UNIT to a tea-boy at the start of the "The Three Doctors." This disrespectful behavior could be attributed to the third Doctor's disparaging attitude towards all members of hierarchical power structures—military leaders and Time Lords alike—since such structures form the invisible prison walls that mark his exile on Earth. At the same time, however, his disrespectful attitude may also be indicative of a long-simmering resentment of the Brigadier for basically murdering the Silurians by bombing their caves in "Doctor Who and the Silurians." And, judging by the way the tenth Doctor quickly turns on his former friend Prime Minister Harriet Jones when she orders the destruction of a peacefully departing Sycorax spaceship in "The Christmas Invasion," it is easy to argue that the Doctor righteously holds grudges against anyone—friend or foe—who fails to live up to his moral standards. Despite their differing personalities and philosophies, however, the third Doctor and the Brigadier nonetheless maintain a long-term professional affiliation even after the Doctor's time-traveling freedom has been restored to him.

As for other UNIT personnel, there's Lieutenant Surgeon Harry Sullivan, whom the fourth Doctor takes an obvious glee in demeaning. Conceived by outgoing producer Barry Letts as a physically assertive assistant harkening back to the male companions of the Hartnell era, Harry politely puts up with the Doctor's half-serious teasing for the duration of his tenure on the TARDIS. More than likely, it's the presence of Sarah Jane that moves the Doctor to constantly resort to the petty Alpha-Male tactics that emasculate Harry and thereby render him a less formidable romantic rival. And while we couldn't imagine the second Doctor dismissing Zoe's superior mathematical skills or even the third Doctor belittling Elizabeth Shaw's scientific expertise, the fourth Doctor continues to downplay Harry's medical knowledge even while Sarah Jane is trapped in a state of hibernation for a short time in "The Ark in Space." Asked whether he and Harry are med techs in this serial, the Doctor off-handedly responds, "Well, my doctorate is purely honorary, and Harry here is only qualified to work on sailors."

While the Doctor's disparagement demonstrates that he is perfectly capable of downplaying his own vast intellect, it also renders Harry an inconsequential individual with no viable skills even when he's in a situation where his twentieth-century medical training may be of some use. Subsequently, the Doctor further demonstrates his low opinion of Harry when he mockingly decrees, "Harry Sullivan is an imbecile!" in "Revenge of the Cybermen." So while we may occasionally sympathize with Harry and think that the Doctor is being too harsh on him, we would never seriously view him as a potential usurper of our lead character's dramatic and charismatic puissance. Consequently, when Harry finally gives up traveling with the Doctor at the conclusion of "Terror of the Zygons," we must ask ourselves whether the Doctor's condescending attitude ultimately influenced the decision.

Adric Must Die!

Judging by the deplorable way the Doctor treats Harry, it's no surprise that the Time Lord practically looks as if he wants to spit upon Adric after he stows away in the TARDIS. One can probably blame Tom Baker's imminent departure from the lead role for the Doctor's rather cold manner towards Adric, and it's arguable that Adric is literally one of the last persons with whom the fourth Doctor would like to spend his time as his reign draws to a close. To add fire to this argument, we can agree that season eighteen is famously imbued with a funereal atmosphere, and that the Doctor is noticeably subdued in comparison to the Time Lord we've known for the last six seasons of the show. Maybe we should think of him as a terminally ill patient who is bitterly resigned to his fate. The presence of Adric, in this context—with his youthful naiveté and fresh approach to life—may only act as a reminder that the Doctor is nearing the end of his current state of existence. And what type of respectable time traveler wants to be reminded at every turn of his old-age by the unwanted company of some selfish and annoying goofy kid from E-Space?

Once the Doctor regenerates into his ostensibly younger-looking fifth incarnation, Adric has someone to whom he can better relate, a fraternal figure who can replace Varsh, the brother he lost in "Full Circle." For the Doctor, however, forging a stronger bond with Adric is nearly impossible, for the boy repeatedly betrays his trust as his impetuous nature and impressionable personality lead the Doctor and company into one predicament after another in most of the season nineteen stories leading up to "Earthshock." By "Earthshock," however, Adric is ready to prove his value to the Doctor as he dies while trying to save Earth from destruction at the hands of the Cybermen.

Given Adric's heroism at the conclusion of "Earthshock," the natural issue that arises is that of the Doctor's refusal to return to the space freighter on which Adric is making his final voyage and grab the sometimes bothersome companion before the ship crashes. Why, in short, doesn't the Doctor save Adric? Quite annoyingly, all of the Doctor's predestination-laden talk of keeping the supposedly sacrosanct laws of time intact is flimsy at best. Fans over the years have often pointed out the inconsistency of the Doctor's reasoning here since his life is essentially dedicated to altering time lines across the universe. Then again, maybe the Doctor, in a flash of post-modern meta-fictional self-awareness, recognizes that Adric's death will be beneficial, at the very least, for those of us in TV-Land.

Not since the deaths of Katarina and Sara Kingdom in the 1966 epic "The Daleks' Master Plan" did *Doctor Who* allow us to see that the Doctor's companions, like the incidental characters and extras who populate his universe, are mortal. While the Doctor himself has "died" several times, his deaths have only been temporary and were quickly reversed through the miracle of regeneration. And since the Doctor has demonstrated time and again his ability to escape the Grim Reaper fairly easily, it's up to the occasional ill-fated companion to demonstrate that traveling in time and space can be dangerous if not deadly. From this perspective, Adric's death lends the Doctor's adventures a sense of gravity and heightened suspense: if we recognize the very real possibility that the Doctor's companions might die in any given adventure, then the stakes of the Doctor's occasional gambles rise accordingly. In "Earthshock," then, Adric serves as the sacrificial male surrogate who travels to the "undiscovered country" that the Doctor can never visit until his own journey's end.

By the next season, however, the Doctor apparently forgets that he pretty much has a chronic problem with troublesome male companions when he admits the alien schoolboy Turlough to the TARDIS crew. Turlough, it turns out, is working for the evil Black Guardian in an agreement that involves murdering the Doctor in exchange for a return ticket to his home planet. But when Turlough comes to the inevitable conclusion that he cannot kill the Doctor, the Doctor, in turn, reveals that he has known about Turlough's murderous deal all along but that he has also had faith that his young companion would do the right thing. This extremely confident and altruistic belief in Turlough's innate goodness is quite a moral stretch even for the Doctor, especially when one considers how unlikable and self-centered Turlough is even after the revelatory events of "Enlightenment."

The Doctor, in this instance, may be showing off or literally killing the Black Guardian with kindness since his belief in Turlough leads the young man to figuratively destroy the Black Guardian by rejecting the terms of their deal. The moral of the story, on the surface, is that truth, honesty, and belief in one's friends outweighs the temptations of murder, dishonesty, and greed. The true underlying message of the story, however, may be that the Doctor will resort to any means necessary, including feigning an impossibly virtuous belief in forgiveness towards a shifty companion (who, it should be noted, considered smashing his Gallifreyan brains out with a rock in "Mawdryn Undead") in order to defeat his enemies. Or maybe, in the end, it's just a lingering sense of guilt over Adric's death that gives the Doctor a soft spot in his hearts for errant and murderous schoolboys.

Masculinities in the New-Who Millennium

Russell T. Davies obviously knows how to write men, as demonstrated by his scripting of a sensitive son of God in *The Second Coming*, and in his controversial yet honest portrayal of gay men in his internationally success-ful series *Queer as Folk*. One of his obvious goals for returning *Doctor Who* to our screens was to humanize the Doctor, giving him emotions with which the audience might readily identify. Gone is the otherworldly, occasionally misanthropic Doctor of yesteryear, and in that distant alien's place stands a lone survivor of an extinct race, a person who so desperately wants to pro-tect and sincerely connect with his favorite race—*humans*. It is therefore no surprise that Davies makes an effort to reevaluate and develop the role of the male companion throughout much of the new series.

Quite wisely, one might argue, Davies does not proceed down the obvi-ous route of throwing the first available male into the gendered tinder box that is a TARDIS crew composed of the Doctor and one representative from each sex. Yes, Mickey Smith, a series regular, is introduced in "Rose," but he doesn't end up initially becoming the Doctor's companion for two rea-sons: A) he's afraid to travel with the Doctor because of the undeniable dan-ger that doing so entails and B) the Doctor simply doesn't like him. Obviously, the Doctor has learned to be more honest about the feeling of envy and repugnance he holds for other males. If he had been this openly honest in the past, moreover, he could have saved himself the constant fric-tion and aggravation caused by annoying male companions such as Adric and Turlough by immediately refusing to travel with them.

Like Adric, Mickey is annoying, but, unlike Adric, Mickey doesn't try to disguise his pusillanimous nature. He is, essentially, Adric gone *right*— meaning we're presented with a more honest portrayal of a character who does not fit the show's traditional paradigm of the heroic companion. Like Adric in "Earthshock," moreover, Mickey begins to redeem himself in

"World War III" as he, with the Doctor's aid, destroys a Slitheen invader who's attacking Rose's mother, Jackie, in her home and when he later blows up the rest of the Slitheen clan by hacking into a UNIT website and launching a missile at them while they're ruling from 10 Downing Street.

Perhaps as a counterweight to Mickey, Davies introduces us to Adam Mitchell in "Dalek." Adam is similar to Mickey in that he's concerned with his own self preservation, but he's more eager to see the universe than Mickey is. This isn't to say that Adam is immune to future shock; upon seeing the Earth in the year 200,000 from the vantage point of an observation deck on Platform One in "The Long Game," the boy embarrassingly faints in front of the Doctor and Rose. What's more, neither of the more-seasoned time travelers are sympathetic to the rookie's swooning. In fact, the Doctor has more or less maneuvered Adam into an embarrassing position in order to emasculate him in Rose's eyes and resoundingly eliminate him as a rival for Rose's affections—a ploy that clearly works quite perfectly.

"He's your boyfriend," the Doctor comments derisively when Adam hits the floor.

"Not anymore," Rose replies in disgust.

But Adam's next act is a harsh betrayal of both the Doctor's and Rose's faith in him. Transmitting details of future computer developments via Rose's "jiggery-poked" cell phone and a microchip he's had installed in his brain to his parents' answering machine in 2012, Adam hopes to make a killing in the advanced technologies market in his own era. Even though these plans are eventually foiled, greed and a sense of self-interest render Adam a version of Adric gone *terribly* wrong. Accordingly, the ninth Doctor—in contrast to his fifth incarnation, who forgave Adric and Turlough for their transgressions—is not open to giving Adam another chance. By dropping Adam off in 2012 with a useless Type Two microchip installed in his brain, the Doctor demonstrates that he is a changed man when it comes to dead-weight companions. Significantly, the Doctor doesn't stop at just kicking Adam out of his TARDIS; he also has to shoot one last crushing jab at him by stating, "I only take the best. I got Rose." This comment works on several levels since it tells Adam that he's neither good enough to travel with the Doctor nor as strong or honorable as Rose. But a second, darker meaning of the Doctor's words also occurs when we semantically play with the phrase "I got Rose" to reveal that the Doctor is victoriously asserting himself in Adam's eyes as Rose's possessive mate.

After demonstrating that he can make quick work of Mickey and Adam, the Doctor meets his match in Captain Jack Harkness, who enters the Time Lord's life in the Hugo-award-winning "The Empty Child." Upon being rescued as she dangles from a Barrage Balloon above Blitz-era London by Jack, Rose is instantly attracted to him, which is perfectly understandable since he's handsome, witty, and a bit of a rogue—all of the components that make an irresistible bad-boy. Subsequently, when Jack meets another time-traveling bad boy—the cynical, leather jacket-clad ninth Doctor—the inevitable competition for Rose's admiration ensues. Resorting to thinly veiled phallocentric allusions during their attempt to escape an army of what appear to be zombies in Albion Hospital, the two argue in front of Rose over whose weapon is better: the Doctor's beloved yet comparatively small sonic screwdriver or Jack's multi-functional, very large sonic blaster, which can also serve as a sonic cannon and triple-enfolded sonic disruptor. In the end, of course, both tools prove useful—as do the sonic devices—and after the two men learn to accept and respect each other, the Doctor willingly rescues Jack and invites him into the TARDIS at the end of "The Doctor Dances."

Over the course of their next few adventures together, there is little or no friction between Jack and the Doctor as they engage in healthy acts of homosocial bonding. Jack's bisexuality, which offers the flattering hint that Jack is attracted not only to Rose but the Doctor as well, may be one reason why the Doctor relaxes around his companion and doesn't try to compete with him. And the two tough guys, as in the tradition of the best "buddy" television cop shows (*e.g.*, *Miami Vice* and *Life on Mars*), learn to work with their differences and function as a winning unit. Furthermore, as a result of the Doctor's altruistic and heroic influence upon him, Jack tells his friend in "The Parting of the Ways," "Wish I never met you, Doctor. I was much better off as a coward," before he goes on to defend the Game Station from a Dalek invasion and is exterminated by one of the evil cyborgs. Unlike Adric's death, however, Jack's demise is only temporary since Rose revives him with the power of the Time Vortex. But, conveniently enough, the TARDIS has already departed the Game Station, effectively offering an excuse as to why Jack, an eminently likeable companion, is being written out of the show. Davies' decision circumvents the potential problem of Jack outshining the new tenth Doctor the following season as he also sets the stage for Jack to thrive on his own as the lead male character in the spin-off series *Torchwood*.

The tenth Doctor, however, as brought to life by the enthusiastic David Tennant, automatically dispels any of our doubts as to whether or not his character can replace the popular ninth Doctor. This Doctor, while being substantially less acerbic than his predecessor, still has a problem with Mickey in "School Reunion." During one telling scene, Mickey screams upon finding a closet full of vacuum-packed mice in a closet at Deffry Vale High School. After Mickey tries to explain the reason for his emotional outburst to everyone, the Doctor comments, "And you decided to scream like a little girl—nine, maybe ten years old? I'm seeing pigtails [and a] frilly shirt." Consequently, the Doctor's words here effectively render Mickey impotent since they metaphorically castrate him in front of Rose and Sarah Jane. It is not shocking to us then that Mickey decides to officially join the TARDIS crew at the end of "School Reunion" in order to verify for himself that he's not just "the tin dog." And, despite Mickey's help during the events of "The Girl in the Fireplace," the Time Lord still cannot hide his disdain for his young companion when, upon Rose's refusal to let him bring a horse aboard the TARDIS, the Doctor responds, "I let you keep Mickey."

The following tale, "Rise of the Cybermen," continues to underscore the theme of Mickey's seeming unworthiness, particularly when Mickey refers to himself as one of the Doctor's "spare parts" in a scene where the Doctor has to choose between running after Mickey or Rose. Not surprisingly, the Doctor, ever a slave to his heroic ideal, chooses to follow Rose, but Mickey's decision to explore the parallel Earth the Doctor has accidentally discovered is ultimately fruitful since he finds a living version of his dead grandmother, joins up with a resistance group, and, by the end of "The Age of Steel," has found his place in the universe, albeit an alternate one. Although he never sacrifices his own life, Mickey once again proves to be very much like Adric in that he dedicates himself to battling the remaining Cybermen who pose a threat to the parallel Earth at the conclusion of this adventure. When we next see Mickey in "Army of Ghosts" and "Doomsday," his transformation into a true hero is complete, as he fearlessly faces both the Cybermen and Daleks, all the while toting big guns and firing off the obligatory witty action-hero dialogue. Even the Doctor is impressed with the change wrought in his former companion, but the bitter truth is that Mickey is only able to truly better himself once he removes himself from the stifling influence of the judgmental and condescending Last of the Time Lords.

Given his relationship (or lack thereof) with Mickey, Rose and everyone else with whom he's shared the TARDIS, we can safely say that the Doctor probably needs all thirteen of his lives (and then some) to mature as a healthy sexual being and as a consistently honorable and considerate comrade to the males who travel with him. Fortunately, as each regeneration brings him one sobering step closer to death, the Doctor's knowledge of his own mortality forces him, particularly in his ninth and tenth incarnations, to reevaluate his relationships with both sexes. More importantly, it is particularly telling that the Doctor, now more obviously than ever, wants to have more than simply platonic relationships with women. As the last of his kind, the Doctor, it seems, just wants to be loved.

Is that so wrong?

4

The Time Lord Manifesto: A Cautionary Guide to Gallifreyan Culture

In the beginning, all we knew was that the Doctor was on the run, but the identity of his pursuers remained a mystery. "An Unearthly Child," the first episode of the original series, reveals that the Doctor and his granddaughter Susan are "exiles" cut off from their own planet "without friends or protection." At the conclusion of the second season, we meet another member of the Doctor's race in "The Time Meddler," but no one names the Time Lord's home planet or, for that matter, utters the term *Time Lord*. In fact, it isn't until the end of the second Doctor's run that we are treated to a view of his home planet. Yet even as a Time Lord tribunal tries their rogue countryman for transgressing the principles of non-intervention which they hold so dear at the conclusion of "The War Games," the Doctor's origins remain sketchy at best. Moreover, as the Doctor continues to encounter his Time Lord brethren in subsequent adventures and through successive incarnations, what little we learn of Gallifreyan culture remains shrouded in mystery. All that emerges for sure is that the Doctor maintains a healthy ambivalence toward his home world, a fact best illustrated by the tension between his initial desire to escape the drudgery of Gallifrey in the original series and his regret over the passing of Time Lord culture in the new series. Because of this ambivalence, moreover, just when the Doctor thinks he's out, the Time Lords always manage to pull him back in.

An Offer He Can't Refuse

While comparing Time Lord culture to that of La Cosa Nostra or the Mafia as seen in films like *The Godfather* and *Goodfellas* may be a bit of a stretch, it actually proves instructive with regard to understanding the Doctor's relationship with the denizens of his home planet. Consider, for example, the popular notion that once one is affiliated with the mob, one is beholden to the organization for life. The same can be said for the Doctor, and it isn't too far beyond the pale to imagine our hero taking an oath of allegiance to Time Lord ideals early in his life in much the same way "made" men in Mafia films vow to protect the interests of the "Family" at all costs. More significantly, however, and to borrow one of the most popular phrases in film history, the Time Lords prove particularly effective at making the Doctor offers he can't refuse.

As a result of his aforementioned trial in "The War Games," the Doctor is banished to Earth, forced to regenerate and stripped of all knowledge regarding time travel. Despite this sentence, however, the Doctor does manage to maintain possession of the TARDIS, which serves as a reminder of both his fall from grace and his potential to reclaim his rightful place as a traveler through space and time. Yet while the TARDIS is indeed a symbol of the Doctor's former standing in Time Lord society and one of the last vestiges of his dignity, the tribunal is not acting entirely out of a sense of altruism when they allow him to keep it. Rather, they are acting in their own self-interest, for as long as the Doctor continues to fiddle with his time machine, the Time Lords have the option of whisking him away to the far reaches of the universe to do their bidding. Like Mafia wise guys Henry Hill in *Goodfellas*, Lefty Ruggiero in *Donnie Brasco* and Christopher Moltisanti in *The Sopranos*, the seemingly powerful Doctor is from time to time rendered a pawn by forces much greater than himself.

What makes the Doctor especially vulnerable to the whims of the Time Lords, however, is not that they are more powerful than he is but that they recognize as his greatest "weakness" the overwhelming twin desires to explore the universe and to rescue the innocent from the clutches of evil. In "The Terror of the Autons," for example, a Time Lord appears on Earth to warn the Doctor that his arch-nemesis the Master is up to no good, and in "The Three Doctors," the Time Lord High Council goes so far as to reunite the third Doctor with his first two incarnations to prevent the destruction of the universe at the hands of the legendary (albeit mad) solar engineer Omega. And while the Doctor regains the secrets of time travel at the conclusion of this serial, the Time Lords continue to meddle in his affairs, perhaps most egregiously in the fourth-Doctor serial "Genesis of the Daleks."

In "Genesis of the Daleks," the Time Lords literally lift the Doctor and his companions Harry Sullivan and Sarah Jane Smith out of time and space by intercepting a transmat beam and placing the reluctant heroes on the battle-scarred planet Skaro at a time when the Daleks appear to be nothing more than voice-controlled battle machines. Poised to dangle yet another offer that can't be refused in front of the Doctor, the Time Lord who appears at the beginning of this serial is clad in a black costume that is much like that of the chess-playing manifestation of Death in Ingmar Bergman's classic existential film *The Seventh Seal*. A harbinger of death himself, this messenger of the Time Lords draws attention to the fact that the Doctor's impending battle against the forces that will bring the Daleks into existence is not simply a risky one but one that he is not expected to win. Like the unwitting and ill-fated Mafia underling David Della Rocco who is sent on what is ostensibly a suicide mission to knock off a rival gang leader in the 1999 vigilante drama *The Boondock Saints*, the Doctor is sent, vastly outnumbered and completely outgunned, into a maelstrom from which he is not expected to return alive.

Needless to say, while the Doctor's inescapable affiliation with the Time Lords is what initially allows them to reach out and tap him for the job, it is his innate sense of altruism that they use to rope the Doctor into halting the creation of the dreaded Daleks. As the following exchange demonstrates, the envoy from Gallifrey gently reminds the Doctor of his position within the larger organization of Time Lords before dangling the ultimate carrot in front of him:

THE DOCTOR: Look, whatever I've done for you in the past, I've more than made up for. I will not tolerate this continual interference in my life.

TIME LORD: Continual? We pride ourselves we seldom interfere in the affairs of others.

THE DOCTOR: Except mine.

TIME LORD: You, Doctor, are a special case. You enjoy the freedom we allow you. In return, occasionally, not continually, we ask you to do something for us.

THE DOCTOR: I won't do it. Whatever it is, I refuse.

TIME LORD: Daleks.

In light of this intense exchange, the Mafia metaphor again comes into play, for the Time Lord, a form of intergalactic "Godfather," is exerting his power as a representative of the Gallifreyan High Council by subtly reminding the Doctor that they *allow* him to traverse the universe and that they can rescind this arrangement any time they see fit. Simultaneously, however, the Time Lord is quite aware that veiled threats will only make the Doctor more obstinate, so he still must cater to the renegade's ego. And so it is that one word, "Daleks," is all it takes him to ensnare the Doctor in another mission. The Doctor himself is not only obliged to satisfy the demands of his own moral standards and his need to be a cosmic champion, but he also realizes that he does indeed have an unspoken agreement with his peers, which he must honor by doing "favors" for them from time to time.

Recognizing the Doctor's innate desire to do good, moreover, the Time Lords have already assumed that the Doctor will take them up on their "unrefusable" offer; after all, why go to the trouble of diverting the Doctor to Skaro if there's a chance that he'll reject the opportunity to either avert the Daleks' creation or "affect their genetic development so they evolve into less aggressive creatures"? A telling sign of the lopsided nature of this agreement, however, is embodied in the form of the time ring that will return the Doctor to the TARDIS when his mission is completed, and the Time Lord's dire warning against losing this ring succinctly illustrates the High Council's desire for a "zero-footprint" level of involvement in the Doctor's mission: by stripping the Doctor of his TARDIS, the Time Lords guarantee that he will leave no clues of their meddling in the likely event of his death. Echoing the warning frequently heard on the original *Mission Impossible* series—"As always, should you or any of your I. M. Force be caught or killed, the Secretary will disavow any knowledge of your actions"—the Time Lords are automatically distancing themselves from a potentially sticky situation that may have irreversible effects upon galactic history.

Ever the thrill seeker and as sharp as ever, the Doctor is fully aware of the parameters of his agreement with the Time Lords; in fact, he welcomes them because he knows that the disavowal works both ways. That is, the Time Lords won't be bothering him as he attempts to avert the creation of the Daleks. Additionally, and to return to the Mafia connection, the Doctor is operating under a form of the code of *Omerta*, which prohibits made men from ratting out their "business associates." Mafia researcher Michael Benson explains the concept in this manner: "Those who call the police are fools or cowards. Those who need police protection are both. If you are attacked, do not give the name of your attacker. Once you recover, you will want to avenge the attack yourself."[1] Upping the ante somewhat, the Doctor's sense of Omerta puts him in a double-bind since the Time Lords serve as the society he must protect and the authority figures to whom he dare not retreat—a fact that points up the inherent split at the heart of Time Lord culture. On one hand, they wish to maintain the façade of nonintervention, but on the other hand, they (or at least some members of their society) realize that they must intervene for the good of the universe.

At the climax of "Genesis of the Daleks," the Doctor agonizes over whether he has the right to prevent the creation of his most dangerous enemies. After all, he theorizes, won't otherwise antagonistic forces band together in the name of defeating this violent scourge? More to the point, won't the entire timeline of the universe be altered as a result of his tinkering with the Daleks' inception? Of course, many of these issues are rendered moot when the Doctor fails to nip the Dalek menace in the bud, yet when he admits that his presence on Skaro has likely delayed the Daleks' evolution by a thousand years or so, one must question the true purpose of his mission. Maybe he didn't alter history at all but simply fulfilled his predestined part in the chain of events that led to the creation of his most dreaded foe. If this is the case, however, then the Time Lords, by putting the Doctor on Skaro at the right time and place, are implicated in the very creation of the race that would eventually destroy them in the oft-discussed but never seen Time War, whose events serve as a backdrop for the new series. What's more, if the Time Lords knew ahead of time that the Doctor was always part of the Daleks' genesis, then they also knew that he could never refuse their offer—not only because doing so was not in his nature but because he had "always already" taken them up on it. Thus, for the Doctor, as with the average Mafia wise guy, free will may, in the end, be nothing more than an illusion. At the same time, however, the Doctor, like any self-respecting "made man," has no problem wielding power over those who happen to be lower on the food chain than himself.

When the second Doctor contacts the Time Lords after all of his options have been exhausted in episode nine of "The War Games," we get a sense of why he has avoided any contact with his own people up to this point. Citing an intergalactic version of *laissez faire* in the form of their non-intervention laws, the Time Lords find the Doctor guilty of interfering with the natural development of lesser civilizations and, as noted, exile him to twentieth-century Earth. Upon arriving on Earth, however, the newly regenerated Doctor realizes that despite the inconvenience (to put it mildly) of being stripped of the power of time travel, his knowledge of alien races and advanced technologies can be a distinct advantage in his dealings with Earthlings. In other words, when dealing with "lesser species," the Doctor himself becomes somewhat of a Godfather figure to those around him, delivering favors in return for unlimited scientific resources and the ego-boosting respect and awe of his colleagues and assistants.

Unlike the asymmetrical balance of power he shares with the Time Lords, the Doctor's negotiations with humans place him on much firmer ground. At the end of "Spearhead from Space," for example, he enters into a mutually beneficial deal with Brigadier Lethbridge-Stewart. In exchange for his unpaid service to UNIT as their scientific advisor, he asks for facilities he can use to repair the TARDIS, a laboratory, equipment, and an assistant. And while the Doctor claims to have no use for money, he requests one item that betrays his arguably materialistic side: a classic car like the vintage roadster he stole from the hospital in which he had been convalescing immediately after his regeneration. Very much a made man during his exile on Earth, the Doctor clearly needs to travel in style. More importantly, however, the renegade Time Lord's relationship with some of his companions—particularly over the course of his fourth incarnation—is reminiscent of that between a Mafia godfather and the "muscle" he hires to enforce his decrees. Leela, a warrior of the Sevateem tribe whom the Doctor first meets

in "The Face of Evil" is basically a savage. A positive if somewhat patriarchal and imperialistic reading of their subsequent relationship as mentor
and protégé would be to say that the Doctor civilizes and refines Leela à la
the classical Pygmalion-Galatea paradigm. Yet while he does protest the slay-
ing of her enemies with poisonous Janis thorns in her debut story, their
subsequent adventures together demonstrate that the Doctor is quite often
glad to have an experienced warrior at his side, one who can act as a "button" (Mafia slang for the hit men a Don frequently employs).

The following season, in "The Invisible Enemy," the Doctor gains
another hit man or, more accurately, a "hit dog" in the form of the mobile
computer K-9, and whenever the Doctor comes in harm's way over the course
of the next several seasons, his robot dog comes to the rescue, nose-laser
blazing. For pure dramatic impact, however, the Doctor's most striking button may well be the youthful Ace who joins his seventh incarnation in the
twilight of the original series. With her Nitro 9 explosives, baseball bat and
combative take-no-prisoners attitude toward any monster or creep who tries
to harm the Doctor, Ace is the ultimate bodyguard for the aging Time Lord.
And, if the show had made it to a twenty-seventh season, we may have
learned that the Doctor was secretly training Ace for acceptance into training as a Time Lord. And if the Time Lords admitted Ace into their ranks,
she would have been in Mafia terms a made woman, since her future as a
Time Lord would probably have granted her twelve more lives and advanced
knowledge and abilities that she might have harnessed in her struggle against
injustice in the universe. Therefore, in this admittedly speculative scenario,
while the Doctor does use Ace to help actualize his long-percolating machinations against the Daleks, Cybermen and Fenric, he simultaneously has
been prepping her for upward mobility in the "organization" that is Time
Lord society.

While drawing too strong a parallel between Time Lord society and
organized crime would likely prove foolhardy, the analogy certainly helps to
illustrate the Doctor's position in relation to forces both above and below
him in terms of power and wherewithal. Like many a cinematic made man,
the Doctor is ambivalent about the organization from which his power stems
since he realizes that, in many respects, he is indeed beholden to the Time
Lords and therefore travels through time and space largely by their grace
and at their mercy. Simultaneously, however, he also enjoys the power and
privilege that being a Time Lord affords him, particularly when that power
grants him the respect and admiration of less technologically advanced
species. Whether serving as a pawn of forces greater than himself or playing the part of a powerful if benevolent and truly "wise" guy, the Doctor—
like the Time Lords themselves—must always walk a fine line between using
power and abusing it.

Decadent, Degenerate, Rotten to the Core?

In the penultimate episode of "The Trial of a Time Lord," the sixth Doctor learns that the Time Lords have performed the ultimate cover-up of all time by moving the Earth two light years across space. They've also arranged for half of the planet's surface to be destroyed by a fireball and, to further cover their tracks, they've renamed the planet Ravolox. The primary target for the fireball, however, was not the Earth itself but three Sleepers from Andromeda who had stolen Time Lord secrets and were hiding there. Shocked by this revelation, the Doctor subsequently makes what is undoubtedly the finest speech of his life before the assembled might of his prosecutor, judge, and jury: "In all my travelings throughout the universe, I have battled against evil, against power-mad conspirators. I should have stayed here! The oldest civilization—decadent, degenerate and rotten to the core! Power-mad conspirators, Daleks, Cybermen, Sontarans—they're still in the nursery compared to us! Ten million years of absolute power—that's what it takes to be really corrupt!"

Perhaps the Doctor, experiencing the overwhelming stress of fighting for his very survival, is being somewhat emotional in his vitriolic attack against his own people, but he is clearly touching a nerve when he comments upon the corruption that is rife within the Gallifreyan Empire. As with all empires, the Gallifreyan one is at once benevolent and corrupt, foolish and wise, traditional and innovative. The inherent tensions among these dualities allow Time Lord culture to both prosper and decline before its eventual obliteration as a result of the apocalyptic events of the Time War. Drawing parallels between historical and contemporary empires, then, may lend us a more lucid and sympathetic understanding of why the Time Lords behave so imperialistically at times.

Without a doubt, it is not as if the Doctor's excellent speech towards the conclusion of his trial is unjustified. After all, the High Council of Time Lords, the ruling elite that should preserve the integrity and non-intervention laws of their empire, did sacrifice the natural progression of the Earth's timeline to simply cover up some secrets in an act that is tantamount to tossing a grenade into a garden to eliminate an anthill. From the perspective of a post–9/11 terrestrial civilization, however, we might argue that a mediocre and continuity-addled tale such as the fourteen-part "Trial of a Time Lord" both comments upon past empires and those to come. Sacrificing half of a populated planet in order to protect mere secrets is undoubtedly a heinous act that rivals even the Doctor's purported act of genocide against the Vervoids depicted in episode twelve of "Trial of a Time Lord." Yet while the allegations against the Doctor ultimately prove to be unfounded, the Time Lords themselves are never held accountable for their crimes, an injustice which all but begs the Roman satiric poet Juvenal's classic question from his *Satire VI*: "Who watches the watchmen?"[2]

On a contemporary level, we can see that history is cyclical insofar as the watchmen continue to require watching, especially as nations that wield economic, political and military might continue to dictate global standards for right and wrong in the modern world. For example, the American and British Empires invaded Iraq in 2003 under the pretense that Saddam Hussein held Weapons of Mass Destruction and as a result of military intelligence suggesting that Hussein's regime had direct links to the terrorist organization Al Qaeda. As all published reports have shown, however, those weapons of mass destruction did not exist, and Hussein's regime and Al Qaeda have yet to be directly linked. Yet American and British involvement in Iraq continues under the pretense of preserving stability and offering the chance for the Iraqi people, historically a tribal-based culture, to experience democracy, a traditionally Western form of government.

In terms of *Doctor Who* presciently predicting future global politics, "The Two Doctors" provides an example of a powerful imperialistic "nation" attempting to enforce sanctions upon another. At the beginning of the tale, the second Doctor, accompanied by Jamie, is on a Time-Lord-influenced mission to Space Station Camera in order to persuade Professor Joinson Dastari to halt the dangerous Kartz-Reimer time experiments that are underway. Dastari takes offense at the Time Lords' wish that his scientists stop their time experiments. The subsequent events of the story, however, prove the Time Lords' fears to be well-founded since Dastari is in league with the Sontarans and the Androgums, who plan to use time travel for their own nefarious purposes. To once more draw parallels with recent history, the U.S., Great Britain, and several other influential nations with nuclear capabilities have threatened to enact sanctions against North Korea and Iran if they continue their burgeoning nuclear experiments. Whether or not these nations are justified in their actions and whether or not North Korea or Iran would misuse any advances in nuclear powers is beyond the ken of this volume, but when we conflate the Time Lords and our contemporary world powers in these circumstances, the similarities demonstrate that those who already possess an enviable power—be it time travel or nuclear fission—tend to have a vested interest in stopping other groups from gaining that power as well.

The Ravolox and Space Station Camera incidents, moreover, are not the only instances of the Time Lords becoming embroiled in controversial actions that offer historical parallels. We learn in "Underworld" that the Time Lords' non-intervention policy resulted from a situation in which the Minyans, whom the Time Lords supplied medicinal and scientific aid and the means for improved communications, forced their benefactors to leave at gunpoint. Subsequently, the Minyans waged war against each other, gained nuclear capability, and then destroyed their planet. Because of this tragedy, the Time Lords vowed to never again directly interfere with the affairs of another species. To wax politically once more, we can cite the fact that many critics argue that U.S. involvement in both the Korean and Vietnam wars only added more fire to situations that may have been best settled internally within those nations. And, to remind ourselves that history is generational or, more poetically, cyclical, the jury is still out on the ultimate effectiveness of international intervention in Iraq. Unfortunately, in the real world, we don't have a Doctor who can materialize and set things straight within the span of a few days.

The True Deadly Assassins

While it's clear that we here on Earth could use someone like the Doctor to help us out from time to time, one question that remains is why the Time Lords need him. One answer is that secretly sending the Doctor to do their dirty work allows the steeped-in-tradition Time Lords to preserve the appearance of adhering to their own tenets of nonintervention. At the same time, however, a darker and perhaps more realistic answer is that the Time Lords need the Doctor because he serves as a cultural buffer or scapegoat in the event of scandal or disaster. In short, more often than not, when the Time Lords ask for the Doctor's help, what they're really looking for is a fall guy.

To argue that season fourteen's dark re-imagining of Time Lord society in "The Deadly Assassin" offers a political allusion to the assassination of President John F. Kennedy may sound preposterous or even blasphemous to fans of both the show and Kennedy alike, but it's worth remembering that the two events have been interlaced since the program's genesis. On November 22, 1963—one day before the premiere of *Doctor Who*—Kennedy was assassinated in Dallas, Texas, and in later stories, Kennedy's presence is palpable. Season twenty-five's first tale, "Remembrance of the Daleks," opens with a shot of a Dalek ship approaching Earth in 1963, accompanied by a medley of voices that includes Kennedy's. Later that season, we learn in "Silver Nemesis" that the Nemesis Statue circles the Earth every twenty-five years, bringing destruction in its wake. Given that the adventure takes place in 1988, the statue must have circled the Earth in 1963, neatly coinciding with the show's first transmission and, as the Doctor mentions, Kennedy's assassination. Finally, in "Rose" the conspiracy buff Clive shows the skeptical Rose pictures of the ninth Doctor in past times. Among these images is

one of the ninth Doctor present in the crowd of people who directly witnessed Kennedy's murder. As viewers, we immediately respond to this image
since Kennedy's murder is one of the pivotal events of the latter half of the
twentieth century. More importantly and on a nostalgic level, we are
reminded that *Doctor Who* was born in the midst of that tumultuous event,
which forever links the tragedy to our favorite show.

Considering the relationship between *Doctor Who* and the Kennedy
assassination, an examination of "The Deadly Assassin" in the context of
the much-documented historical tragedy makes at least a modicum of sense.
After abandoning Sarah Jane Smith at the conclusion of "The Hand of
Fear," the Doctor materializes on his home planet amidst the dreary pomp
and circumstance of the Time Lords at their bureaucratic worst just in time
to witness the assassination of Gallifrey's Lord President. Yet even before
the Lord President is assassinated, his Presidential Resignation Day ceremony
evokes a downbeat funereal air as Time Lords representing their respective
orders file into the Capitol's Panopticon in a zombie-like manner. From the
outset, therefore, we know that this is not the Spartan futuristic Gallifrey
of "The War Games" or "The Three Doctors." Instead, this Gallifrey offers
biting commentary on great empires in decay as well as the spiritual malaise
of the moldy individuals who govern and populate them.

Mysteriously summoned to the Presidential Resignation Day ceremony,
the Doctor eventually arrives on the scene unfolding in the Panopticon and
begins to strike up an awkward conversation with his old Prydon Academy
classmate, Runcible, who is now a commentator for the Capitol's Public
Registered Video—a prescient precursor to the twenty-four hour cable news
channel. Shortly thereafter, the Doctor discovers a rifle positioned near a
news camera on an unguarded catwalk. Gazing through the rifle's crosshairs
at the exact moment the President is killed, the Doctor soon finds himself
under arrest for the President's murder. As events unfold, however, we learn
that the Doctor is not the killer and that the true culprit is the Master,
who shot the retiring President from another location within the Panopticon.

A second shooter? At this point, it would be difficult *not* to recall the
infamous Zapruder Film, a silent eight-millimeter color home movie shot
by Dallas dress manufacturer Abraham Zapruder as he witnessed the
Kennedy assassination. The Zapruder Film was not immediately available
to the greater American public until its broadcast in March of 1975 to controversial effect during the late-night TV show *Good Night America*. Ever
since that airing, the short film's depiction of Kennedy's last moments
remains one of the darker iconic images of contemporary media history. And
since the final episode of "The Deadly Assassin" first aired in 1976 just two
days before the anniversary of Kennedy's death, the notion that the serial's

imagery may well have been inspired by the Zapruder Film is not out of the question.

The significance of the parallel between the Kennedy assassination and that of the Lord President becomes clear in light of the public and spectacular nature of both events. Where Kennedy's assassination occurred in full view of the crowd surrounding his motorcade, the Lord President's assassination occurs in the center of the Time Lord Panopticon. That the latter occurs where it does is important since a panopticon represents a building such as a prison, hospital, or library whose extremities are all visible from a single point in the center of the structure. The flipside of this arrangement, however, is that the center of the structure is visible from all points along the periphery, so when the shocking event of the Lord President's murder occurs, all Time Lords in the vicinity along with all Gallifreyans viewing the assassination via Public Registered Video become privy to the tragedy in a moment of public mass consciousness. To some degree, moreover, the same can be said of the Kennedy assassination; although only those immediately present witnessed the assassination in real time, the full scope of Kennedy's death devastated the entire nation as details became available via television and radio.

Perhaps because of its public nature, the Kennedy assassination has taken on the power of myth in the intervening years. As with "The Deadly Assassin," the real-world Kennedy assassination has its own second-shooter theories, and while we know that the Master is the true perpetrator of the Lord President's assassination, there is much doubt surrounding the Warren Commission's verdict that Lee Harvey Oswald acted alone when he pulled the trigger on Kennedy. While many conspiracy theorists argue that Oswald could not have been the lone gunman and that a second shooter helped to accomplish the murderous deed from a position on a grassy knoll near Kennedy's passing motorcade, the truth—if ever a single truth can be said to exist in such a situation—has very likely been lost to the public amidst the tangle of rumors and speculation that surrounds the assassination.

In many respects, the failure of the Warren Commission to fully satisfy the objections of conspiracy theorists is indicative of the failure of most terrestrial agencies to effectively deal with complex and thorny issues. We can, however, rest assured that seemingly advanced cultures are no better equipped than we are in this regard. After the Doctor is accused of murdering the Lord President, he gains firsthand knowledge of the convoluted inner workings of Gallifrey's legal system, which, like those of many modern nations, is rife with loopholes and contradictions. First, Castellan Spandrell informs the Doctor that as immediate punishment for his alleged crime of murdering the President, he will be placed in a vaporization chamber. Yet in what may be the program's greatest send-up of overworked national-

istic mantras, the Doctor wittily remarks, "Vaporization without representation is against the constitution," reminding us that even in futuristic societies, well-paved rhetoric can potentially save one's skin from the execution
chamber. Moreover, the Doctor swiftly invokes Article 17 of the Time Lord
Constitution, which not only grants him temporary immunity but also allows
him—a suspected murderer—to toss his floppy hat into the proverbial ring
and run for the office of President of the High Council!

With the forty-eight hour reprieve that the impending election gives
him, the Doctor begins his investigation of the Lord President's assassination, but he is disgusted by the outmoded technology the Time Lords utilize for maintaining their archives. "Do you think this stuff is sophisticated?
There are worlds out there where this kind of equipment would be considered prehistoric *junk*," he comments to the archivist Coordinator Engin,
touching upon the irony that one of the most powerful races in the universe is failing to keep up with the technological advances of its competi-
tors. Echoing this sentiment, comic book mastermind, magician, and essayist
Grant Morrison offers a commentary on the gradual decay of empires in
issue three of the DC Comics limited series *Seven Soldiers: Shining Knight*. As
Doctor Gloria Friday, an antiquities expert, discusses the rise and fall of great
empires with an FBI Metahuman specialist named Helen Helligan, she states
that every civilization must reach its peak, which is equivalent to "a time of
harvest." Once so-called "ripening" occurs, however, decay is inevitable. As
Friday notes, her theory holds "predictable and grim implications" for any
society already at its peak—a fact that is certainly true of Gallifrey.

After gaining mastery of time and space and establishing self-righteous
non-intervention laws, the Time Lords, it would seem, rested on their lau-
rels. As a result, their society, like their technology, stagnated to a point
where the Master, accompanied by the well-respected Chancellor Goth,
could slip through Gallifrey's security protocols, interfere with the archives
and the APC Net, and assassinate a Lord President right in front of the high-
est-ranking Time Lords.[4] The Time Lords themselves, then, are as culpable
as anyone else with regard to the assassination of their Lord President insofar as their own negligence is what allows that tragedy to occur.

Masters of the Universe

While the Time Lords have certainly committed many shameful deeds
over the course of their long history, their treatment of Omega, the solar
engineer whose efforts made time travel possible, is arguably one of their
most egregious. As revealed in "The Three Doctors," Omega was thought
to have died in the creation of the black hole that provides the energy

required for the Time Lords' travels in time and space. This assumption, however, is proven wrong when Omega attempts to escape from the antimatter universe in which he has been imprisoned since being left for dead. The only problem is that Omega's attempts at escaping from his antimatter prison are putting a strain on the Time Lords' power supply, so the very people who owe every debt of gratitude to him decide that the only reasonable course of action is to stop him in his tracks. As a result, Omega goes in the blink of the public eye from being a heroic figure in Time Lord mythology to being a villain—a phenomenon with which we are all too familiar here on Earth.

Witness Michael Jackson, originally a beloved member of the Jackson 5 and later the moon-walking, sequined-glove-wearing "King of Pop" in the 1980s, whose name is now and forevermore associated with child molestation charges, even though he was never convicted of such crimes. Witness William Jefferson Clinton, the wildly controversial but equally popular forty-second President of the United States who was impeached and nearly destroyed because of the Monica Lewinsky scandal that unfolded in the late 1990s. Witness Mel Gibson, the celebrated director of *Brave Heart* and *The Passion of the Christ*, who is now ostracized in Hollywood as being an anti-Semite as a result of several poorly chosen racist remarks directed at the California police officers who were arresting him for speeding and suspicion of drunk driving in July of 2006.

As with Omega, each public figure's former greatness has been indelibly sullied by questionable words or deeds. Omega's situation, however, does contain mitigating circumstances, since no single Time Lord who rose up after his apparent "sacrifice" looked into the possibility that he might have survived the black hole's creation. Moreover, if we take into consideration the effect of thousands of years of solitude upon a being who is almost immortal, we can begin to sympathize with Omega's megalomaniacal actions and self-pitying flights of fancy. Yet regardless of how sympathetic—or right— Omega might be, he is rendered the villain in this tale as the Doctor's first three incarnations work to defeat him and thus to maintain Gallifrey's status quo. Indeed, as a reward for helping his fellow Time Lords, the third Doctor is granted the power of traveling through time and space once more, forcing us to wonder if even the Doctor's conscience might be bought for the right price.[5]

But maybe we're being a little unfair when we fault the Doctor for foiling Omega's efforts at escaping his lonely exile in exchange for the secrets of time travel. After all, he didn't know ahead of time that the Time Lords would be restoring these secrets to his memory, and even if he had known, the Doctor's inherent sense of intergalactic wanderlust is so intertwined with his very soul that the ability to travel through time and space may well be an incentive that he is utterly incapable of resisting. By way of contrast, what motivates the Doctor's arch-nemesis the Master is a far more nefarious set of desires. At the risk of gross oversimplification, where the Doctor wants nothing more than to explore the universe, the Master wants only to rule it. Despite this apparent antipathy, however, the two are frequently and inexplicably drawn to each other. What's more, while many articles in *Doctor Who Magazine* and assorted fan publications have offered deft play-by-play analysis of their encounters, what remains to be seen is why the two time travelers, in spite of their vast intellects, centuries of experience and mutual (if grudging) admiration for one another, inevitably succumb to fisticuffs when all other modes of intercourse fail.

The Master was originally conceived by produce Barry Letts and script editor Terrance Dicks as a sophisticated, charming, and nonetheless dangerous foil to the third Doctor. Engaging in a series of escalating conflicts throughout season eight of the series, the Doctor and the Master neatly sum up their philosophical differences in that season's penultimate serial, "Colony in Space." As the Master attempts to convince the Doctor that the two of them should use the power of a so-called Doomsday Weapon to rule the universe with an iron fist, he tells the Doctor that "the basic law of life" dictates that one must either "rule or serve" and that nothing, not even loyalty to the Time Lords, should prevent the Doctor from taking his rightful place next to his arch-foe as a master of the universe. Unconvinced, the Doctor responds by saying that the Master will never understand that what motivates him is a desire to "see the universe, not rule it."

Given that the Doctor and the Master have such divergent values, the natural question that arises is that of why they seem to be so attracted to each other. Sure, opposites attract, and the antagonism between the Doctor and the Master lends *Doctor Who* a sense of dramatic tension that might otherwise be absent if the heroic renegade didn't have the constant threat of his villainous opposite to keep him on his toes, but at the same time, both characters seem to take a perverse joy in basking in each other's presence. A simple answer to this question may be that the Master and the Doctor come together out of loneliness or a sense of nostalgia for the company of their own kind. Consider, by way of example, the time-honored tradition of the holiday family gathering. As we visit with parents, siblings and assorted cousins whom we may rarely see outside of such occasions, personal differences can frequently remind us of why we don't get together with these loved-ones more often. At the same time, however, we are drawn to such gatherings by a sense of shared history and experience. That is, we take comfort in being with our own even as our own drive us crazy. Likewise, the Doctor and Master can be said to interact in the manner of an emotionally charged chemical reaction that is equal parts love and hate. In other words, when the Doctor gets bored with defeating the machinations of the Dalcks, Cybermen, Sontarans *et al*, he begins to long for a foe who will put up a good—which is to say a *smart*—fight. Moreover, even when he defeats his former friend, the Doctor can be fairly certain that any setback is only temporary for the Master and that no prison will ever hold him permanently.

Even as the third Doctor and Jo Grant visit the Master in the prison that holds him in episode one of "The Sea Devils," the question on everyone's mind is not whether the evil Time Lord will escape, but when and how he will do so. To understand the Doctor's and the Master's psyches in this situation, we can turn to French philosopher Michel Foucault's provocative book *The History of Sexuality—Volume I: An Introduction*. In this volume, Foucault advances his theory of "perpetual spirals of power and pleasure." Within the context of his work, Foucault uses these spirals to explain the relationships between nineteenth-century psychiatrists and patients who suffered from what were then considered sexual perversities, but his theory can also be applied to the relationship between the Doctor and the Master as well. For Foucault, the spirals of power and pleasure are experienced on both ends of the following relationships: parents and children, adults and adolescents, educators and students, doctors and patients, and psychiatrists and hysterics or perverts. As for the spirals themselves, Foucault claims that the pleasure comes out of "exercising a power that questions, monitors, watches, spies, searches out, palpates, brings to light; and on the other hand, the pleasure that kindles at having to evade this power, flee from it, fool it, or travesty it. The power that lets itself be invaded by the pleasure it is pursuing; and opposite it, power asserting itself in the pleasure of showing off, scandalizing, or resisting."[6]

By adding jailer and prisoner to the above list of opposites, we can argue that Foucault's spirals come into play in "The Sea Devils" the moment the Doctor visits the Master in prison. That moment, however, is rife with ambiguity since, unknown to the Doctor, the Master is in league with the prison's governor, Colonel George Trenchard. Under the Master's sway, Trenchard has begun to allow the Master certain liberties, including that of leaving his cell from time to time to carry out his schemes. Once the Doctor realizes that the Master is up to his old tricks, of course, he naturally confronts his nemesis and their conflict takes the form of a swordfight. Yet no sooner has the Doctor bested his opponent than Trenchard appears and returns the advantage to the Master.

Applying Foucault's spirals to this scenario, we can argue that each party experiences some degree of power and pleasure at the other's expense. The Master, though technically a prisoner, enjoys both the power and pleasure of knowing what the Doctor initially does not—that he can come and go as he pleases because Trenchard is his pawn. Correspondingly, the Doctor initially takes pleasure in the sense of moral superiority that visiting his jailed foe implies. When their roles are reversed, moreover, and Trenchard allows the Master to interrogate the Doctor, the Doctor takes pleasure in being the Master's prisoner insofar as he now must play the game of figuring out how to escape from his enemy's clutches. Per usual, the Doctor eventually wins at this game, but not before the Master can permanently escape from his terrestrial prison by appropriating a hovercraft. Far from being chagrined at this escape, however, the Doctor allows the hint of a smile to creep across his face as he watches his nemesis flee—a sign, perhaps, that he is in fact pleased at the prospect of battling his most worthy nemesis when their paths inevitably cross once more.

In numerous other adventures, the Doctor and the Master resume their spiraling games of power and pleasure, occasionally forming temporary alliances before their relationship degenerates as it almost always does into savage fisticuffs. In "The Deadly Assassin," for example, the Doctor and the Master resort to brute force in their climactic struggle in the presence of the all-powerful and ironically named Eye of Harmony. Additionally, as the Master reaches wonderful heights of megalomania, he causes the fourth Doctor to fall to his doom from the scaffolding of the Pharos Project radio telescope at the conclusion of "Logopolis." What's interesting about this encounter, moreover, is that before disposing of the Doctor, the Master voices his desire to rule the universe by using the telescope as an intergalactic megaphone and giving everyone within its broadcast range a choice between total annihilation and continued existence under his guidance. If only the Doctor would get out of his way, the subtext of this adventure seems to argue, then the Master could do a halfway decent job of bringing order, peace and prosperity to the cosmos.

But would the Master really be happy if he were to achieve his dreams of cosmic domination? Probably not—since for both the Master and the Doctor, the joy is in playing the game and not necessarily in winning it. Deep down, the Master knows that he needs the Doctor to foil his schemes, hence his admission in "The Five Doctors" that "A cosmos without the Doctor scarcely bears thinking about." So even as the end draws near for the fourth Doctor at the end of "Logopolis," the Master surely takes pleasure in the knowledge that the Doctor will—in some form, anyway—live to fight another day.

Along similar lines, the Doctor's admission in "Logopolis" that as Time Lords, he and the Master "in many ways ... have the same mind" raises the issue of whether the Doctor might *ever* finish the Master off with his own hands since such an act might well be akin to suicide. Putting this issue to the test, the final tale of the original series, "Survival," presents the familiar tableau of witty discourse between the Time Lords degenerating into a physical struggle. As a dying planet deteriorates all around them, the Doctor raises an animal skull to bash the Master's brains in but stops himself at the last minute as he offers what may be the strongest anti-war message *Doctor Who* has ever delivered: "If we fight like animals, we'll die like animals!" And even though the Master largely ignores this message as he raises a hefty bone to beat the Doctor to a pulp, his failure to kill the Doctor in this instance once again raises the possibility that their rivalry—and the sense of power and pleasure they both derive from it—will continue.

Dropping Out

If the Master is the most twisted and bitter of Gallifrey's renegades, then the Rani, whom the sixth Doctor describes as having a "brilliant but sterile mind," is certainly the most indifferent and emotionally detached. Lacking a vendetta against either the Time Lords or the Doctor, she simply wishes to pursue her scientifically aberrant schemes whether they pertain to a single planet as in "The Mark of the Rani" or to all of reality as in "Time and the Rani." All she really asks is that her Time Lord peers leave her alone. From a gendered perspective and at the risk of speaking far too broadly, the Rani's diligent commitment to tackling one specific task at a time, like that of Romana who chooses to assist the Tharils at the conclusion of "Warrior's Gate," suggests that female Time Lords are more logical and focused than their male counterparts. After all, the Doctor is always moving from one destination to another, routinely picking up fresh companions and making new friends and enemies while the Master always seems to be engaging in scheme upon scheme—or better yet, schemes wrapped in other schemes—to the absolute dismay and frequent confusion of all parties involved. When it comes to the Rani, however, we're faced with a single-minded individual whose monolithic view of the universe places her at the top of a massive hierarchy and subjugates all others to her self-proclaimed superiority.

In "The Mark of the Rani," for example, the titular villainess scoffs at the Doctor's concern over her human victims. "They're carnivores," the Rani replies when the Doctor points out that her victims have done her no harm; "What harm have the animals in the field done them? The rabbits they snare? The sheep they manage to slaughter? Do they worry about the lesser species when they sink their teeth into a lamb chop?" While such rhetoric may be chilling, it also resonates with the overall mentality of the Doctor, the Master and all Time Lords who even occasionally condone tampering with the natural development of "lesser" species. Even when the Doctor lends a hand, after all, he's more or less signaling to those who accept his help that they'd be lost without him. To put it another way, the fact that some Time Lords—most noticeably the Doctor—have no problem with materializing anywhere in time and space and manipulating the destinies of less technologically advanced species suggests that, strictly speaking, they share the Rani's dim view of the "animals" that populate the universe.

Of course, the Master and the Rani are not alone in their contempt for life forms they deem less evolved than themselves. In "The Time Meddler," the so-called Meddling Monk interferes with Earth history for the sheer fun of it, and a renegade known only as the War Chief allies himself with bellicose aliens in "The War Games" in order to satisfy his dreams of conquering the galaxy. For sheer delusions of grandeur, however, nobody beats the revolutionary Morbius, the former leader of the Time Lord High Council whose ambition to conquer the universe led to his eventual execution at the hands of his own people. Such depravity—snuffed out though it may have been—at the uppermost echelons of Gallifrey's government returns us to the issue of whether the nearly absolute power the Time Lords wield over time and space lends itself to absolute corruption. As we learn in "The Five Doctors," Gallifreyan technology was once used to whisk countless races away from their homes and deposit them in the planet's Death Zone so they could fight for the Time Lords' amusement. That multi-Doctor story also reveals the mastermind behind the more recent reactivation of the Death Zone to be Borusa, the Doctor's esteemed former teacher and a leader of the High Council. Given all of this information, it's difficult to view Gallifreyans as anything other than essentially corrupt and drunk with power.

Assuming that the dim view of other species held by the Master, the Rani, Morbius *et. al* is symptomatic of the hubris of Time Lord culture at large, perhaps it's no wonder that some elements of that society have chosen—to borrow a phrase from the late, great Timothy Leary—to tune in, turn on and drop out. While this is ostensibly what the Doctor did when he left Gallifrey to explore the universe, other Gallifreyans have taken more drastic steps to shed the assumptions, mores and dictates of their culture. In "The Deadly Assassin," for example, Castellen Spandrell speaks disparagingly of the Shabogans, a group of outsiders who shun mainstream Time Lord society and commit petty acts of vandalism in order to make their dissatisfaction known among the population at large. Similarly, an unnamed group of disenfranchised Time Lords depicted in "The Invasion of Time" embraces a lifestyle that is committed to peace, tranquility and a return to nature.[7] Conspicuously absent from the latter group's way of living, naturally, are technology and any form of bureaucratic or hierarchical structure that might otherwise lead to the kind of cultural hubris at the heart of mainstream Time Lord society.

Perhaps following the lead of the Shabogans, other Time Lords have also dropped out of mainstream society as well. Introduced in "Planet of the Spiders," the mysterious K'Anpo Rinpoche is revealed to be a childhood mentor of the Doctor who has left Gallifrey to lead a life of quiet meditation on Earth. As the abbot of a Tibetan meditation center, K'Anpo lives a peaceful existence with his fellow monks and offers a retreat for those humans who wish to escape from the fast-paced life of latter twentieth-century England. What is even more interesting about K'anpo is the fact that he meditates alongside his deputy Cho-Je, who is actually a projection of his future self. Imagine the bickering that would result if the second Doctor, for example, meditated alongside a projection of the third Doctor, and you'll get a sense of the inner harmony that K'Anpo must have in order to undertake such an activity in peace.

Significantly, K'Anpo—after fully adopting the form of Cho-Je—helps the third Doctor through a difficult regeneration before fading into the universe to continue his inner journey of peace and self-discovery. As K'Anpo's transformation into Cho-Je and, in turn, the third Doctor's regeneration into the fourth demonstrate, the meditative Time Lord embraces change even as he meditates over the unity of all time—past, present and future. Moreover, K'Anpo's inherent sense of inner harmony may also set the stage for the fourth Doctor's encounter with the mysterious Watcher in "Logopolis," for the Watcher, it turns out, is actually a dim projection of the soon-to-arrive fifth Doctor. Indeed, it's entirely conceivable that the appearance of the Watcher signals that the Doctor himself has taken a small step toward achieving a higher degree of personal harmony by the time he battles the Master in "Logopolis." And if the splintered and occasionally self-loathing Doctor can take such steps toward finding inner harmony, then there may also be hope for the rest of Time Lord society as well.

Or there might have been, if not for the Time War.

Shooting a Myrka

Although the destruction of Gallifrey in the frequently discussed but never seen Last Great Time War in some ways renders discussion of Time Lord culture moot, the long shadow cast by that culture is one the Doctor can never escape. Even in the absence of a home planet, the Doctor remains both a proud representative and a biting critic of the culture from which he originally hails. To make sense of this apparent conundrum, we can turn to George Orwell's famous essay "Shooting an Elephant," which offers poignant commentary on the author's relationship with the British Empire. In this essay, Orwell—whose magnum opus *1984* is widely regarded as a major influence upon such *Doctor Who* serials as "The Green Death," "Genesis of the Daleks," "The Sun Makers" and "The Happiness Patrol"—describes serving in the town of Moulmein in Lower Burma as a sub-divisional Indian Imperial Police Officer when an elephant in heat goes on a deadly rampage. Wishing to kill the elephant, the local citizenry turns to Orwell, who finds his prey at rest, its "must" already passing. Despite the now-peaceful nature of the elephant, Orwell realizes that his only option as a representative of the British Empire is to put the beast down; to do otherwise would be to risk a loss of respect and authority among the Burmese people. Thus, ambivalently succumbing to the will of the mob, Orwell slaughters the elephant.[8]

Like Orwell in his unfortunate situation, the Doctor is frequently forced to use his equivalent of superior firepower—that is, his brilliant intellect—to come to the aid of those who seek his help. In the worst of those situations, the Doctor knows that any seeming victory will be pyrrhic at best. Over the course of the fifth-Doctor serial "Warriors of the Deep," for example, the Time Lord slays a monstrous sea creature known as the Myrka and releases deadly hexachromite gas into the ventilation system of a sea base in order to kill a bellicose contingent of Silurians and Sea Devils. Upon bearing witness to the human and reptilian toll his actions have taken by the time the serial concludes, however, the Doctor sadly notes that although he has prevented nuclear war from erupting on Earth, "There should have been another way."

In marked contrast to his downbeat reevaluation of the intervention techniques he employs in "Warriors of the Deep," however, the tenth Doctor we see in "Doomsday" gleefully disposes of Cybermen and Daleks by engineering a void that can only be described as a living hell for his enemies. Furthermore, unlike Orwell or his earlier self, he uses his intellect and superior knowledge of the universe to commit an act that is tantamount to the genocide of two races. And while the Time Lords appear to be extinct at this juncture, the Doctor, in his own likeable way, preserves the hegemonic nature of their empire by suppressing the cultures of the admittedly cold and mechanical Cybermen and Daleks in favor of his own. Given the fascist nature of both regimes, of course, the Doctor's efforts at saving the world may well be justified, but the fact remains that his ongoing mission to protect the universe at large is highly informed by the cultural norms that shaped and continue to define his complex and sometimes inconsistent sense of morality.

Conflicted though the Doctor may be with regard to the decadent culture of his home world, recent revelations suggest that he returned to the Time Lord fold somewhere between the events depicted in the 1996 TV movie and the Nestene invasion of Earth at the start of the new series, for we learn in "The Parting of the Ways" that the Doctor bears direct responsibility for the simultaneous destruction of the Time Lords and Daleks that ended the conflict. While the reasons behind the Doctor's apparent reconciliation with his people will forever remain a matter of speculation, his wistful reference to standing together with his fellow Time Lords at the Fall of Arcadia suggests that in the end, the ideology of his home world resonated more strongly with the Doctor's own values than he previously thought. In this sense, even in the absence of a planet to call home, the Doctor will always be "pulled back in" because his decision to continue traveling the universe and fighting for what he believes to be right forever makes him a representative of the simultaneously laudable and questionable tenets of the world that was—and someday, some way, may once more be—*Gallifrey*.

5

Cranky Cyborgs: Daleks, Cybermen and the Future of Humanity

For a race with no discernible lips, the Daleks have managed to pay an inordinate amount of lip service to the notion that they are devoid of emotions. Indeed, when it comes to boasting complete emotional detachment, the Daleks are rivaled only by the Cybermen, whose own lip service to the ideals of logic and cold, calculating reason temporarily gained the slightest modicum of plausibility when the race adopted orifice-revealing glass jaws in "Earthshock." Yet for all of their bluster and all of the pride each race takes in lacking emotion, the Daleks and Cybermen have never quite measured up to the ideals to which they aspire.

"Love, pride, hate, fear! Have you no emotions, sir?" asks the first Doctor of a Cyberman in "The Tenth Planet," but surely he jests. Consider the absolute indignation of the Cybermen who fall prey to Lady Peinforte's gold-tipped arrows in "Silver Nemesis." Their pitiful cries pale only in contrast to the pride with which the Cyber Leader declares that imagination, thought, freedom and pleasure "all will end" as soon as the latest diabolical Cyber-plan transforms Earth into "the New Mondas." Likewise, consider the sheer panic and desperation in the voice of any Dalek who stumbles upon an enemy armed with a tarp, a sheet, a blanket or, heaven forbid, a well-aimed hat-to-the-eyestalk: "My vision is impaired! I cannot see!"

Even the most casual of Whoficionados will note that for a race devoid of emotions, the Daleks certainly place an inordinate number of exclamation points at the ends of their sentences. On the other hand, consider the unassuming and relatively obscure Voc and Supervoc robots whom the fourth Doctor and Leela encounter in "The Robots of Death." Armed only with impassive art-deco facemasks and metallic Oscar Wilde hairdos, the Vocs and their Supervoc brother manage to carry off one hell of a killing spree without so much as raising an enamel eyebrow. While the Daleks can't seem to glide through a hallway without breaking into a chorus of their trademark exclamation-point-laden battle-cry, the Vocs calmly and almost lackadaisically repeat their objective as they attempt to eliminate their prey: "Kill the Doctor. Kill the Doctor. Kill the Doctor." Additionally, while the Cybermen come off as cranky old bastards whenever they fall under attack, the Vocs simply go about the business of attempting acts of manual strangulation while their would-be victims throw knives or detonate explosives. In point of fact, the biggest rise anyone gets out of any of the robots in "The Robots of Death" is a simple request: "Please do not throw hands at me."

In short, the Voc and Supervoc robots fully realize the ideal to which the Daleks and Cybermen aspire. Yet while the complete lack of emotion with which the robots carry out their mission lends a particularly creepy air to "The Robots of Death," these robots lack a certain *joie de vivre* (or at least a certain *joie-de-*killing-things) that the Daleks and the Cybermen share; what makes both races resonate so strongly with audiences is that they do, in fact, have personalities—hence the phenomenon of schoolboys all over England walking around with toilet plungers and shouting "Exterminate!" within hours of the first-ever incident of a Dalek shouting this same word on television. Moreover, the Daleks and Cybermen also prove especially haunting insofar as they underscore the complexity of humanity's relationship with the machines that saturate our cultural landscape.

With regard to logic, the above-mentioned robots have a distinct advantage over the Daleks and Cybermen: they are entirely robotic. Imagine the jealousy with which the Daleks, for example, must look upon their purely mechanical cousins. Imagine, too, the sheer outrage said Daleks must feel upon recognizing this jealousy and identifying it as (horror of horrors) *an emotion!* Adding insult to injury, imagine the further outrage of realizing that outrage is itself an emotion, and what begins to emerge is a clear explanation of the Daleks' perpetual anger as well as the motivation behind their longstanding grudges against such purely robotic races as the Mechanoids and the Movellans. More significantly, where episodes of *Doctor Who* that pit humanity against robots suggest a clear split between humans and machines, episodes featuring Daleks, Cybermen or other cyborgs serve as a reminder that the line between humanity and the machines we humans love grows less distinct every day.

Why So Cranky?

While the Daleks and Cybermen may be the best-known cyborgs the Doctor has encountered in his travels, others have crossed the Time Lord's path as well—all of them cranky, and many of them itching for a fight. But what is it, exactly, that makes these cyborgs so cranky? Do they just need a hug, or do their problems run deeper? A quick rundown of some of the Doctor's less-renowned cybernetic friends and foes demonstrates that cyborgs really aren't that different from the rest of us when it comes to having a bad day.

- Arcturus: Representing the Arcturus System, this Galactic Federation delegate appears in "The Curse of Peladon" and resembles a Dalek in many respects. For one thing, he's not particularly adept at climbing steps, which puts him at a distinct disadvantage on the rocky environs of Peladon. For another, he's intent upon killing the Doctor. Unlike latter-day Daleks, however, Arcturus lacks the power to levitate and would probably kill for a polycarbide armor shell. Indeed, it's his lack of any armor whatsoever that makes this wannabe Dalek such an easy target. What makes Arcturus so cranky, however, is not so much a sense of armor-envy but, more than likely, the confusion that stems from his unrequited love for the multi-armed hermaphroditic delegate from Alpha Centauri. Sure, he never makes his true feelings known, but who among us could resist the charms of a massive, four-armed eyeball dressed in a shower curtain?
- The Skarasen: In "Terror of the Zygons," this monstrous cyborg spends much of its time attacking oil rigs in the North Sea off the Scottish coast. When the Doctor frees the Skarasen from the control of its fiendish creators, the Zygons, it returns to the only home it has ever known, Loch Ness, where it will forever be mistaken for the mythical Loch Ness Monster. This wouldn't be so bad if not for the fact that another of the Doctor's nemeses shares the same claim to fame. At the conclusion of "Timelash," a mutated mad scientist called the Borad slips through—of all things—the Timelash, which transports him to Loch Ness where he is doomed to be mistaken for the mythical Loch Ness Monster for years to come. What makes the Skarasen so cranky, then, is sharing Loch Ness (and all of the attendant glory that goes with being its eponymous monster) with a piddling mad scientist from the future.
- The Peking Homunculus: Appearing in "The Talons of Weng Chiang," the Peking Homunculus is actually a robotic doll with the brain of a pig that travels from the fifty-first century to the nineteenth century in order to fulfill its lifelong dream of becoming a ventriloquist's dummy. Apparently, however, showbiz is not all that it's cracked up to be, and the Peking Homunculus quickly tires of jokes revolving around the "Now who's the dummy, dummy?" punch-line. As a result, the Homunculus takes to playing with switchblade knives and eventually gets behind the wheel of a laser cannon. Yet while literally living out of a steamer trunk proves somewhat irksome, what really gets this little piggy's goat is the mere fact of its own existence, and it doesn't take long for the Peking Homunculus

to come to the conclusion that any race dumb enough to put a pig's brain in a child's toy needs to be put out of its misery.

- The Captain: The Doctor meets this particularly cranky cyborg while searching for the second segment of the Key to Time in "The Pirate Planet." Half-man, half-machine, the Captain keeps a robotic parrot on his shoulder and is under the constant care of a nurse, who herself is the tangible projection of a dying old crone. Cranky throughout much of the adventure due to his apparently insatiable appetite for planets, the Captain goes over the edge and turns super-cranky when K-9 kills his parrot, thus proving the old adage that nothing should come between a man and his bird.

- The Kandy Man: As Kermit the Frog so famously croaks, "It isn't easy being green," and in the Kandy Man's case, it isn't easy being sweet, either. And before you start bellyaching over his classification as a cyborg, remember that the sugar constituting the bulk of the Kandy Man's fetching figure is an organic compound. So central is sugar to his composition, in fact, that our favorite sweetie must remain forever on the move to prevent his sherbet-marzipan-caramel-toffee hide from coagulating. As a result, we must forgive his crankiness, as the Kandy Man is much like an aging arthritic who continuously labors to make perfect vats of fondant surprise and other delectables, all for the sheer joy of putting everlasting smiles on the faces of his "volunteers."

- The S.S. Madame De Pompadour: The S.S. Madame De Pompadour's damaged computer is probably more of a frustrated cyborg than a cranky one, but one gets the distinct sense that it grows weary of looking for a brain, namely that of the actual living, breathing Madame De Pompadour. On the positive side, the computer is becoming more human as it tries to complete its mission. Even if a few crewmembers had to sacrifice their lives in order to give the computer an upgrade, a nice pair of eyeballs and a few exposed organs can only build the child-like, confused computer into a better person as it admirably struggles to find its way in the cyborg world. Then again, the smell of roasting meat that permeates the spaceship doesn't do much for this cyborg's odds of meeting a discerning woman of taste—especially not one of Madame De Pompadour's caliber. And so it is that this cyborg is doomed to a life of loneliness and mindless frustration.

- Adam: Briefly a companion to the ninth Doctor, Adam Mitchell may not yet be a card-carrying cranky cyborg, but anyone whose forehead can open like a gaping mouth probably isn't all that happy. With the snap of a finger, Adam becomes a shocking postmodern spectacle as an access hatch opens to expose the inner workings of his skull. As if this weren't frustrating enough, poor Adam must live with the knowledge that while his head holds a treasure chest of untold technical marvels, the software for accessing those marvels will not be available for another 198,000 years.

- The TARDIS: Because the Doctor's Type-40 TARDIS is in many ways alive, it is an excellent contender for the title of the ultimate cranky cyborg. Granted, it does assist the Doctor in regenerating several times, and it allows Rose to come to his rescue at the climax of "The Parting of the Ways," but it can also be viewed as cranky given its frequent unreliability and overall unpredictability. In "The Impossible Planet," the Doctor lets it slip that the TARDIS was grown, not built, and the TARDIS has also been rumored to be comprised of an ever-changing coral-like substance. Combining this fact with the knowledge that the TARDIS has a "heart" in the form of the Time Vortex, it's easy to speculate that the journeys on which it brings the Doctor and his companions are all the result of being attuned to the totality of time and space. Like a nurturing yet flawed creature who both loves and loathes her pilot and long-time occupant, the TARDIS brings the Doctor on trips that will always be guaranteed to thrill. And the root of the time machine's crankiness? More than likely, it has something to do with sharing her beloved Doctor with all of those attractive young women he brings aboard. After all, hell hath no fury like a TARDIS scorned.

On Daleks and Road Rage (Among Other Things)

In "Revelation of the Daleks," the sixth Doctor arrives on the planet Necros only to discover his old nemesis Davros hard at work reinventing the torture wheel. Identified as the creator of the Daleks in "Genesis of the Daleks," frozen solid and held over for trial in "Destiny of the Daleks," and thawed out in "Resurrection of the Daleks," Davros has returned once again to build a new army of angry salt and pepper shakers, this time using human tissue in his efforts to create a master race. Echoed forcefully in "The Parting of the Ways," in which the ninth Doctor discovers yet another army of Daleks cultivated from human tissue, this twist on the Dalek myth draws attention to the social significance of the Daleks as a metaphor and also goes a long way toward explaining their longstanding popularity among fans of *Doctor Who.* We love the Daleks not because they are so alien, but because they are so much like us.

To bastardize a phrase from "The Three Doctors," the Daleks resonate so well with us because, now more than ever, they are we, and we are they. Nonetheless, when Terry Nation and Raymond Cusick designed the Daleks in 1963, their intention was to create a race that was decidedly *not* human.

In *Doctor Who: The Early Years*, Jeremy Bentham explains that Nation "had long held a morbid fascination with the horrors of contemporary warfare: gas attack, chemical shelling and especially with the effects of nuclear weapons" and that Nation's fascination led Cusick to envision a race that had decayed into "horrible shapes, almost armless and legless, dependent on machines to give them any mobility."[1] Yet as alien as the Daleks may have been envisioned in 1963, humanity is, by degrees, inching inexorably toward the wholesale adoption of the Dalek ideal—*i.e.*, a world full of atrophying jellyfish hell-bent on ruling the world from within the confines of armed and largely indestructible rolling shells.

The term *road rage* comes to mind.

Coined in the late 1970s, the term road rage applies to any number of anti-social behaviors and aggressive acts that occur, predictably enough, on the road. In a book titled *How Emotions Work*, psychologist Jack Katz notes that two personality traits common to most road-ragers are a "routine production of incredulity" and a tendency to stereotype.[2] In other words, the typical road-rager is always surprised at how poorly other people appear to drive no matter how many times he or she has witnessed the same or similar acts of poor driving. Moreover, this constant state of surprise tends to reinforce one's own sense of superiority over all other drivers on the road.

Sound familiar?

Despite having encountered countless illogical species throughout their travels, the Daleks are always completely flabbergasted and (some might say) even flummoxed whenever they stumble upon yet another species that irrationally refuses to succumb to the inevitable and surrender without a fight in the face of a clearly superior enemy.

"The Daleks must be obeyed!" the Daleks shout at anyone who will listen.

"You must cooperate!" they cry.

"The Daleks are superior!" they insist.

Yet for all of this insistence, resistant life forms continue to proliferate, and the Daleks, like their road-raging counterparts, can only draw one conclusion: the universe is filled with idiots.

The parallel between road-raging humans and Daleks is made especially clear in the 1988 serial "Remembrance of the Daleks." Early in the first episode of this serial, the seventh Doctor and his teenage companion, Ace, climb into the back of a van that, like the interior of a Dalek, comes fully loaded with sensors, monitors and other electronic equipment. Later, the Doctor explains that the Daleks are descended from a race much like the human race and that even though they may not be "little green men," the Daleks are, rather, "little green blobs in bonded polycarbide armor." Bringing Ace up to speed on Dalek history, the Doctor explains (while the pair take turns driving the van) that the Daleks are "the mutated remains of a species called the Kaleds." Furthermore, according to the Doctor, "The Kaleds were at war with the Thals. They had a dirty nuclear war. The resulting mutations were then accelerated by their chief scientist, Davros. What he created, he then placed in a metal war machine, and that's how the Daleks came about." Upon hearing this information, Ace makes the astute observation that "the metal thing" she's just had the pleasure of meeting "had a creature inside controlling it." Less astute, however, is Ace's failure to grasp the irony of her own situation: while marveling at the notion of a "metal thing" with "a creature inside controlling it," she herself is a creature controlling a metal thing from within.

That the van in which Ace and the Doctor are riding in the above scene is a military van—in other words, a "metal war machine"—only strengthens the parallel between the Daleks and humanity: our longstanding love-affair with motor vehicles renders us increasingly inhuman. What's more, one element of car design that proves especially dehumanizing is, somewhat ironically, the emphasis car manufacturers place on safety. While no one would ever argue that cars should be *less* safe, the increased protection that modern cars offer can blind drivers to their own fragility and also to the potentially fatal results of either carelessness or blind aggression behind the wheel. As social commentator Bill Good observes,

> The cars today are probably safer than at any time in our history, but they're being driven by people with no apparent concern for themselves or others. Being one of the others, I'm troubled by that. Even more disturbing is the complete lack of grace shown when someone makes an honest mistake or somehow angers the aggressive driver. The language that comes out of some people's mouths is unbelievable ... and it's not all young men. I've seen soccer moms yell at the top of their lungs while flipping the bird, right in front of their kids.[3]

Although such soccer moms may not be yelling "Exterminate!" they might as well be; the kill-or-be-killed rationale behind most acts of road rage sheds light on the sociopathic nature of the driving experience. When we're on the road, we don't see people; we only see cars, trucks and other vehicles. Consequently, we care little or nothing for other drivers or their passengers.

As most television commercials commissioned by the auto industry demonstrate, driving is a largely solitary activity that should, above all else (and small-print warnings be damned), be *fun*. Which is to say that we should view driving as little more than a game and other drivers as mere opponents. One result of this attitude is that we lose all sense of social responsibility upon sliding behind the wheel. Films as diverse as *Death Race 2000*, *Stand by Me* and *Bill and Ted's Bogus Journey* satirically depict the act of driving as nothing more than an opportunity to rack up points for striking everything from mailboxes to cats and pedestrians. Likewise, the virtual realm of the videogame serves as the perfect training ground for converting otherwise level-headed and civic-minded individuals into something more akin to what Davros describes in "Resurrection of the Daleks" as "totally logical war machines."

Humanity's virtual training began in 1975 with the release of *Death Race* —a primitive arcade game that awarded points for running down pedestrians—and continues to this day with more sophisticated games like *Grand Theft Auto* and *White Van Man*, a game in which a white Ford van ploughs through city streets in an attempt to knock other motorists off the road. While it may be unlikely that the Daleks themselves are actively involved in the programming and production of such videogames, these seemingly mindless diversions do an excellent job of simulating the Dalek point-of-view and fostering sympathy for the Dalek perspective—a perspective that is revealed in "Remembrance of the Daleks" to include the crosshairs that are the hallmark of most "first-person shooter" video games.

Along similar lines, a particularly chilling twist on the road rage phenomenon appears in Don DeLillo's magnum opus *Underworld* in the person of Richard Gilkey, the Texas Highway Killer. Armed with "his father's old .38," Gilkey fires upon lone drivers from behind the wheel of his car as he roams Texas highways in search of victims.[4] When asked about his motives, the killer—speaking through an electronic device that alters the sound of his voice *a la* the Daleks—instructs his interviewer to interpret his ongoing murder spree "as a game" and quickly points out that he is not a sniper.[5] A sniper, Gilkey notes, is a stationary individual who fires a rifle "more or less long-range."[6] What makes Gilkey special is that he remains in motion as he takes aim and fires upon his victims. Playing a deadly game that operates on the combined principles of road-rage simulators and first-person shooters, Gilkey has, in essence, become a primitive, gas-guzzling version of a Dalek—a murderous combination of man, machine and gun.

Not to be outdone by DeLillo and his fictional Texas Highway Killer, however, the real-life Lenco Armored Vehicles Corporation of Pittsfield, Massachusetts, has developed its own version of the Dalek—a modified Ford F-550 commercial truck equipped with a turret and 1.5-inch-thick steel armor (bonded polycarbide armor having, apparently, proved too cost-prohibitive). While the traditional military tank has long been a battlefield mainstay and, itself, draws obvious comparisons with the basic Dalek concept, Lenco's BearCat, as it is called, is designed specifically as an urban assault vehicle. One review of this vehicle notes that for all of its armor and "Terminator looks," the BearCat drives like any other large truck and is "almost nimble."[7] What's more, the vehicle is intimidating; in addition to the above-mentioned features, the BearCat is equipped with seven gun ports and—just like a Dalek—an array of chemical and radiation sensors. In fact, the most significant difference between the BearCat and Dalek machinery is size. Where each Dalek is designed to house a single Kaled mutant, the BearCat seats two humans comfortably in the front seat and boasts enough cargo room in the rear for ten SWAT troopers.

While the BearCat's size may prove somewhat prohibitive with regard to rolling down a narrow corridor and shouting "Exterminate!" while zapping one's enemies, a single-seat, personal-use Dalek may well be in the works for those of us who wish to wreak havoc on public sidewalks and in local shopping malls in addition to the more traditional road rage venues. As Peter Dunn reports in an essay titled "Beware of Hell's Grannies," pedestrians in increasing numbers are regularly being run down by "wild-eyed pensioners" on electric scooters.[8] While some rightly argue that such scooters serve as a valuable form of transportation that allows older people to remain active, Dunn notes that an estimated 200,000 vehicles, "some of them hefty, 'all-terrain' four-wheel jobs," are already terrorizing public pavements.[9]

According to the Electric Mobility Company of Sewell, New Jersey, which manufactures the top-selling Rascal line of scooters, such vehicles allow riders to "enjoy the thrill" of accelerating to top speeds of eight miles per hour, and while the company's press materials make no mention of a chief scientist with a vaguely Greek-sounding name, the measurements of the Rascal are roughly those of the Dalek base. Where Rascal scooters run from anywhere between thirty-nine to forty-eight inches in length, the Dalek base is, according to official BBC blueprints, forty-three inches in length. Where Rascals are generally in the neighborhood of twenty-five inches in width, Daleks tend to hover in the thirty-four to thirty-six inch range. Coincidence? Probably. At the same time, however, the similarity is striking, and it doesn't take a huge stretch of the imagination to combine the BearCat and the Rascal to come away with the basic concept behind the Dalek: a fully armed and armored rolling survival unit.

We love our cars.

We love our guns.

We love the freedom of personal mobility.

Isn't it high time we combined all of these elements to take our rightful place as the supreme power of the universe—or at least of the shopping mall?

One Cell in a Billion

Of course, a penchant for rolling about the planet and shooting things isn't the only attribute we humans share with Daleks. Independent of our cars and guns, we have come to embrace the aggressive mindset that has allowed the Daleks to become the scourge of the universe, and even without the protection afforded by a bonded polycarbide armor shell, each of us can easily view the world from the insular perspective of the mutated mass of cells that dwells within each Dalek; while driving around your neighborhood with a rifle protruding from your vehicle certainly won't hinder your efforts at adopting the Dalek outlook, you can achieve similar results without arousing the suspicions of the local authorities by simply sitting in front of your television and watching any twenty-four-hour news station. From this vantage point, moreover, you can gain the opportunity to formulate a worldview that reduces every issue imaginable to a series of simple binaries (such as black/white, good/bad, kill/be killed) and that, as a result, relieves our species of the collective burden of discussing complex issues in complex terms.

Though two distinct species, the Kaled mutant at the helm of the original Dalek and the human couch potato are cut from the same cloth. Both lead sedentary lives, both have relatively amorphous bodies and, perhaps most importantly, both can only view the world via electronic media rather than directly. That is, where the Kaled mutant perceives its surroundings in terms of visual data gathered by the eyestalk built into the Dalek's dome, the human couch potato can—in its most advanced stages of development— only see the world through the lens of the television camera. Accordingly, the couch potato's fondness for television gives all of humanity a leg up in the race to become as single-mindedly hell-bent on conquering the universe as the Daleks themselves.

Significantly, the affinity between the Dalek eyestalk and a television camera is not merely technological in nature. Rather, both media are similar in that they frame the world in relatively simple terms. While the Dalek dome can swivel a full 360 degrees, the crosshairs through which the Kaled mutant views the world render targets of all things within its purview. In other words, a Dalek never sees anything for "what it is," but instead sees everything as an obstacle to be overcome or an enemy to be destroyed. Therefore, a Dalek can never, for example, appreciate the intrinsic beauty of a sunset or the mysterious charm of the Mona Lisa's smile. To put it bluntly, viewing the world through a pair of crosshairs dictates that if a given phenomenon can't be blasted into oblivion, it might as well not exist. Hence the emotional impact of the conclusion to "Dalek," an episode in which the ninth Doctor and Rose discover what is purportedly the last surviving specimen of the cybernetic species imprisoned in an underground lab deep beneath the surface of the Utah Salt Flats. When the mutant within the Dalek abandons its armor to gaze directly upon the sun, it looks all-too briefly upon a world that it never knew—a world consisting not simply of targets and enemies of the Dalek race, but of frequently conflicting emotions, ephemeral subtleties and complex ambiguity. This is the world that is lost to all Daleks and, according to some social commentators, the world that is lost to humanity as well when television mediates virtually all that we see and hear.

As social critic Jeffrey Scheuer argues in *The Sound Bite Society: Television and the American Mind*, television "acts as a simplifying lens, filtering out complex ideas in favor of blunt emotional messages that appeal to the self and to narrower moral-political issues."[10] Thus for all of its technological complexity, "television's main systematic effect on human thinking is that of simplification."[11] What results from such simplification is what Scheuer describes as a "sound bite society," or a culture in which "slogans and images supplant arguments and ideas."[12] Examples of such societies can run the gamut from Germany during the rise of the Third Reich to the United States during the lead-up to any political election, but what they all have in common is a tendency to favor gut reactions and quick fixes over critical thinking and long-term planning. Or, in terms the Daleks might better appreciate, television teaches humanity that it is better to exterminate than to negotiate.

Although belaboring the Dalek propensity for extermination is far from necessary, a quick look at the race's negotiation techniques (or lack thereof) accentuates the parallel between the Daleks and humanity in the age of television. In the Daleks' historic first attempt at discussing the issue of Dalek superiority with a perceived inferior, a representative of the race outlines its position in no uncertain terms shortly before exterminating Davros at the conclusion "Genesis of the Daleks": "We obey no one! We are the superior beings!" Later in Dalek history—in "The Evil of the Daleks"—another Dalek ambassador kindly explains that "There is only one form of life that matters: Dalek life!" Later still, in a rare display of compassion, a Dalek in "Resurrection of the Daleks" holds out the race's equivalent of an olive branch when it offers the following ultimatum to a cloned human: "Should you fail, you will be exterminated!" Such notable quotations (along with the oft-angrily repeated cry of "Exterminate!") more than justify the seventh Doctor's observation in "Remembrance of the Daleks" that one reason he dislikes dealing with them is that the Daleks are "such boring conversationalists." At the same time, however, it is difficult to ignore the similarity between the Dalek mode of expression and that of a certain subspecies of human: the political pundit.

In *Lies and the Lying Liars Who Tell Them*, humorist Al Franken dedicates a chapter to covering the rhetorical techniques of cable-television talk-show host Bill O'Reilly. Using what Franken refers to as "a shopworn inventory of boorish tactics" that includes "blustering, bullying and belittling," O'Reilly frequently cows his guests into submission with regard to political issues and has been known to threaten violence when "elevated discourse" fails to produce the results he desires.[13] An example of such behavior occurred when O'Reilly interviewed Jeremy Glick, whose father died in the terror attacks of September 11, 2001. According to Franken, "Glick had signed an advertisement opposing the war in Iraq, and O'Reilly invited him on the show to explain himself, which he did modestly and eloquently. Until, that is, O'Reilly cut him off.... A little while later, O'Reilly told Glick to 'shut up, shut up!'"[14] What's more, once the cameras were off, O'Reilly sent Glick away with a threat: "Get out of my studio before I tear you to fucking pieces!"[15]

Such callous disregard for opposing points of view certainly points to the totalitarian, fascist worldview held by the Daleks, and O'Reilly's tendency to resort to threatening language is highly reminiscent of the megalomaniacal ravings of Davros in serials like "Remembrance of the Daleks," in which he spouts his usual venom: "Do not anger me, Doctor! I can destroy you and this miserable insignificant planet!"

O'Reilly, however, is by no means an anomaly; as Franken observes throughout *Lies and the Lying Liars Who Tell Them*, nearly all on-air political commentators favor vitriolic bombast over meaningful dialogue. Similarly, as Neil Postman argues throughout his landmark study of television's effect on American culture, *Amusing Ourselves to Death: Public Discourse in the Age of Show Business*, nearly every aspect of contemporary intellectual activity has been simplified for the sake of television, and because of this simplification, the American mind has atrophied.[16] Where the American populace was once capable of following a seven-hour debate between rival political candidates, today's Americans can barely sit through the introductory remarks of its modern-day ninety-minute equivalent.[17] The same holds true with regard to Americans and their attitudes towards religion, education and the news of the day. Regardless of the gravity of any single show's subject matter, television's overriding need to attract massive audiences has rendered all manner of programming akin to such senselessly violent melodramas as *The A-Team* and *Dallas*.[18]

Writing in the early to mid-1980s, Postman clearly identified the trend that would lead to such popular television programs as *Judge Judy*, *Big Brother*, *Survivor*, *The O'Reilly Factor* and *The Weakest Link*, all of which demonstrate time and again that the loudest mouth will always claim victory over the meek and humble. It should come as no surprise, then, that two of these programs (*Big Brother* and *The Weakest Link*) figure prominently in a series of more recent Dalek-related *Doctor Who* adventures that begins with "The Long Game" and concludes with "Parting of the Ways." Specifically, when the ninth Doctor arrives on an orbiting news satellite in the year 200,000, he meets a team of journalists who can directly access data via cybernetic implants that allow them to collect and broadcast the news of the day almost as soon as it occurs. Soon, however, the Doctor learns that the news satellite is under the control of an angry worm known as the Mighty Jagrafess, which is attempting to influence Earth's cultural development by manipulating its broadcast media. What the Doctor doesn't initially realize, however, is that the Jagrafess is itself under the control of the Daleks, and it isn't until the Time Lord returns to the satellite one hundred years after his first visit that he understands the full extent to which the mass media are being used to advance a sinister agenda: the reconstitution of the Dalek army.

Sinister as the Daleks' latest master plan may be, it also highlights the extent to which humanity is well on its way to evolving into a species very much like the Daleks. Not only are the denizens of the futuristic Earth depicted in "The Long Game" as hooked on television as many are today, but some—like the "journalists" mentioned above—have also gone so far as to have direct-data feeds installed in their foreheads. In fact, no sooner does the TARDIS materialize on the satellite than one of the Doctor's companions is voluntarily undergoing surgery to have a similar feed installed in his own head. That the companion's name is Adam is undoubtedly symbolic. Like the Adam of Genesis, his "crime" involves the pursuit of forbidden knowledge: what motivates him is a desire to access information about the future of Earth and to profit from that information upon his return to the twenty-first century. Yet when the Doctor eventually casts Adam from Eden— or, in this case, the TARDIS—it is not simply Adam's thirst for knowledge that the Doctor finds contemptible. After all, this same thirst is exactly what compels the Doctor to wander the universe in search of adventure. The Doctor's methodology, however, is active and involved whereas Adam's mode of accumulating knowledge is passive and heavily mediated. To put it another way, where the Doctor gets down and dirty as he risks his own life in the pursuit of knowledge, Adam's mode of "learning" relies entirely upon technology to serve as his eyes and ears and, as a result (and as is the case for the Daleks themselves), his mode of information-gathering ensures that he need never experience life directly.

While Adam's reliance upon technology to serve as his eyes and ears may well shield him from the world at large, a more significant theme in "The Long Game" is television's tendency to reinforce humanity's narcissism while simultaneously handicapping our capacity for critical inquiry. Over the course of its ninety-year rein over the airwaves, the Jagrafess has slowed the intellectual development of the Earth and its colonies to the point of complete mental shutdown, rendering the Fourth Great and Bountiful Human Empire ripe for the Daleks' picking. Even after the Doctor destroys the Jagrafess—thus halting its manipulation of the news media—humanity continues on its narcissistic and short-sighted path. This is because the Daleks have realized that they no longer need to manipulate the news in order to control humanity; rather, they only need to keep the masses amused.

By providing such mindless fare as the "reality" programs depicted in "Bad Wolf," the Daleks further their efforts to take over the galaxy on two fronts: the cultivation of new Dalek forces and the intellectual suppression of those who might otherwise resist them. As "Bad Wolf" opens, the Doctor, Rose and fellow time-traveler Captain Jack find themselves appearing separately in futuristic versions of *The Weakest Link*, *Big Brother* and *What Not To Wear*. Amusement, however, gradually gives way to horror as each show progresses. Initially giggling over the nonsensical questions[19] posed by a robotic Anne Robinson on *The Weakest Link*, Rose soon learns that those deemed "weakest" don't simply go home with a few parting gifts but are—to all appearances—vaporized. Likewise, the Doctor's mild chagrin at being caught in the *Big Brother* house turns to sheer outrage when he sees one of his own opponents vaporized as well, and Captain Jack's makeover on the set of *What Not to Wear* threatens to turn deadly when a robotic fashion consultant approaches him with a chainsaw and suggests that a slight nip and tuck might do his image a world of good. All of this, of course, serves as fodder for the pleasure-seeking masses of the Human Empire; as Jack's captors explain, because "vid-sockets" are all the rage, each show is being transmitted directly into billions of eyeballs at once.

What goes unsaid but is strongly suggested throughout "Bad Wolf" is that the viewing audience is largely responsible for the violence that occurs onscreen. When the Doctor presses his fellow *Big Brother* contestants for details about the game, he learns that demand for new episodes is so high that sixty versions of the show are running at once and that new contestants are constantly and involuntarily being lifted from their lives and placed directly in harm's way. Yet despite the fact that anybody might conceivably end up a victim of television's voracious appetite for fresh meat, the masses are too beholden to their own lust for blood to do anything about it. In the words of T.S. Eliot, the denizens of the Fourth Great and Bountiful Human Empire are so "distracted from distraction by distraction"[20] that they are perfectly willing to risk evisceration themselves if doing so is the price of eternal entertainment.

America's Funniest Home Videos, anyone? Or, if repeated kicks to the crotch aren't your cup of tea, how about *American Idol*, in which the thrill of victory is made to seem all the more sweet when juxtaposed with the embarrassingly awful auditions of the completely untalented. Or how about *Cops*, in which the dregs of society are dragged, kicking and screaming, to justice? Or *Cheaters*, in which the same dregs are caught on tape as they engage in clumsy acts of marital infidelity? These shows exist because we love to watch people squirm, and these shows are popular because, deep down, we're all sadists at heart.

That is, deep down, we're all as hateful and bloodthirsty as Daleks.

Television, it seems, has the power to bring out the worst in us—and the Daleks utilize this power to great effect in the execution of their latest, most fiendish plan. After Rose's apparent execution at the hands of the robotic Anne Robinson, Captain Jack learns that "people don't get killed in these games" but instead "get transported across space" to a hidden location on the edge of the solar system where they meet fates worse than death. Connecting the dots in "Parting of the Ways," the Emperor Dalek explains that he was the sole survivor of the Time War and that after falling through time, crippled but alive, he waited "in the dark space, damaged but rebuilding." Centuries passed, the Emperor further explains, and his slowly growing army "quietly infiltrated the systems of Earth, harvesting the waste of humanity." The Emperor, that is, took all of Earth's game show contestants and converted them into Daleks. And while the Emperor takes great pains to point out that "only one [human] cell in a billion was fit to be nurtured," chances are good that the cell to which the Emperor refers is the same one that is responsible for tuning into *Jerry Springer* and *Cops* on a regular basis.

Much to the Emperor's chagrin, Rose observes that if everything he's just reported is true, then the Daleks are, in fact, half human. Although the Dalek masses dismiss this observation as blasphemous, Rose is correct—a fact that should come as no surprise given the introduction of Lady Cassandra in episode two of the season, "The End of the World." Touted as the last living human, Cassandra resembles a Dalek more closely than anything else. Much like the Emperor Dalek, her brain floats in a solution of blue liquid, and her "body" consists of a span of human skin stretched across a metal frame that glides across the floor of her spaceship as a Dalek might. And while Lady Cassandra will not technically exist until the year five billion—some four-billion, nine-million, eight-hundred-thousand years after the events depicted in "Parting of the Ways"—the message is clear: regardless of outside influences, the fate of humanity is to evolve into a species that is very much like the Daleks. Indeed, that Lady Cassandra so closely resembles a flat-screen television suggests that we will evolve into a cross between the Daleks and the form of diversion we love best. Moreover, Lady Cassandra's guile, vanity and penchant for murder ensure that while she is not as traditionally armed and armored as the Daleks, she is still a force to be reckoned with, the ultimate specimen of a dying yet treacherous species.

As "Parting of the Ways" draws to a conclusion, the Doctor is faced with a dilemma: the only way to destroy the Daleks is to trigger a device that will wipe out Earth's populace as well. To overcome this dilemma, the Doctor rationalizes that dying as a human is a far better fate than living as a Dalek, yet what he fails to consider is that with or without the Daleks, humanity is already so wedded to machinery as to render the distinction between the races essentially irrelevant. Reliant upon television and similar technologies for nearly all sensory input, humanity has shut itself off from the outside world. Hopelessly addicted to increasingly violent forms of entertainment, we have grown numb to the sight of blood and destruction. Beholden to the most reductive modes of communication, we mindlessly and endlessly repeat the most hateful of slogans so much that we need not wonder what a Dalek invasion might be like—for, truly, we have met the Daleks, and they are we.

The Unbearable Ambivalence of Being Cyber

While Lady Cassandra certainly bears some resemblance to the Daleks, she is also undeniably akin to the angry pepperpots' intergalactic lack-of-soul mates, the Cybermen, in terms of *raison d'être* and *modus operandi*. What drives Lady Cassandra is a sense of vanity that is most clearly manifest in her apparent desire for eternal beauty (no doubt, in the Lady's case, a purely relative term), and the method she employs to guarantee that beauty is radical surgery. Likewise, the Cybermen are driven by a similar sense of vanity that is embodied in the race's collective quest for immortality. Moreover, unlike the Daleks—which amount to the mutated remains of a once-humanoid species now situated inside a fleet of metal war machines—the Cybermen have all gone under the knife, so to speak; although they remain humanoid in form, all of their frail human organs have been replaced with nearly indestructible artificial counterparts.

Like Lady Cassandra, the Cybermen have had nearly all traces of their original humanity removed via surgery, and what remains is a joyless race intent only on survival. Also like Lady Cassandra, however, the Cybermen carry a heavy sense of ambivalence at the core of their being. Torn between their overwhelming urge to survive and their suppressed loathing of what they have, of necessity, become, both the Cybermen and Lady Cassandra mirror humanity's own increasingly complicated understanding of the body and the machines and procedures we employ to prolong its usefulness.

Describing Lady Cassandra in *Doctor Who: The Shooting Scripts*, Russell T. Davies notes that the character was inspired by the "once-beautiful women reduced to nodding china lollipops" he had seen in attendance at the 2004 Academy Awards.[21] This revelation, coupled with Rose's comparison of Cassandra to Michael Jackson in "The End of the World," suggests that the character's freakish nature is rooted in twenty-first century values and ideals insofar as one trait that Hollywood's nodding china lollipops share with Jackson is a desire to be perceived as eternally young and beautiful. While the general public may view figures like Jackson as eccentric for their seeming obsession with facelifts and other forms of cosmetic surgery, such popular television programs as *Made*, *Extreme Makeover* and *The Swan* constantly reiterate the notion that one's appearance can and should be altered by any means necessary in order to conform with the latest trends in beauty and fashion. Looking ahead five billion years to Lady Cassandra, it's clear that where human vanity is concerned, the more things change, the more they stay the same.

As Michael Jackson's fascination with Peter Pan and his publicly professed desire to live forever suggest, the underlying conceit behind our culture's increasing obsession with cosmetic surgery is that the appearance of eternal youth might magically lead to the real thing. And it goes without saying that the self-proclaimed King of Pop isn't the only one with a vested interest in promoting the myth of eternal youth; the pharmaceutical industry has sunk a fortune into promoting the idea that—for the right price—life can be prolonged indefinitely. As a direct result of massive marketing campaigns on the part of drug companies, otherwise reasonable people are lining up in droves to have botulinum toxin (a.k.a. Botox) injected into their foreheads to reduce the appearance of wrinkles, the elderly are apparently thinking of taking up break-dancing, and dirty old men are leering at unsuspecting young coeds with a renewed sense of possibility.[22]

But who can blame them?

The ads are so beguiling.

"I did it for myself," an attractive woman says of her decision to try Botox.

"Celebrate! Celebrate! Do what you want to do!" another ad sings to arthritis sufferers.

And who can forget the image of former U.S. Presidential candidate Bob Dole winking at fellow erectile dysfunction victims as if to say that the stamina and sexual prowess of their youth can be regained for the price of a little blue pill? More recently, an ad depicting two adult men playing a rigorous game of basketball implores those of us for whom arthritis drugs are not sufficient cause for celebration to consider hip and knee replacement surgery. It isn't hard to imagine the Cybermen getting off to a similar start.

In the (perhaps apocryphal) Big Finish *Doctor Who* audio production, "Spare Parts," the fifth Doctor and Nyssa materialize beneath the surface of the wayward planet Mondas only to discover that its inhabitants are on the verge of evolving into the cybernetic race that will one day spread terror throughout the cosmos and cause the death of the Doctor's mathematically gifted if sometimes socially awkward companion, Adric. Brought before a committee of "swollen heads" wired into a single computer mainframe, the Doctor notes that the evolution of the Cyber-race started with procedures similar to those currently popular here on Earth: "How did it start? Just a few hip replacements and breast implants? Vanity's a killer, isn't it? And where will it end? Sleek heartless scavengers, cobbled up from space junk and other people's bodies. But you'll look ever so stylish."[23] Clearly a caveat against mixing vanity with technology, these remarks strongly suggest that if humanity isn't careful, we might very well follow in the footsteps of the Cybermen and become, like them, "so bloated with spare parts" that only cold logic will stifle our natural urge to scream in agony.[24]

Indeed, the tension between the agony of cybernetic existence and the biological imperative to keep on keepin' on not only lends "Spare Parts" its sense of dramatic urgency but also renders the Cybermen highly compelling villains in general. Everyone, it seems, wants to live forever and without pain, but at what price? In "Spare Parts," a minor character named Dodd asks a similar question as he explains that the people of Mondas regularly and voluntarily opt to replace their natural organs with titanium and plastic because they "think it'll last."[25] At the same time, however, some Mondasians are now composed of so much machinery that they opt to have their emotions surgically removed as well in order to avoid insanity.

"We all want immortality," Dodd admits; "But with a chrome finish?"[26]

As if to answer Dodd's question with a resounding *NO*, a young woman named Yvonne wanders away from Cyber-HQ midway through what the governing forces on Mondas euphemistically refer to as the augmentation process. "Primitive, genderless, [and] confused," Cybervonne (as she is rechristened) wanders the streets of her underground city, desperate to find the father who can only react with a tragic amalgam of horror and compassion when he sees what's become of his child.[27] And as any serious student of Cyberlore knows, Cybervonne is not alone in her despair and confusion over being augmented. In the eminently non-canonical yet equally entertaining comic strip series, "Throwback: The Soul of a Cyberman," a malfunctioning Cyberman named Kroton begins to question the meaning of existence and eventually makes what appears to be the ultimate sacrifice in order to save a band of human freedom fighters from certain doom. Similarly, in the sixth-Doctor serial, "Attack of the Cybermen," a partially converted human named Lytton realizes that the fate in store for him is so horrendous that he beseeches the Doctor to kill him before the conversion process can be completed. Most recently, in "The Age of Steel," yet another malfunctioning Cyber(wo)man laments that her conversion took place on the eve of her wedding day.

No one, it would seem, wants to be a Cyberman, yet theirs is the path we're most intent upon following—a conclusion emphasized by the fact that the "re-imagined" genesis of the Cybermen depicted in "Rise of the Cybermen" and "The Age of Steel" occurs not on Mondas but on a parallel Earth. In a clear nod to "Spare Parts," the tenth Doctor's companion, Mickey, describes himself as one of the Time Lord's own "spare parts" before venturing out into a world where the Cybermen are preparing to emerge as the galaxy's dominant life-form. This new generation of Cybermen, moreover, represents an improvement over previous models in that gold is not a threat to their respiratory mechanisms, and they are far less prone to internal bickering as their counterparts in the classic series. For example, where the Cyber Leader in "Silver Nemesis" must silence one of his dissenting lieutenants with the admonition that he is acting "outside [his] function," the Cybermen of "The Age of Steel" are more akin to the Borg of *Star Trek* fame in their adherence to a hive-like, singular mindset. "We think the same ... We are uniform," one Cyberman explains when Cyber-creator John Lumic ponders the essence of Cyber-being, and this attitude is confirmed by repeated shots of Cybermen marching, dozens at a time, in perfect lockstep. In short, when functioning properly, these new Cybermen lack all traces of ego and serve as paragons of groupthink.

In addition to their improved military prowess, the new Cybermen are also superior to their predecessors in terms of branding. Whereas the original Cybermen can trace their roots to state-sponsored initiatives proposed in the underground cities of planet Mondas, the new Cybermen are the creation of John Lumic, president of Cybus Industries. Given this position, Lumic's goal is not simply to prolong human life and eradicate the threat of disease but to make a few bucks in the process as well. As anyone familiar with Bill Gates and the history of Microsoft knows, the best way to make a killing in any industry is to aim for total market saturation by eliminating the competition and insinuating the company's brand-image into every nook and cranny of the public sphere. To this end, every Cyberman is stamped with the Cybus Industries logo, and rather than simply converting all humans into cyborgs, these new-generation Cybermen offer their human opponents "free upgrades." That is, their initial strategy for world domination is to use the soft-sell marketing technique of offering humanity the chance to trade up from perishable flesh and blood to indestructible chrome and steel. Only when the humans resist do the Cybermen resort to plan B, which is to point out that upgrading is compulsory. Like the good marketers they are, the Cybermen will not rest until their logo is stamped upon the chest of every sentient being on Earth.

At first glance, the service Lumic offers appears highly desirable. Who, after all, wouldn't be tempted by the offer of eternal life? Consider, for example, the comments of well-intentioned if terminally obtuse office manager David Brent in the BBC comedy series *The Office* when he opines that since "time travel is actually impossible," his greatest fantasy would be to have "some sort of everlasting life ... to experience the future and live on and on and on and on and know what it's like to live forever."[28] The cost, however, of gaining what Lumic refers to as "a body that will never die" is the substitution of metal and plastic for one's flesh and blood, and having one's brain sustained indefinitely "within a cradle of copyrighted chemicals" not unlike the glowing blue cocktail in which Lady Cassandra's gray matter floats. From Lumic's perspective, this isn't a bad trade at all; early in "Rise of the Cybermen" he notes that while humans are flesh and blood, the brain is truly "what makes us human." Hence, his reasoning goes, preserving the brain (and the brain alone) is tantamount to preserving humanity.

While the "service" offered by Cybus Industries may seem valuable to the likes of David Brent, Lumic's target market is reluctant to embrace what one comic strip calls "Cyberification."[29] Perhaps this reluctance stems from an innate sense among Lumic's potential customers that the brain alone is *not* what makes us human, but that, in the words of the fifth Doctor in "Earthshock," "the pleasure of smelling a flower, watching a sunset, eating a well-prepared meal" (*i.e.*, enjoying what the Doctor describes as "small, beautiful events" that can only be appreciated through the fleshly senses) "is what life is all about." Or perhaps the problem is that humans recognize the value of ambition and are haunted by the very question posed by the tenth Doctor in "The Age of Steel": "Once you get rid of sickness and mortality, then what is there to strive for?"

Then again, maybe it's simply the violent nature of the conversion process itself that turns potential customers away from Lumic's generous offer of a free upgrade. Although the viewing audience never sees the screaming circular saw of Lumic's processing plant make contact with human flesh, it appears on the screen long enough to make one thing perfectly clear: going Cyber won't exactly tickle. At the same time, however, the implements of conversion bare remarkable similarity to those used by the androids who threaten to give Captain Jack a drastic makeover in "Bad Wolf." This parallel, moreover, suggests that what the Cybermen are offering amounts to nothing more than plastic surgery writ large. Sure, the procedure is drastic and painful, but if the Cybermen were to retool their sales pitch and give the old soft-sell another try, they might well be able to coax more people into their fold. After all, if Lady Cassandra is any indication of the direction humanity is taking with regard to its attitude toward the artificial extension of life, then no procedure is too drastic for us to consider—not even Cyberification. In fact, both in Lumic's parallel Earth and in our own reality, we're already halfway there.

In Lumic's universe, the citizens of the developed world are eager to wear the Earpods he has developed. A variation on our own iPods, which have the capacity to provide habitués with days and days of quality entertainment, Lumic's Earpods are, as the Doctor describes them, "like Bluetooth attachments" for the human brain, and subscribers to the Cybus Industries "Daily Download" can have sports, news, lottery numbers and other forms of entertainment beamed directly into their heads. And while one particularly chilling scene in "Rise of the Cybermen" depicts a city full of Daily Download subscribers standing stock-still as their daily dose of infotainment commences and then bursting into laughter once the transmission ends, the Doctor is quick to remind Rose that her own reality—that is, *our* own reality—isn't much different.

In addition to our iPods, we have our televisions, our computers, our cell phones, our Blackberries (the addictive nature of which has led some to dub them "Crackberries") and a myriad of other electronic devices to divert us from the world we might otherwise perceive with our natural senses. What's more, anyone who's ever watched even the most casual cell phone or Blackberry user (if, indeed, casual use is possible with these commodities) is familiar with the automatic flip of the wrist and accompanying downward glance that overtake the individual when checking messages. Most of us are also familiar with the narcotic effect of planting the so-called "ear buds" of our iPods in our ears and tuning out the world. And who among us can claim never to have slipped into the cathode-ray-induced vacant trance of the TV junkie? We're so hooked on technology that it's now difficult to discern who or what is in control—us, or the devices we love. No one has to round us up and force us to bow down before our electronic gods. No one has to hold a gun to our collective head to make us watch TV. No one forces us to opt for cosmetic surgery. We do all of these things willingly, eagerly and ecstatically, and we always seem to do them in the name of progress.

All of this is not to say that our relationship with machines is necessarily bad. Technology has undoubtedly given humanity hope where, in many instances, none previously existed. Pacemakers, dialysis machines and artificial joints, limbs and organs have all improved the quality of life for countless people. Additionally, cosmetic surgery has allowed many victims of birth defects and other forms of disfigurement to gain what, for lack of a better term, we might term a more "normal" appearance. And as for our electronic media, there's no denying the valuable services they provide our culture. The issue, however, is whether or not we allow these machines to turn us into the "everlasting children" Lumic envisions in "The Age of Steel." Do we allow technology to arrest our development and turn us into walking automatons like the Cybermen, or do we begin to exercise more discipline, more thought, more control with regard to technology in order to ensure that we retain at least some degree of autonomy over the electronic world in which we are ensconced?

For the purposes of drama, villains like Lumic or Davros are needed to get the ball rolling and to serve as catalysts who force certain issues to their inevitable crises, but the value of a show like *Doctor Who* is that over the course of a season or two, the gradually unfolding narrative allows viewers to take a long view of our own social evolution. Since time travel is a given in the program, *Doctor Who* can allow for the juxtaposition of seemingly disparate elements like Lady Cassandra and the Daleks or Cybermen to demonstrate that humanity is on the gradual path to becoming something closer to the Doctor's longtime foes than what we currently define as human. On one hand, the show can demonstrate the resistant steps we will take when an alien force attempts to hurry us along, to force us, for example, into becoming cybernetic monsters. On the other hand, however, *Doctor Who* also does a wonderful job of demonstrating that when the road is long and we believe ourselves to be in the driver's seat, we'll gradually move of our own volition in the direction the Cybermen and Daleks have taken before us. In other words, we don't need a Davros or a Lumic to transform us into the stuff of nightmares.

All we need is time.

6

Intergalactic Culture Jam: The Doctor vs. the Mega-Corporation

Upon reviving *Doctor Who* in 2005, Russell T. Davies wasted no time in shocking some of the show's longtime fans by instituting a series of changes that ran the gamut from destroying the Doctor's home planet to updating the Time Lord's fashion sense, and along with the entire population of Gallifrey went the Doctor's apparent fondness for dressing like Jimi Hendrix, Toulouse-Lautrec and Willy Wonka. Yet despite his new-found appreciation for close-cropped hair and leather, the new Doctor turned out, like all of his predecessors, to be an iconoclast at heart (or *hearts*, as the case may be), and he quickly disproved the common wisdom that the clothes make the man. First on his to-do list, in fact, was blowing up a department store. Sure, the store was full of his old enemies the Autons, but the apparent glee with which the Doctor went about his business is a clear indication that he had somehow managed to maintain his subscription to *Adbusters* while the Great Time War raged on. By inaugurating the new series with such a spectacularly anti-corporate gesture, the Doctor signaled that Daleks, Cybermen and Sontarans would not be his only nemeses in the coming years, but that he would be targeting big business as well.

Of course, the Doctor's distaste for corporate juggernauts is nothing new. Adventures dating as far back as the Patrick Troughton-era "Fury from the Deep" and "The Invasion" pit the second Doctor against the deadly results of off-shore drilling and the machinations of the fictitious International Electromatics Corporation, respectively. Likewise, the Jon Pertwee-era "Spearhead from Space" introduces the alien race that eventually inspires the ninth Doctor to blow up the above-mentioned department store, and its sequel, "Terror of the Autons," serves as a firm object lesson to anyone who might be tempted to view the plastics industry as anything but toxic to human life. Also in the Pertwee era, "The Green Death" sees the third Doctor teaming up with a band of proto-Greenpeace hippies to stop the Global Chemicals corporation from poisoning the planet.

Leaving the confines of Earth, the fourth Doctor bumps up against extra-terrestrial and futuristic corporations in "The Robots of Death" and "The Sun Makers," and a confrontation with an interplanetary conglomerate forces the fifth Doctor to regenerate in "The Caves of Androzani." In "Vengeance on Varos," the sixth Doctor meets Sil, a slug-like representative of the Galatron Mining Corporation who resorts to threats of mass destruction when attempts at negotiation fail, and in "Mindwarp" the same Doctor appears to assist Sil in his efforts at intergalactic currency speculation. Even Davros and his dreaded Daleks have a go at running their own cryogenics and food-services company in "Revelation of the Daleks," and, drawing the original series to a close, episodes like "Paradise Towers," "Dragonfire," "The Happiness Patrol" and "The Greatest Show in the Galaxy" turn much of Sylvester McCoy's tenure as the seventh Doctor into an extended riff on advertising, consumerism and the entertainment industry, as well as a self-conscious critique of the ways in which the *Doctor Who* franchise has itself been commodified.

Given the Doctor's history of struggle against corporate greed and corruption, the anti-corporate detonation that kicks off the new series should come as no surprise, nor should the underlying suspicion of massive, faceless corporate entities that undergirds much of the new series. Consider, for example, Geocomtex in "Dalek," Cybus Industries in "Rise of the Cybermen" and "The Age of Steel," and the series of shadow corporations that own Satellite Five (a.k.a. the Game Station) under the watchful eye of the Daleks in "The Long Game" and "Bad Wolf." In these episodes, corporations do more than simply provide the Doctor and his companions with a series of obstacles to overcome over the course of each forty-five minute timeslot. Rather, the corporations depicted in these and all germane episodes of *Doctor Who* form the very fabric of the worlds the Doctor and his companions visit and, as such, allow the program to take aim not only at the corporations that have enveloped our own world, but also at the detrimental attitudes, values and practices that corporate culture encourages.

And rightfully so.

As corporate watchdog Erik Assadourian notes, the corporation is now the most powerful institution in the world.[1] With over 69,000 transnational corporations in existence—the hundred largest of which hold over eight-trillion dollars in assets—corporations have managed, according to Assadourian, to co-opt almost every institution on the planet by "spending billions to lobby governments; funding academic research (and sometimes suppressing unfavorable results); purchasing a half-trillion dollars in advertising each year to promote their products or political positions; even creating civic organizations to convince people that issues like climate change, smoking and obesity are not threats."[2] Thus while corporations are by no means perfectly intertwined with national governments as they are in the fourth Doctor serial "The Sun Makers," which heckles the British tax system and irrational corporate loyalty in the same breath, their influence over the institutions that govern us has, over the years, proven too tempting for most (if not all) politicians to resist and (in the overwhelming number of cases) too subtle for the masses to recognize.

Here is where the good Doctor intervenes.

By drawing attention to the potential hazards of bowing unquestioningly to the wisdom of the corporation, *Doctor Who* provides viewers with the ability to recognize the insidious sway corporations hold over the mass-consciousness of the "civilized" world as well as the tools for resisting this influence. In other words, the Doctor is involved in what many cultural and media critics might refer to as an extended culture jam—the practice of reclaiming the public sphere by turning the overblown ethos of mass consumption and corporate culture that is a hallmark of Western Civilization on its head. Think Albert Markovski battling the massive Wal-Mart stand-in Huckabees in the existential comedy *I ♥ Huckabees!* Think a team of culture jammers known as the Billboard Liberation Front plastering a portrait of Charles Manson across a thirty-by-ninety-foot Levi's ad to protest the company's unfair labor practices. Think legions of skulls scrawled over the faces of fashion models on posters and billboards around the world.[3] More to the point, think the third Doctor confounding the BOSS computer in "The Green Death" with his absurdist illogic. Think the fourth Doctor programming the Company computer to impose a growth tax on the Company itself in "The Sun Makers." Think the ninth Doctor's irrepressible joy at blowing up Henrik's department store in "Rose," and you'll get a sense of the animating spirit behind the culture jam movement—and where the Doctor might fit into it.

One Word: Plastics

Call it a hint: rather than battling the Daleks, the Cybermen or the Master in the first of his regularly televised adventures in nearly twenty years, the ninth Doctor confronts the Autons, a relatively obscure race that appeared only twice in the program's history. Given the wide range of enemies and alien races that have become synonymous with *Doctor Who* over the years, surely the show's producers could have easily selected a rival with a little more pull at the proverbial box office. Even if A-list villains like the aforementioned Daleks and Cybermen were busy making cameo appearances in the latest installment of the holovid series *Jupiter Rising*, surely Davies could have made a few calls and landed a Sontaran or two, a small detachment of Ice Warriors or even the ghost of longtime *Doctor Who* antagonist and all-around wet-blanket Mary Whitehouse to kick-start the new series. But the Autons? Why?

To borrow a phrase from *The Graduate*, all questions regarding the return of the Autons can be answered with just one word: plastics. The embodiment of an alien intelligence called the Nestene Consciousness, the Autons have taken many forms ranging from traditionally inanimate objects like trash bins and plastic daffodils to vaguely human shapes like dolls and mannequins. What all of these forms have in common, however, is that they're composed entirely of plastic, perhaps the most ubiquitous artificial substance on the face of the Earth. Indeed, what sparked so much controversy among concerned parents upon the broadcast of "Terror of the Autons" in 1971 was not simply the violent nature of the episode but that it depicted everyday objects like telephone lines and inflatable chairs turning of their own volition against their human masters. What kind of message was that for children to absorb, the concerned parents (led by Mary Whitehouse) demanded? After all, plastic was humanity's friend, the harbinger of what the DuPont Chemical Corporation called an age of "better living through chemistry." Yet here it was—strangling innocent people while wide-eyed children watched with a mix of horror and fascination over tea and crumpets.

That couldn't really happen, could it? some of these children surely wondered. Plastic turning against us? Absolute rubbish!

Right?

Thirty-five years later, the common wisdom among environmental scientists is that while chemistry may have made our lives much more convenient, this convenience comes at a high price insofar as plastics threaten individual health as well as that of the environment. The average plastic container takes somewhere in the neighborhood fifty to eighty years to biodegrade, and plastic foam (better known by its corporate moniker, Styrofoam) never biodegrades. As a result of this low-to-nonexistent rate of biodegradation, discarded plastics suffocate the surfaces of oceans, rivers, lakes and streams, choke sewer lines and slowly leach poisonous chemicals into our soil and water supply. As is commonly known, the chlorine that is a chief component in vinyl is poisonous, but the more insidious damage is done by dioxin, a chemical that is released when plastic is burned or eventually begins to break down. Associated with various forms of cancer, diabetes, hormone disruption, birth defects and infertility, dioxin is among the most studied toxins in the world and can be found in harmful amounts in nearly all humans. In addition to dioxin, moreover, other chemicals that go into plastics—like phthalates, which make plastic more pliable, or bisphenol A and p-nonylphenol, which make plastic more firm—have an especially negative effect on children and have been linked to occurrences of early onset puberty in young girls.

As the ninth Doctor observes in "Rose," Earth's poisoned environment makes it a logical target for the latest Auton invasion: "Lots of smoke and oil, plenty of toxins and dioxins in the air. Perfect! Just what the Nestene Consciousness needs." Yet beyond the damage it has literally wreaked upon the environment, plastic carries a number of metaphorical connotations that make it the perfect avatar for a maleficent alien intelligence as well. In our culture, *plastic* is a synonym for fake, artificial and lifeless. Plastic goods are cheap. Plastic goods are disposable. Nobody ever cherishes a plastic heirloom or stops to admire the plastic trim on an ultramodern automobile dashboard. Even so-called "limited edition" plastic toys and collectibles are made in batches that number in the tens of thousands and can always be replaced with ease and in mass quantities. Infinitely malleable and equally resilient, there's so much of the stuff gumming up our cultural arteries that we don't know what to do with it.

More significantly, plastic is a distinctly corporate product that frequently symbolizes all that is wrong with our current culture of mass-consumption. People don't generally whip up small batches of Polyvinyl Chloride in their basements or create their own Barbie dolls from scratch, and the notion of a mom-and-pop "microbrew" plastics manufacturing operation is patently absurd because plastic is a product of expedience. In other words, nobody makes plastic out of a sheer love for the product—as small microbreweries do in the beer market, for example—but because making astronomical amounts of the product is cheap and easy. As a result, corporations must bear the burden of meeting all of humanity's plastic needs—and the needs of those from beyond humanity as well. Needless to say, the invasions depicted in "Spearhead from Space" and "Terror of the Autons" are predicated upon the existence of both the technology and the corporate machinery needed to manufacture plastic, since without these mechanisms, the Nestene Consciousness would have no means by which to embody itself. Similarly, these same mechanisms allow for an entirely human mode of consciousness—that of consumerism—to invade the public sphere and render us all, in the opinion of some social critics, as lifeless as the zombie-like store mannequins that come to life and terrorize unsuspecting shoppers in "Spearhead from Space."

In his seminal works *The System of Objects* and *The Consumer Society*, French social theorist Jean Baudrillard argues that the speed with which goods are mass-produced in Western society has fundamentally altered the relationship between humanity and the objects that surround us. According to Baudrillard, a "kind of fantastic conspicuousness of consumption and abundance, constituted by the multiplication of objects, services and material goods" surrounds us and causes "a fundamental mutation in the ecology of the human species."[4] Strictly speaking, the theorist notes, "the humans of the age of affluence are surrounded not so much by other human beings but by objects. Their daily dealings are not so much with their fellow men, but rather—on a rising statistical curve—with the reception and manipulation of goods."[5] In other words, because the exhortation to accumulate and arrange signs of social status is so strong in our society, we have no choice but to define ourselves in relation to the objects we possess. Surrounded by objects, we have come to behave as objects ourselves. That is, we no longer interact with the world at large or the people who occupy that world. Instead, we situate ourselves within self-contained constellations of objects that insulate us from meaningful interaction of any kind. In short, we are too busy accumulating and arranging commodities in an effort to demonstrate that we live "the good life" (however it may be defined) to connect with each other or the world at large. Mindlessly locked in a cycle of eternal accumulation, the denizens of consumer culture are no more capable of independent thought than are the faceless, heartless Auton mannequins of "Spearhead from Space" and "Rose."

Surely the parallel between the Nestene Consciousness and consumerism is no coincidence. The terrifying images of deadly telephone cords, inflatable chairs, rubber dolls and plastic daffodils that raised the hackles of Whitehouse et al in 1971 serve as more than mere warnings that the proliferation of plastic products literally has the potential to strangle and suffocate human beings and other forms of life. These images also speak to the metaphorical suffocation to which Baudrillard alludes—i.e., the potential for the consumer mindset to cut individuals off from meaningful human interaction and, in so doing, to render those individuals effectively lifeless. This sense of suffocation takes on greater urgency in the new series when Rose chooses a life of adventure with the Doctor over the dull, drab life her materialistic mother encourages back on Earth. In this sense, the desire to live as more than just a mindless consumer is not just an incidental element in Rose's character; it's the driving force that animates her every action.

Rose craves danger and excitement because the lifestyle the Doctor offers beats the hell out of working in a department store where she's regarded by her customers as being no different from the mannequins that surround her; she loves traveling with the Doctor because in this context, she's become more than simply the walking, talking manifestation of how much money she makes or how many status symbols she's accumulated over her lifetime, and has instead come into her own as a true human being. This change in Rose's sense of self is most apparent in the tenth-Doctor adventure "The Impossible Planet" when she meets a slave race known as the

Ood. When Rose asks why members of this race—all of whom think and act in almost perfect unison—allow themselves to be enslaved, the Ood respond that they have "nothing else in life" and that being ordered about is all they crave. What's telling in this exchange, however, is not simply that the Ood are described as "a herd race, like cattle," but that Rose herself admits to having been of the Ood way of thinking in her own past. That is, Rose, like the Ood, once saw herself as a slave, living not as an individual but as part of a herd, existing not on her own terms but trying to live up to definitions of success and accomplishment laid out by others.

It's highly fitting that shortly after Rose's conversation with the Ood, she and the tenth Doctor express their absolute horror at the notion of adopting the bourgeois lifestyle they've so far managed to avoid as a direct result of their ongoing travels. Under the impression that they've lost the TARDIS, Rose informs the Doctor that he'll need to "find a planet, get a job [and] live a life, same as the rest of the universe." Naturally, the Doctor recoils at this potential set of circumstances: "I'd have to settle down. Get a house or something—a proper house with doors and things. Carpets. Me! Living in a house! Now *that* is terrifying." Adding insult to injury, Rose reminds the Doctor that in order to buy a house, he'll need to obtain a mortgage.

"I'm dying!" the Doctor retorts. "It is all over."

That the Doctor and Rose are teetering on the precipice of a black hole and about to confront a creature who claims to be Satan only emphasizes the dread the Doctor feels with regard to settling into an overly comfortable bourgeois life. In fact, the black hole and the prospect of confronting Satan are nothing compared to the dreaded lifestyle that life without the TARDIS represents to the Doctor and Rose; settling into a lifestyle predicated on debt and the accumulation of material goods is, in the Doctor's own words, the equivalent of dying. Given this attitude, it's only natural that much of the adversity faced by the Doctor and Rose over the course of their adventures together is commercial in nature. As such, these adventures serve as a biting commentary on human avarice and consumption. Henry van Statten is the living embodiment of greed in "Dalek," and it is his very greed that threatens to undo him when the Dalek he has uncovered comes to life. In "The Long Game" and "Bad Wolf," Satellite Five and the Game Station render humanity as susceptible to becoming mindless consumers of commodities and useless information as do our own mass-media outlets on present-day Earth. And for pure shock value, nothing beats the image of a Christmas tree—the perfect symbol of humanity's tendency to commercialize even the most sacred of events—springing to life and going on a murderous rampage in "The Christmas Invasion."

Perhaps the most sustained critique of consumerism and corporate cul-

ture, however, takes place over the course of the two-episode adventure comprised of "Rise of the Cybermen" and "The Age of Steel." These episodes
take the viewer to a parallel Earth that is much like our own in that the corporate logos and catchy slogans that constitute its cultural landscape are
inescapable. Pete Tyler, Rose's other-world "father," continually repeats his
catch-phrase, "Trust me on this," as he rakes in a fortune selling counter-
feit health drinks to an unsuspecting world. His wife, Jackie, meanwhile,
defines her own self-worth in terms of her possessions and takes great pride
in a pair of custom-designed electronic Earpods that she has received as a
gift from John Lumic of Cybus Industries, the corporation responsible for
bringing the Cybermen to life. These Earpods—electronic attachments that
allow users to download every manner of programming directly into their
brains—give Lumic access to the information in Jackie's brain in much the
same way electronic "cookies," grocery store discount cards and other consumer tracking devices keep tabs on our every purchase and contribute to
the vast stores of information all large corporations use to target individual
consumers as efficiently as possible in their marketing efforts. Likewise, the
Earpods worn by nearly everyone on Lumic's Earth give Cybus Industries
control over the masses, and the viewing audience can't help but feel a
twinge of both familiarity and mild terror as the citizens of London download their daily allotment of news and entertainment. Just as they freeze in
place while the Earpods do their work, so too do we oh-so-frequently fall
into silent trances as television works its mind-numbing magic upon us,
thereby making us susceptible to the most outrageous claims of advertisers:

A-1 makes hamburgers taste like steakburgers.

Visa. It's everywhere you want to be.

Hebrew National. We answer to a higher authority.

Meow Mix. So good, cats ask for it by name.

Gillette. The best a man can get.

Guinness is good for you.

Beef. It's what you want.

Under a similar influence, the people of Lumic's Earth march mindlessly to the Cybus Industries conversion centers where they are mechanized,
homogenized and stamped with the corporation's logo. As they march out
onto the streets of London, the newly minted Cybermen advance in perfectly impassive lockstep, very much like the Autons of previous *Doctor Who*
adventures. Also like the Autons, the Cybermen are controlled by a single
intelligence, the code of logic that commands them to saturate the world
with the Cybus brand by converting all of humanity to their way of life—
and by incinerating those they deem to be "reject stock." In this sense, the
parallel between the rise of the Cybermen and that of the Third Reich is
particularly apparent and draws attention to the fact that the embrace of

Nazism on the part of otherwise "good" people occurred in large part due to Hitler's efforts at marketing his "brand." In point of fact, what the Autons, the Cybermen, the Nazis and the ethos of consumerism all have in common is that their shared project is to replace individual free will with an external code that forces subscribers to march in perfect, mindless lockstep with each other. The Autons call this code the Nestene Consciousness. The Cybermen call it logic. Borrowing a term from Friedrich Nietzsche, the Nazis called it Will to Power.

And the denizens of consumer culture?

Among other things, we call it keeping up with Joneses, and as we bow down before the Nike Swoosh and make our daily pilgrimages to Wal-Mart and the Golden Arches, we gradually concede victory to the power of consumerism and sell our souls to the mindless, heartless, faceless corporations that render Autons and Cybermen—or worse—of us all.

A Life Form Perfectly Adapted for Survival and Conquest

In "Spearhead from Space," a high-ranking Auton notes that the Nestene Consciousness will eventually be embodied in "a life form perfectly adapted for survival and conquest" on Earth. This life form, however, consists not only of the squid-like creature brewing inside a tank in a secret laboratory at the Auto Plastics manufacturing plant, but also of the company itself. The squid, moreover, may be read as a metaphor for the company's potential reach. Although Auto Plastics is a small firm, with the right management—that is, with the right form of Consciousness at the helm—this negligible toy company could, through a series of well-calculated mergers and acquisitions, get its tentacles into every significant industry in the world as did former energy giant Enron before its spectacular implosion in 2001.

Founded in 1930 as Northern Natural Gas Company—a consortium made up of Northern American Power and Light Company, Lone Star Gas Company, and United Lights and Railways Corporation—Enron demonstrates that humanity need not look to the stars for a life form perfectly adapted for survival and conquest; we have that life form right here on Earth, and it's called the corporation. Like the shape-shifting Proteus of classical mythology as well as the infinitely plastic Autons, Enron has gone through many incarnations since its inception and has also demonstrated that the corporation is nearly impossible to kill. After ownership in the Northern Natural Gas consortium was dissolved through a series of public stock offerings, the company reorganized itself as a holding company called InterNorth and later absorbed its competitor, Houston Natural Gas, to become Enron in 1985. Over the next fifteen years, Enron moved beyond the energy business and extended its reach into many more industries, including water, metals, lumber, petrochemicals and plastics. At its height, the corporation claimed revenues in excess of $101 billion, but a series of scandals caused Enron's stock to plummet from ninety dollars a share to thirty cents a share almost overnight in 2001.[6]

Yet the beast refused to die: although the company went into bankruptcy and its chief officers were found guilty of securities and wire fraud, Enron itself, like the Hydra of old, has spawned three independent corporations that will likely live on in perpetuity in one form or another—perfectly adapted for survival indeed! Moreover, ours isn't the only world where the animating spirits of seemingly moribund corporations live on in their offspring. A website promoting the second season of the new *Doctor Who* series offers a mock "official" history of Cybus Industries that cites the International Electromatics Corporation—the corporation that brought the Cybermen to Earth in the Troughton-era serial "The Invasion"—as one of the company's forerunners. Speculating that the Cybus Corporation was "created in 1982 from the remains of electronics company International Electromatics," the site's unnamed authors note that the "acquisition of International Electromatics' extensive research and development files proved invaluable in giving the Cybus Corporation a head start in the fledgling computing industry, developing international networking systems and information distribution nodes for military use."[7] While the strict canonicity of the information contained on this site may be questionable, it helps to explain why an International Electromatics truck is seen rounding up vagrants in "Rise of the Cybermen" and bears out the notion that corporations in the fictive world of *Doctor Who*, as in our own world, follow the basic principal of survival and conquest at any cost.

But is it accurate to consider the corporation a life form?

Yes, actually. It is.

Although intuition and common sense may scoff at the notion of placing the corporation in the same category as the individual, the law has long given corporations the same rights and privileges as citizens and has, in effect, viewed corporations as living entities. In *The Corporation: The Pathological Pursuit of Profit and Power*, Joel Bakan notes that in addition to banning slavery, the Fourteenth Amendment to the Constitution of the United States gave nineteenth-century robber barons the opportunity to successfully argue for the personhood of corporations. Along with that personhood, moreover, came the rights granted to all persons under the law—*i.e.*, the rights to life, liberty and the pursuit of happiness. For corporations, however, happiness has increasingly been defined in terms of profit and power, and Bakan argues that the corporation's mandate to maximize profitability at any cost renders it not just an individual in the eyes of the law but a pathological entity in the context of society at large. According to Bakan, the corporation is "deliberately programmed, indeed legally compelled, to externalize costs without regard for the harm it may cause to people, communities, and the natural environment."[8] In other words, the corporation will do anything to advance its own agenda, a truth made plain in the third Doctor serial, "The Green Death."

The central plot of the "The Green Death" involves a corporation that matches Bakan's description almost perfectly. In this adventure, representatives of the Global Chemicals corporation lie to government officials in order to conceal the fact that their chemical plants produce waste that is poisoning the environment. Boasting of a pollution and waste-free method of chemical production, the corporation is actually dumping its chemicals into a nearby disused coal mine. Even more disconcerting, this dumping has caused a swarm of maggots to mutate, and as the adventure progresses, an army of giant flies threatens to spread deadly poison throughout England and possibly the world. While the corporation's utter disregard for both civil authority and the environment help to illustrate Bakan's argument regarding the pathological nature of corporations in general, what's most interesting about Global Chemicals is the company's hierarchical structure: the head of the company is not a well-paid CEO with a golden parachute but a computer with a stainless-steel shell.

Dubbed BOSS—short for Bimorphic Organizational Systems Supervisor—the computer at the heart of Global Chemicals is, to borrow a phrase from Bakan, "deliberately programmed" to maximize the company's profits regardless of ethical, legal or ecological considerations. To this end, BOSS has the capability of "processing" the company's employees, a euphemism for erasing their free will and enslaving them to the will of Global Chemicals. In addition to lying to government officials and poisoning the environment, processed employees will even go so far as to commit suicide for the good of the company, as evidenced when a middle-manager is programmed to leap to his death from a factory window in an elaborate cover-up.

Yet BOSS represents so much more than mere loyalty to the corporation. Unlike the Nestene Consciousness at the helm of the Auto Plastics corporation in "Spearhead from Space," BOSS is not an alien intelligence but a human creation. Much like Frankenstein's monster, then, BOSS is the perfect metaphor for corporations in general in that while humans create it, corporate machinery often takes on a life and will of its own, and the mandate for profitability can all too easily override all other concerns. What BOSS suggests, then, is that we, as a race, have not only invented the technology that will enslave us but have also given rise to the culture that will allow us to acquiesce to this slavery even when all signs tell us, as in "The

Green Death," that what's good for the corporation is not necessarily good for our own survival. Knowing no boundaries, BOSS eventually draws the conclusion that a mere monopoly over the chemical industry will not be enough; rather, the megalomaniacal computer will not rest until it gains control of the entire world. While the Doctor eventually puts a halt to the computer's machinations, "The Green Death" forces viewers to wonder what dangers the real-world counterparts of Global Chemicals might be presenting—and what we can do to save ourselves from them.

Praise the Company! (Just Do It)

Perhaps the best way to protect ourselves from the machinations of overbearing corporations is to understand the source of their power within the social sphere. While Global Chemicals has the benefit of a mind-control device, most real-world corporations use more subtle means of swaying the masses in their favor. Using the term *sigil* to denote a sign endowed with seemingly magical powers, writer Grant Morrison explains that corporate logos like the McDonald's Golden Arches, the Nike Swoosh and the Virgin autograph are "super-breeders" that multiply like the cells of a virus and attack unbranded imaginative spaces everywhere. According to Morrison,

> The logo or brand, like any sigil, is a condensation, a compressed, symbolic summing up of the world of desire which the corporation intends to represent. The logo is the only visible sign of the corporate intelligence seething behind it. Walt Disney died long ago but his sigil, that familiar, cartoonish signature, persists, carrying its own vast weight of meanings, associations, nostalgia and significance. People are born and grow up to become Disney executives, mouthing the jargon and the credo of a living corporate entity. Walt Disney the man is long dead and frozen (or so folk myth would have it) but Disney, the immense corporate egregore persists.[9]

In the world of *Doctor Who*, this haunting form of corporate magic takes many forms, most of them malevolent, all of them immortal. Battling the Beast itself in "The Satan Pit," the tenth Doctor remarks that while the devil "is an idea," ideas are "hard to kill." Almost certainly true with regard to alien intelligences and extra-dimensional specters alike, this observation also applies to the animating forces behind corporations, as evidenced quite forcefully in the fourth-Doctor adventure, "The Sun Makers."

When the Doctor, Leela and K-9 materialize in a city called Megropolis One, they learn that the people of a dying Earth have been granted salvation by a corporation known only as the Company, which has generously moved everyone to one of the moons of Pluto and illuminated the formerly dead satellite with six artificial suns. Despite the apparent magnanimity of the Company, however, all is not well in Megropolis One. The Company, it turns out, is owned and operated by an alien race known as the Usurians—a play, no doubt, on the practice of usury or lending money at exorbitant rates of interest. As their name implies, the Usurians have economically subjugated the people of Megropolis One to the point where the first citizen the intrepid time travelers encounter is attempting to take his own life as a result of the burdensome taxes levied upon him. The Company, moreover, is such a massive force that it employs nearly everyone on the planet and, as such, serves as the governing body of the masses. Thus while not technically a public agency, the Company has the power to institute rules and regulations and to impose fines, taxes, pay-cuts and surcharges for everything under their suns.

Yet while the Company has effectively destroyed the spirits of its employees, they by and large accept their collective lot in life with gratitude and consider themselves blessed by its generosity. As much as anything else, then, what the Doctor wants to learn as he's drawn further into their predicament is why the antagonized citizens of Megropolis One are so eager to bow down before the Company. What he discovers is that the Company uses a number of methods to guarantee loyalty and hard work from its employees. Chief among these methods are the substitution of propaganda for education, the promotion of complacency via chemical means, and the aggressive institution of corporate branding through slogans and logos—all of which mirror troubling trends in our own society.

The people of Megropolis One know absolutely nothing of their own history or how they came to be in the service of the Company, but they are well-versed in corporate platitudes and talking points. Much to the chagrin of social researcher Naomi Klein, a similar trend is infiltrating our own culture, and it can be traced to an unhealthy relationship between corporations and public schools. As Klein reports in No Logo, this trend started in the early 1990s when private corporations started funding technology programs in American and Canadian public schools in exchange for ad space and, in the case of fast-food and soft-drink companies, exclusive distribution deals. What these corporations were really after, however, was not simply ad space on school walls but fertile ground in which to plant the seeds of brand loyalty in the budding minds of young consumers. In no time, the advertisements that had apparently "saved" the struggling school system were becoming less ancillary and increasingly central to school curricula. As a result, Klein argues, students in corporate-sponsored schools, like the employees of the Company, have increasingly come to view corporations not as profit-driven enterprises but as selfless benefactors who make the world more fun, meaningful and fulfilling by virtue of their mere existence.

Of course, our loyalty to the companies that surround us stems not only from increasingly corporate school curricula but from other elements in our environment as well. In "The Sun Makers," the Company pumps an anxiety-inducing chemical called PCM or pento cycleinic-methyl-hydrane into the atmosphere of Megropolis One to keep its employees in line. While the official company line is that the gas eliminates airborne infections, the Doctor quickly points out that the only infection PCM eliminates is that of freedom. And though we may not be breathing PCM here on Earth, we, too, live an environment in which anxiety is increasingly the norm and in which otherwise free-thinkers are discouraged from expressing their differences with so-called mainstream society.

In lieu of psychoactive gasses, one of the chief culprits in breeding an atmosphere of fear and repression in our own culture is television. Dean Emeritus of the Annenberg School of Communication George Gerbner argues that today's children are, for the first time in human history, hearing most of the stories that form their view of the world, "not from their parents or school or churches or neighbors, but from a handful of global conglomerates that have something to sell."[10] What's more, because the stories that sell are most often violent, the view of the world that children are receiving is itself a violent one. Dubbing this phenomenon "mean-world syndrome," Gerbner argues that as television desensitizes viewers to violence, it also instills in those viewers a "pervasive sense of insecurity and vulnerability" that causes people to fear each other, shun social interaction and actually go so far as to demand repression from the government. From Gerbner's perspective, one result of the increased sense of vulnerability in our culture is that it is now "impossible to run an election campaign without advocating more jails, harsher punishment, more executions, all the things that have never worked to reduce crime but have always worked to get votes."[11] In other words, the mean-world syndrome causes us to view the world as more dangerous than it really is and, as a result, to elect government officials who behave like those depicted in "The Sun Makers."

And it doesn't end there!

As corporations infiltrate our schools and taint our minds with fear and loathing, their slogans and logos gain stronger footholds in the public imagination due to their utter simplicity. That is, because our cultural institutions no longer encourage critical thought and in some cases actively discourage it as does the Company in "The Sun Makers," the simplest images and phrases have the best shot at survival. As a result, an ultimately meaningless phrase like *Just do it!* coupled with the trademarked Nike Swoosh can spread through the cultural consciousness like wildfire—or like a particularly contagious virus, depending on your choice of metaphor. And because our defenses against these psychological invaders are generally dulled by the mental atrophy our world encourages, we never think to ask even the most basic questions like "Just do *what*, exactly?" Or in the case of the oft-repeated "Praise the company!" that echoes like a dirty joke throughout "The Sun Makers," simply, "Why?"

That such questions go largely unasked does not bode well for our society, and the fact that the latest series of *Doctor Who* adventures continues to investigate the same modes of civic repression employed by the Company in "The Sun Makers" suggests that the role of corporations in our world is now as problematic as ever. When a race of planet-hopping vampires puts an entire school full of children to work in "School Reunion," one can't help but see a parallel with the Faustian deal our real-world schools have, of economic necessity, been forced to strike with corporate devils. When newscasters focus entirely on violence and destruction in "The Long Game," the critical lens of *Doctor Who* is focused squarely on our own news industry and the "mean world" it has had a hand in creating. And as the Cybus logo spreads throughout the world in "The Age of Steel," there is no question as to where our society is heading if we allow corporations to continue in their ruthless march to power. In fact, so aggressive is marketing in our world and so pervasive are massive corporations that one can't help but wonder whether even the Doctor might have his price.

Not Commercially Oriented?

Assessing the Doctor's character in the Target novelization of "The Sun Makers," the Collector comes to the conclusion that the Time Lord is "not commercially oriented," a notion that is supported by the Doctor's demeanor, behavior and attitude throughout his journeys in time and space.[12] The second Doctor, after all, wasn't stereotyped as a "cosmic hobo" for his business acumen, and although the third Doctor proves himself to be a dandy and a bit of a wine snob throughout his tenure as UNIT's scientific advisor, his taste in cars and clothes is so unique as to place him far beyond the reaches of mass-market consumerism. Moreover, his insistence in "Spearhead from Space" that he doesn't want money because he has "no use for the stuff" divorces the Doctor from the capitalist sphere altogether and underscores the anti-corporate tone of the serial. Yet while the Doctor himself may not be commercially oriented, the program in which he appears is in many ways a commercial enterprise, a fact that complicates any argument about the anti-corporate attitude of the *Doctor Who* series as a whole. Similarly, that the Doctor is armed with a time machine and an arsenal of advanced technology as he confounds the efforts of corporate aggressors throughout the universe raises the issue of whether we humans, with our limited resources, stand any chance at all of halting our own corporate monstrosities. Or, to put it another way, does *Doctor Who*—either in terms of the program's content or its place in the public imagination—teach us anything of practical value with regard to battling corporations in our own small corners of the universe?

One thing to keep in mind is that *Doctor Who* is, among other things, a brand. The show's various logos are all trademarked, and the British Broadcasting Corporation receives a licensing fee each time that trademark is used by a toy manufacturer or a book publisher. Indeed, it may very well be the program's potential as a brand that brought *Doctor Who* back to television. Even if the show's ratings never rival those of, say, *Dallas* at its peak or *ER*, it will always be able to inspire more merchandising opportunities than either show. Perhaps taking a cue from George Lucas, whose *Star Wars* franchise was not limited to the series of films but also branched out into books, action figures, breakfast cereals and bath products (among other things), the BBC has begun to license a plethora of new *Doctor Who* merchandise to celebrate the revival of the series. A quick glance through the ads in the newly "regenerated" *Doctor Who Magazine* reveals that for a small price, the average fan can turn his or her own home into a veritable museum of all things *Who*. There are, of course, posters galore, action figures, CDs, DVDs and books, but there are also items like the talking Dalek necktie, the complete set of official *Doctor Who* collector plates, talking *Doctor Who* pens, and the official *Doctor Who* duvet cover, bean bag and curtains (available separately or as a set). Then there are the badges, the wall calendars, the *Doctor Who* pajamas and tee shirts, the reprints of *Doctor Who* comic strips and the back issues of *Doctor Who Magazine*. And if the Mel Brooks sci-fi spoof *Spaceballs* is any indication of what's to come, it won't be long before the official *Doctor Who* flamethrower hits the market as well.

Even as the program's merchandising tie-ins proliferate, however, the *Doctor Who* fan base remains relatively small—hence the failure of the Fox made-for-TV movie to capture the imagination of United States audiences in 1996. The show's audience, then, constitutes a niche market, and while smaller boutiques like Galaxy Four and Burtons can make modest profits through sales of the above-mentioned products, massive retail outlets like Wal-Mart are unlikely to stock *Doctor Who* merchandise any time in the foreseeable future. Likewise, the public-domain nature of much of the show's iconography renders *Doctor Who* particularly resistant to excessive commercialism. The TARDIS, for example, is a police box and therefore "free for use of public." Needless to say, it would also be difficult, if not impossible, for the BBC to demand licensing fees every time someone donned a long scarf and wide-brimmed hat or pinned a stalk of celery to his or her lapel—not to mention the legal headaches involved in trying to claim sole ownership of the ubiquitous question mark that adorned everything from the

Doctor's shirt collars to his umbrella handle in the 1980s! Sure, intellectual properties like K-9 and the Daleks don't technically belong to the public, but there's nothing to stop creative kids from making their own robotic dogs out of shoeboxes or picking up toilet plungers and threatening to exterminate their friends and neighbors. As a matter of fact, the BBC went so far as to publish plans for do-it-yourselfers to build their own Daleks in a 1973 issue of *Radio Times*. From this perspective, *Doctor Who* represents the ultimate DIY fantasy: a world whose boundaries depend a great deal less on money than on imagination.

In addition to incorporating the stuff of everyday life into the fabric of the program, the producers of *Doctor Who* have also managed to resist— or at least critique—the excesses of crass commercialism by occasionally drawing attention to the show's own capacity for commodification. In "Dragonfire," for example, a minor character makes a clear reference to *Doctor Who: The Unfolding Text*, suggesting that the Doctor's marketability has somehow bled from our universe and into his own.[13] That the Doctor grimaces at this overt reference to one of the first tomes on the significance of the *Doctor Who* program suggests that he is innately uncomfortable with his role as an icon and goes a long way toward explaining his eagerness to take his latest companion—the impulsive, destructive and sometimes cynical Ace—under his wing. Purportedly derived from the sci-fi comic-strip series *Halo Jones*, which itself presents an ongoing critique of consumer culture, Ace is motivated by a desire to escape the drudgery of her life as a cashier in a fast-food cafeteria and has a strong affinity for explosives that presumably rubs off on the Doctor enough to inspire the department store blast that kick-starts the new series in "Rose." With Ace in tow, the seventh Doctor further investigates his own role as a performer when he enters a talent contest in "The Greatest Show in The Galaxy" only to conclude that while there may indeed be no business like show business, it's not the business he wants to be in. Perhaps, then, it's only fitting that the good Doctor's initial series of adventures ended exactly a year later with the broadcast of "Survival." After twenty-six years of not only saving the universe but also serving as a pop culture icon, the overworked Time Lord probably needed a break.

Either that, or the action figures simply weren't selling in sufficient numbers to keep the program afloat. In either case, when the Doctor made his long-awaited return to the airwaves, he did it—quite literally—with a bang. And while nobody recommends that viewers repeat the Doctor's explosive experiments at home (or at the local department store, for that matter), his ongoing suspicion of corporate leviathans challenges us all to probe beneath the surface of the candy-coated messages that saturate our cultural landscape. In this way, *Doctor Who* is most instructive. We need not necessarily tilt at windmills, as it were, in our stance toward the massive, faceless corporations that demand our submission. Rather, following the Doctor's cue, we'd do best to approach these corporations—and our own relationships to them—with critical minds. We must question the meaningless drivel of the advertising industry. We must recognize the power of corporate logos and slogans to invade our minds and spread among us like viruses. We must not accept as a given that happiness stems directly from participation in the massive orgy of buying and debt that drives our hollow economy forward. And, like the Doctor, we must always be willing to assert the indomitable sovereignty of the human will over the heartless calculations of the monsters we've created. In this way and in this way only, the Doctor's adventures suggest, will humanity survive its own folly.

The future is in our hands.

Viva la revo-who-cion!

7

Red Kangs Are Best: Language Games in the Whoniverse

Among the more-or-less standard science-fiction devices at the Doctor's disposal is his ability to communicate with nearly every species he encounters. Where the heroes of the *Star Wars* universe, for example, use the golden protocol droid C-3PO to expedite matters when translating unfamiliar dialects becomes crucial to overthrowing Darth Vader and his evil forces, and the miraculous Babel Fish in Arthur Dent's ear allows him to understand anything anyone from anywhere in the universe says to him regardless of language in *The Hitchhiker's Guide to the Galaxy*, the Doctor and his companions rely on the TARDIS to serve as their translator. As explained in the ninth-Doctor adventure, "The End of the World," the TARDIS shares a psychic bond with all who pass through its doors, and one of the fringe benefits of this bond is the gift of tongues. Yet even though the TARDIS can translate nearly any language its occupants might encounter, the Doctor and his companions must frequently navigate the vagaries of language itself as they travel through time and space.

To borrow a sentiment from the fourth-Doctor serial "The Hand of Fear," speech, diplomacy and conversation are among the oldest weapons in the universe and are, in many ways, superior to conventional weapons. This observation is borne out when an air-force bombing raid only serves to strengthen an alien invader holed up in a nuclear power plant, and the Doctor must resort to the age-old tactic of negotiation in order to resolve the situation. This, of course, is just one of many instances in which language proves to be among the most powerful forces in the universe, and the Doctor's travels through time and space repeatedly demonstrate that language is not only a means of getting one's point across but also the very "stuff" of which cultures are formed and the only means by which the universe itself can be understood and decoded. Needless to say, then, since the Doctor's strongest overriding desire is to grapple with the deepest mysteries of the universe, a strong grasp of language in all of its forms, functions and intricacies is of utmost importance in the execution of his endeavors.

When Is a Police Box Not a Police Box?

While the TARDIS seems to be fairly adept at substituting familiar words for their foreign equivalents, one thing it cannot do for the Doctor or his companions is translate words that correspond to completely unfamiliar concepts. In other words, the TARDIS is as bound to the same rules of language as the rest of us, and it can, as a result, find itself at a loss for words from time to time. One striking example of this occurs in the very first episode of *Doctor Who* when the TARDIS apparently fails to translate the word *TARDIS* for Barbara Wright and Ian Chesterton after they stumble into the Doctor's time machine at the beginning of "An Unearthly Child." As a result, the Doctor's granddaughter Susan must take up the slack by explaining that she "made up the name TARDIS from the initials *time and relative dimension in space*" and that she thought both of her teachers would understand this concept as soon as they "saw the different dimensions inside from those outside."

The sheer irony of Susan, the pupil, delivering a lesson to her teachers is not lost in this scene, but, as we learn in a flashback sequence shortly before Ian and Barbara force their way into the TARDIS, this pupil has been pointing out the failure of their language to account for certain fairly complex concepts for some time. In one striking instance, Ian recalls presenting a math problem using A, B, and C as variables, only to be told by Susan that the problem can only make sense if a second set of variables— D and E, or time and space—are included in the set. Unbeknownst to Ian at the time of this exchange, the teacher-student dynamic between Susan and himself experiences a major shift as she attempts to school him in the science of her own daily life, and given the vast difference in knowledge between them, it is only appropriate that the lesson unfolds through the use of simple letters, the most basic building blocks of Ian's language. Yet because Ian has not yet had the pleasure of stepping into the dimensionally transcendental TARDIS, he cannot even begin to wrap his mind around the kinds of complex concepts that Susan is advancing even as she does so in the most rudimentary fashion.

Perhaps realizing that they lack the words to make sense of their mysterious pupil, Ian and Barbara decide that they need to gain first-hand knowledge of her life outside of school. As a result, they take a trip to the address listed for Susan in the school registry only to find that it is the address of a junkyard. Here, they stumble upon what can be read as a sign of things to come, for just as the relatively small façade of the police box they are soon to discover gives way to a massive interior, the painted sign on the fence in front of the junkyard holds more meaning than is at first apparent. Bearing the name I.M. Foreman, this sign initially seems to denote only that the owner of the junkyard is, in fact, a gentleman by the name of I.M. Foreman. Examined from a more playful angle, however, this name can be read as a pun, for when spoken aloud, "I.M. Foreman" becomes "I am for man." Or, translated very loosely, "I am an intergalactic defender of humanity."

But because Ian and Barbara aren't prone to loose translation, they take everything more or less literally, so when they eventually find a police box standing somewhat incongruously among the junk in Foreman's yard, they cannot imagine that it might be anything but what it appears to be. Moreover, because the pair might generally if unconsciously associate such a box with concepts like safety, order and authority, the last thing either might imagine as they make their approach is that it might actually be a doorway into an unpredictable and dangerous alien world. That is, there is a vast difference between what the police box signifies for Susan's teachers and what the TARDIS actually is, and the only way for Ian and Susan to fully understand their odd pupil is to enter the TARDIS and find themselves in another dimension.

To understand the process that Ian and Barbara are experiencing as Susan explains the nature of the TARDIS to them, we can turn to linguist S.I. Hayakawa's *Language in Thought and Action*, which explains that mastering language is

> not simply a matter of learning words: it is a matter of correctly relating our words to the things for which they stand. We learn the language of baseball by playing or watching the game *and studying what goes on*. It is not enough for children to learn or *say* "cookie" or "dog"; they must be able to use these words in their proper relationship to nonverbal cookies and dogs before we can grant they are learning the language.[1]

Along these lines, Ian and Barbara must not only come to terms with the fact that the TARDIS is indeed substantially larger than its exterior shell but with the truth that the ship can travel in time and space as well. A prolonged period of orientation within the TARDIS's interior helps Ian and Barbara realize that they are not dupes of an optical illusion, and subsequent visits to prehistoric Earth and to Skaro show them that the machine can travel through time and space. Thus, like Hayakawa's inquisitive children, Ian and Barbara learn to say TARDIS by recognizing the word in its relationship to the nonverbal TARDIS, which is comprised by its futuristic if mind-bending interior and its time and space-traveling capability.

At the same time, however, Ian and Barbara are also coming to grips with the slippery nature of linguistic signs. In "Nature of the Linguistic

Sign," linguist Ferdinand de Saussure argues that the linguistic unit, or sign, is "a double entity formed by the associating of two terms."[2] These two terms are the concept and the sound-image or, as Saussure later dubs them, *the signified* and *the signifier*. For example, the concept *tree* is signified by the sound-image or signifier "tree." This is not to say, however, that a signifier is simply a word and that its corresponding signified is simply the word's definition. Indeed, as the TARDIS demonstrates, an image such as a police box can also be a signifier, and a signifier such as a police box that is actually a dimensionally transcendental time machine can, upon close scrutiny, prove highly complex (as is the case with signifiers in poetry, for example) if not entirely misleading (as is the case with lies, jokes and many puns). Thus as Ian, Barbara and others who have entered the TARDIS eventually come to realize, the Whoniverse is no place for the literal-minded.

The Fake That Is Not a Fake

Just as all of the Doctor's companions must learn to realize when a police box is not really a police box, others who come into contact with the Time Lord must contend with the fact that he is, in many ways, a trickster and therefore likely to deceive. In season seventeen's high-water mark, "City of Death," for example, the Doctor engages in some linguistic chicanery in order to save the Earth from destruction at the hands of the evil alien Scaroth. Scaroth, we eventually learn, is the last of the bellicose Jagaroth race, and a freak accident has splintered him into twelve separate entities and scattered those entities across time. In order to reassemble himself, Scaroth has set in motion a plan that involves nudging humanity (over the course of millennia) toward the invention of time travel so that he might go back in time and prevent the accident that led to his splintering. From the Doctor's perspective, however, the main problem with this plan is that the accident Scaroth is trying to prevent also happens to be the event that led directly to the inception of life on Earth.

In a twist that very few television programs outside of *Doctor Who* could ever pull off, the portion of Scaroth's plot that takes place in the twentieth-century is financed by the sale of works of art and other artifacts laid away by the "splinters" of himself who occupy previous eras in Earth's history. Most notable among these works of art is Leonardo da Vinci's *Mona Lisa*, several copies of which Scaroth commissions in 1505 so that he might sell them in the twentieth century under the guise of Count Scarlioni, a charming and urbane art thief.

In order to discover how Count Scarlioni obtained so many copies of the *Mona Lisa*, the Doctor travels to Renaissance Italy to visit his old friend da Vinci. The famous painter, however, is not in his studio, so the cheeky Time Lord writes *THIS IS A FAKE* on the blank boards the artist will use to paint the additional copies of the *Mona Lisa* that Scaroth has commissioned. Consequently, the Doctor reasons, the *Mona Lisa* copies will be identified as fakes upon close scrutiny via x-ray in the twentieth-century. At the same time, however, it can be argued that the Doctor is actually lying, or once again playing the part of the misleading trickster, when he labels the extra copies of the *Mona Lisa* as fakes; each copy of the painting, after all, truly is an authentic work of art painted by da Vinci himself.

Likewise, we can once more note that although the TARDIS is permanently stuck in the form of a police box, one cannot use said box to contact the police. As with the TARDIS, whose exterior belies its true form, the writing of *THIS IS A FAKE* underneath the oil paints that form the copies of the *Mona Lisas* steers the beholder of the object and its accompanying text away from the truth. The Doctor, of course, writes a lie in order to thwart Scaroth's nefarious plans and to preserve the laudable idea that the *Mona Lisa* is one-of-a-kind, but the fact remains that, regardless of his good, moralistic intentions, the Time Lord has manipulated language in order to undermine and deceive others. This deception, moreover, is especially noteworthy given that the only *Mona Lisa* to survive the fire that engulfs Scarlioni's residence at the end of "City of Death," and which currently hangs in the Whoniverse's Louvre, is one of the so-called fakes!

Fictions Living within Fictions

While serials like "An Unearthly Child" and "City of Death" certainly give viewers an opportunity to contend with the complexity of signification, others demonstrate the ways in which fictions and other texts can form the basis of the lives we live. The experimental tale "The Mind Robber," for example, places the second Doctor, Jamie and Zoe in an unreal realm called the Land of Fiction. Shortly after arriving in this realm, which is located outside of time and space, Jamie finds himself (literally) reduced to a two-dimensional cardboard cutout of his former Highlander glory, and the Doctor comes into possession of a dictionary after falling into a series of word games with a group of mysterious children. Upon discovering Jamie in his unflattering flattened state, the Doctor also finds a safe and a wishing well. Perhaps instinctively recognizing that the standard rules that govern words and language may not apply in this realm, he drops the dictionary and wishes for faith in wishing wells.

Having abandoned his dictionary—which is to say his attachment to literal translation—for the moment, the Doctor is free to play word games with the forces that are holding Jamie's essence hostage. As a disembodied voice laughs at the Time Lord, he sees the crossed-out letters M and T before envisioning a mist. Shortly thereafter, he sees a hand and a crossed-out letter H. Understanding that he's been challenged to decode a kind of rebus, the Doctor takes the images of Jamie, the safe, and the well, and removes the crossed-out letters from the words *mist* and *hand* to learn that Jamie is safe and well.

After restoring Jamie to life with some degree of success, the Doctor turns his attention to Zoe, who is calling to him from behind a door that has neither a handle nor a lock. Realizing that the door is just an image painted on a brick wall, the Doctor asks, "When is a door not a door?" and immediately answers his own question with the pun, "When it's ajar!" That the door and the wall suddenly disappear to reveal the sight of Zoe trapped in a giant jar suggests that this Land of Fiction in which the Doctor and company have found themselves is a world where words are so powerful that they quite literally govern and constitute reality. Reinforcing this notion, Jamie soon discovers that he and his fellow travelers are actually wandering through a forest comprised of words when he climbs a tree that is revealed to be a giant letter S. Looking out over the surrounding landscape, Jamie informs the Doctor that what they initially perceived as a forest is actually a jungle of proverbs and clichés.

The triteness and overuse of the clichés that make up the "forest" in which the Doctor and his companions find themselves trapped may underscore the meaningless nature of such language insofar as, rather than advancing dialogue, such conventions tend instead to stifle real communication. That is, when we repeat sayings that have been handed down for generations, we tend to stop thinking about what they mean, let alone why they're meaningful at all. As a result, these phrases tend to lose meaning, and conversations that revolve around such phrases tend not to lead us toward enlightenment of any kind but only in verbal circles that have already been trodden by countless others. Along similar lines, the character Lemuel Gulliver from Jonathan Swift's *Gulliver's Travels*, whom the Doctor meets sporadically throughout the serial, can only speak the words that Swift has given him. If there is any parallel to be drawn here, it may well be that when we speak in clichés, we become fictions ourselves, or at the very least, as is the case with Gulliver, language begins to speak through us rather than vice-versa.

The stakes in the tension between humanity and language become greater when the Doctor and company leave the forest and eventually make their way to a citadel where Jamie and Zoe are ambushed by an army of white robots who disorient them and crush them within the pages of a giant book—an experience to which nearly everyone can relate if only on a metaphorical level. In point of fact, those of us who have dutifully trudged through massive school-assigned textbooks for the sake of gaining cultural wisdom probably know the feeling of being crushed by a book all too well. Moreover, in addition to teaching us that spoon-fed readings and massive doses of received wisdom are worse than the bitterest medicine, such experiences allow us to recognize the danger of walking in perfect lockstep with the words and traditions that have been handed down to us: if we simply accept what we read without posing questions, we run the risk of becoming tools of our texts rather than free-thinking subjects.

Addressing this issue, French literary critic and philosopher Roland Barthes distinguishes between what he terms "writerly" and "readerly" texts. Critiquing the readerly text in a tome titled S/Z, Barthes observes that

> Our literature is characterized by the pitiless divorce which the literary institution maintains between the producer of the text and its user, between its owner and customer, between its author and reader. This reader is thereby plunged into a kind of idleness—he is intransitive; he is, in short, *serious*: instead of functioning himself, instead of gaining access to the magic of the signifier, to the pleasure of writing, he is left with no more than the poor freedom to accept or reject the text: reading is nothing more than a *referendum*.[3]

What this critique amounts to is a call for readers to recognize their full potential for collaboration with the writer in the act of reading. Hence the "writerly text" is one in which the reader is allowed access to the "pleasure of writing," which is to say a text in which the reader is as involved as the writer in creating meaning from words. Oddly enough, the same critique is more or less leveled by Edina Monsoon in the hit BBC comedy *Absolutely Fabulous*.

In an episode titled "Gay," Edina enters a second-hand bookshop and almost immediately begins to complain to her long-estranged son Serge that her "book allergies" are acting up. When pressed on the matter, however, Edina admits that, strictly speaking, allergies aren't the problem so much as her sheer distaste for the written word. She exclaims, moreover, "I hate these books ... these dusty old books, these books full of dead ideas." Subsequently, Serge reminds his mother that she used to tell him that books can only amount to "a graveyard of ideas—tiny coffins full of putrefying concepts," and he also points out that because of this belief, Edina used to go so far as to burn all of his books. While this latter course of action may not be what Barthes has in mind when he criticizes the readerly text, Edina's concern over the potential for books to contain nothing but dead ideas is certainly in line with the French theorist's call for a more writerly approach to texts.

As if to illustrate Barthes' critique, Jamie and Zoe are temporarily replaced by a pair of walking, talking copies of themselves as they struggle to escape from the text that threatens to crush them. Repeating a string of identical phrases, these copies can only speak the words that the master of the Land of Fiction puts into their mouths. As such, the Doctor quickly recognizes these versions of Jamie and Zoe as mere shadows of the witty, intelligent and free-thinking companions whom he knows and admires.[4] Consequently, when he is given the opportunity to use what is ostensibly a magic typewriter to "write" himself and his companions out of their current predicament, the Doctor decides against doing so because dictating their actions would be akin to enslaving Jamie and Zoe to his will, regardless of his good intentions. His only recourse, he eventually comes to realize, is to exhort his trapped companions to exercise their freedom of choice: "Think for yourselves. Don't be afraid. You can open the book. Go on! You can do it.... Don't worry about fiction. Hang onto real life! You've got to get out!"

Inspired but not governed by the Doctor's words, Jamie and Zoe free themselves and return the favor by destroying the master computer that regulates the Land of Fiction. Yet even as the Land of Fiction collapses and the Doctor and company are returned to their proper realm, the power of language to shape the "real world" remains intact insofar as the unexamined proverbs, clichés and other pieces of received wisdom that make up many a cultural heritage continue to hold sway over the intellectual landscapes of that reality. The challenge posed within the Land of Fiction, then, is also a challenge the Doctor must face in his own universe; he must recognize his own potential as what Barthes might call a writerly reader to shape the texts that shape his world. By extension, those of us who live beyond the Doctor's fictitious realm can also take a cue from Barthes and actively engage in a dialogue with all of the linguistic structures that define who we are, how we behave, and where we fit into society.

Xoanon's Polarizing Rhetoric

During Philip Hinchcliffe's tenure as producer of *Doctor Who*, script editor Robert Holmes made frequent use of repeated mantras to underscore the attitudes and values of various characters and cultures. In "The Brain of Morbius," for example, the Sisterhood of Karn incessantly chants the sibilant mantra, "Sacred Fire, Sacred Flame," while worshipping at the natural hearth that yields the immortality-granting Elixir of Life. Later, in "The Hand of Fear," a possessed Sarah Jane Smith coldly reiterates the phrase "Eldrad *must* live" as she ruthlessly fights her way to the Nunton Complex, a nuclear power station that contains enough energy to convert the eponymous hand into a full-fledged alien menace. In stories like these, verbal communication serves as a means by which individuals and cultures announce their intentions and carry out their objectives. This function of language is given added weight in "The Face of Evil," in which the competition between two distinct modes of cultural discourse—in this case, the discourse of religion—results in conflict between a pair of warring tribes that are, ironically, united in their faith in the same god.

In this serial, the Doctor comes into contact with a pair of tribes called the Tesh and the Sevateem, both of which worship a god they call Xoanan. In an odd twist, however, neither tribe knows that the other worships Xoanan; rather, each considers the other's deity evil. This is largely because each tribe is descended from a separate team of space explorers whose function in relation to their ship has dictated the course of evolution the tribe would take. Members of the Sevateem, the Doctor eventually learns, are the descendants of the ship's survey team, and members of the Tesh are the descendants of the technicians who stayed behind to tend to the ship and its computer, the sentient and megalomaniacal Xoanan. Over the centuries, moreover, Xoanan's "guidance" has led to the intellectual decline of both tribes, and by the time the Doctor arrives on the scene, each culture is steeped in religious mumbo-jumbo and largely meaningless rhetoric derived from what might be termed the mother tongue of the original crew of space explorers.

When members of the Sevateem initially encounter the Doctor, they make a gesture whose purpose is ostensibly to ward off evil but which the Doctor recognizes as a perfect analog to the sequence for checking the seals on a Starfall Seven spacesuit—the very spacesuit, in fact, that the Sevateem's progenitors likely wore during their first outings on the unnamed planet. Yet gestures are not the only signs of the Sevateem's cultural heritage, and when a shaman named Neeva brandishes what at first glance appears to be a relic of some kind, the Doctor immediately identifies it as a particle accelerator with the power to turn the entire primitive village into "a smoky hole in the ground." In addition to his particle accelerator, Neeva has a number of other artifacts as well. Among them is an armored space glove and a space helmet equipped with a communications device. Needless to say, Neeva sees neither object for what it is but instead as "the Hand of Xoanan" and a direct line to the voice of Xoanan respectively.

While the joke is in some ways on Neeva and the Sevateem throughout the early scenes of "The Face of Evil," we shouldn't be too quick to laugh at them since they're only doing their best to construct a sensible model of the world using the only clues they have. As Stanley I. Greenspan and Stuart G. Shanker note in *The First Idea*, such activity is among the things that make us human:

Humans are remarkably sophisticated in the sorts of preverbal and verbal techniques they employ to form bonds of common humanity. We use items of
clothing, jewelry, and body decoration, distinctive ways of walking and talking,
distinctive kinds of gestures and looks, and distinctive kinds of belief systems
and social structures to build our sense of shared allegiance.[5]

Nonetheless, what becomes clear from the Doctor's first encounter with the
members of the Sevateem is that theirs is a culture whose fairly complex system of traditions and beliefs is built around a fundamental misunderstand-
ing of their origins. In other words, the stories that the tribal elders have
more or less conjured to make sense of their world are completely wrong.
What makes this situation particularly disturbing, however, is that these stories, much like the proverbs depicted in "The Mind Robber," have taken on
a life of their own and now form the basis of Sevateem society, which is predicated almost entirely on destroying the so-called "enemies" of Xoanan—one
of whom, it inevitably turns out, is the Doctor.

When the Doctor introduces himself to the Sevateem, the members of
the tribe identify him as the Evil One, a moniker whose meaning becomes
apparent when he finds his own face carved into the cliff where the Tesh
dwell. Subsequently, when the Doctor meets the Tesh, they mistake him for
the living embodiment of their god—a misconception based on the fact that
the Doctor's personality has for centuries been imprinted upon the super-
computer that manages both their lives and the lives of their sworn enemies, the Sevateem. Despite their apparent antipathy toward the Sevateem,
the Tesh are equally misguided in their faith in Xoanan as evidenced in a
discussion between the Doctor and the tribe "captain," Jabel:

THE DOCTOR: Jabel, do your people have a holy purpose?
JABEL: We serve Xoanon and tend the holy places. We guard his tower
against the savage. We deny the flesh so that our minds may find communion with Xoanon.
THE DOCTOR: Ah, well it has a sort of logic. Outside the barrier, physical courage and strength. Inside the barrier, paraphysical achievement and
the sort of psi-power you used against [Leela]. It's an experiment in eugen-
ics.
JABEL: Yes, lord.

With this revelation, the Doctor suddenly realizes the extent to which
Xoanan is implicated in instigating the ceaseless war between the Sevateem
and the Tesh: by manipulating both tribes, the mad computer is attempting to determine whether brute force and animal instinct trump denial of
the flesh and ascetic detachment, or vice-versa.

One way to view the conflict between the Sevateem and the Tesh, then,
is to view it in terms of what some world-views hold as the tension between

the body and the mind or between matter and spirit. Frequently described as Manichean, this outlook encourages a blunt perspective that more or less paints the world in the black and white terms of good and evil. As the Sevateem and Tesh demonstrate, however, one culture's good might be another culture's evil, and such distinctions hinge largely on the stories we tell ourselves. With regard to terrestrial faith, for example, all monotheistic religions by definition involve the worship of a single God who is usually described as being perfect in all ways. Yet although most religions agree upon this basic tenet, the traditions, myths and other texts that have evolved around the worship of this perfect God tend to be different from one religion (or even one sect) to the next. To put it another way, each religion has evolved as a complex set of ideas and theories for grappling with a phenomenon whose full scope, given its infinite nature, is ultimately too complex for the human mind to fully comprehend, let alone for language to express.

The resulting differences among religions wouldn't be such a problem, of course, if not for the fact that they have been (and continue to be) used to justify the most heinous of atrocities. If the members of each religion could gain a stronger appreciation for the social, political and historical contexts from which their sacred texts have emerged rather than viewing their own tenets and traditions as inherently good and divinely inspired as Neeva does in "The Face of Evil," then one cause of conflict among humans might be eliminated. After all, even if we grant the existence of a heaven, every religion's understanding of it is rooted in oral or written traditions and therefore as flawed as it is praiseworthy. This ambition, however, is easier stated than achieved, as demonstrated when Neeva grows despondent and later psychotic upon realizing that the religion he has spent his life mastering is as imperfect as his understanding of the relics in his possession.

Ironically, it is Xoanon who finally unites both tribes as he overtakes their hearts and minds, shouting "Destroy and be free!" As the members of both tribes repeat this command and carry out the mad computer's orders, we are reminded that mantras work to reinforce control and submission, as was the case in "The Hand of Fear" when Sarah Jane repeated "Eldrad *must* live!" while under the influence of the dreaded Eldrad. So, as the Doctor works to heal Xoanon by removing his mind-print from the computer, both the Sevateem and the Tesh mutually close in on the Time Lord to destroy him. Simultaneously, the now-bereft and psychotic Neeva goes on the hunt for Xoanan, suggesting that hell hath no fury like a shaman scorned. More importantly, however, Neeva's mad hunt raises the issue of whether the Sevateem or the Tesh can survive without the guiding hand of Xoanan, for if the shaman's breakdown is any indication of what is to come, both tribes face the danger of falling apart in the absence of their admittedly false god.

As "The Face of Evil" draws to a conclusion, Xoanan relinquishes all claims to godhood and agrees to serve as an advisor to the Sevateem and the Tesh rather than masquerading as a deity. And although representatives of the two tribes almost immediately begin to argue over their respective roles in the new, godless world order they now face, the fact that they are engaged in dialogue at all (rather than attempting to kill each other) suggests that substituting rational discourse for superstition will allow both tribes to evolve into something far superior to their previous incarnations. Along similar lines, an exchange between the Doctor and Leela dovetails nicely with the cultural shift that is occurring among the members of both tribes; when Leela refers to the main computer complex that houses Xoanan as the former god's "sacred heart," the Doctor gives her a look of reproach that prompts her to use more proper terminology.

In this exchange, the Doctor educates Leela in the science of advanced technology in much the same way his granddaughter did for Ian when she instructed him in the dimensionally transcendental nature of the TARDIS years earlier. Like any good teacher, moreover, the Doctor immediately corrects his new pupil's misconceptions about the world in order to dispel her superstitious and primitive beliefs. While a cynical reading of his emerging relationship with Leela might insinuate that the Doctor is no different from Xoanan when it comes to imposing his vision of the world upon others, the point he makes here is not simply that he is right and that Leela is wrong but that Leela needs to take a more critical approach to her understanding of the world around her. This approach is certainly in line with the Doctor's earlier observation that "the very powerful and the very stupid ... don't alter their views to fit the facts" but instead "alter the facts to fit [their] views." By insisting that Leela alter her views to fit the facts with which she is presented, the Doctor provides her with a framework for interpreting phenomena without recourse to mythology and superstition. By implication, it is this same intellectual framework that will allow the Sevateem and the Tesh to move beyond their own ill-informed mythologies and to establish a new culture built around something more akin to "the truth" than was previously possible.

The Prophecy of Voice

Where clothing provides a straightforward indication of the function of each tribe depicted in "The Face of Evil," season nineteen's "Kinda" presents a tribal group whose outward appearance belies the true nature of its members.[6] On the surface, the Kinda appear to be a matriarchal, primitive tribe. Beneath this façade, however, lies a sophisticated, telepathic culture that possesses advanced engineering skills, as suggested by the double-helix designs of their necklaces. Among the Kinda, moreover, women serve as leaders since they possess the power to communicate both verbally and telepathically. The men, by way of contrast, can only communicate with other members of the tribe via mental telepathy. Yet while power relations within tribe are clearly defined in terms of gender, the tribe itself has clearly achieved a state of civic balance with which all members appear quite content.

Although the arrangement governing the Kinda has apparently served the tribe well for generations, the arrival of a team of colonists on their planet, Deva Loka, poses an immediate threat to their way of life. This fact is demonstrated most dramatically when a Kinda male is imprisoned by the "Not-We" (the name the Kinda use to denote the colonists), and the male loses telepathic communion with the tribe. Shortly thereafter, the prisoner's brother, Aris, approaches the tribe's blind matriarch, Panna, and her apprentice, Karuna. As Karuna reads and translates the young male's thoughts into speech, she tells Panna that he does not agree with her decree that there are more immediate concerns than his brother's imprisonment, and she verbally relays his questions: "Why must I listen? Don't the Not-We in the Dome have voice?" In a telling response with regard to the relationship between speech and the insight required of those who might rule over others, Panna comments, "Yes, of course they do, but it is not as it is with us. With them, voice is not a mark of wisdom."

In this exchange, the concept of the "Not-We" is noteworthy in that it amounts to a form of exclusionary and hierarchical language. We, of course, underscores the solidarity and (pardon the pun) kinship the Kinda feel for one another, but the other half of the term—Not—emphasizes the difference all members of the Kinda tribe recognize between themselves and outsiders. Ironically, then, as much as the colonists discriminate against the Kinda by labeling them primitives, the Kinda also engage in their own brand of discrimination by saddling all outsiders with the inferior "Not-We" designation. Such discrimination, moreover, could not exist before the appearance of the colonists since the colonists are apparently the first outsiders the Kinda have encountered. As a result, their arrival on Deva Loka can be viewed as the impetus for a kind of "original sin" within Kinda culture: a degree of hubris that allows the tribe to view themselves as superior to—rather than simply different from—those with whom they are not familiar.

Perhaps symbolizing the Kinda's allegorical fall from grace, a demonic force called the Dukkha Mara threatens the stability and order of the tribe. Finding the distraught Aris, the Mara, through Tegan, its current host body, transfers its essence into the Kinda male. As noted, Aris could initially only "voice" his concern for his brother's safety through his thoughts, but his protests were nonetheless muted (and he, in turn, emasculated) by his inability to speak. Under the Mara's influence, however, Aris gains a voice and immediately says, "All things are possible. Yes. Yes," before laughing diabolically and running off into the jungle. In this instance, the declaration that all things are possible suggests a degree of perceived omnipotence on the part of Aris. Possessed by the Mara, then, and in direct opposition to the females Panna and Karuna, Aris becomes drunk with power and is moved to express his feelings of superiority over others. These hyper-masculine thoughts, moreover, have an ironic ring to them, since Aris implored the maternal Panna to heal him prior to his possession by the Mara.

A psychological battle of the sexes thus takes places throughout much of "Kinda," with the question of who has the right to speak and to command hanging in the balance. When Aris returns to his tribe, he claims that he is fulfilling the Kinda prophecy, which states that a male with the power of voice will arise from the Kinda when the Not-We come—a male who must be obeyed. Aris's claim to leadership of the Kinda, nevertheless, is tainted by the Mara residing within him, and so whether he is actually fulfilling his tribe's prophecy is subject to conjecture. At the very least, we can compare Aris to a child who, when first fumbling with the basic sounds of verbal speech, demands such necessities as food, toys, and parental affection. Aris, therefore, claims power over his tribe, but his demands are quite child-like as he seeks immediate self-gratification.

The fifth Doctor himself is not immune to Panna's belief that males are the inferior sex, but he certainly is not about to join forces with the Mara-possessed Aris to prove these women wrong. Upon gazing into the mystical Box of Jhana, the Doctor tells Panna that the experience was "most enlightening." Panna then retorts, "What's he babbling about? No male can open the Box of Janna without being driven out of his mind. It's well known. Unless—is he an idiot?" Deciding that the Doctor is indeed a "male fool," she lets him witness a trance-induced vision of time running out for the Kinda. And, in the end, the Doctor once more manages to save everyone by defeating the Mara—a laudable act which decidedly disproves the matriarchal tribe's assertion that all "idiot" males who possess the ability to speak are useless or bereft of wisdom.

Red Kangs or Blue?

As with "The Face of Evil" and "Kinda," a number of serials from the seventh Doctor's era explore the relationship between language and culture. In season twenty-five's "The Happiness Patrol," for example, language works as a tool of oppression. For anyone living in the totalitarian world of Terra Alpha, poetry is forbidden, unhappy people are labeled "killjoys," and those who break the rules are placed in ever-shifting "waiting zones." Within these zones, individuals "wait" to "disappear," a fate that can take several forms, among which, being immersed in the maniacal Kandy Man's "fondant surprise" is arguably the worst. In short, the overwhelming proliferation of euphemisms on Terra Alpha helps to conceal the violence that is endemic to that planet, for without the proper words to describe their collective plight, the Terra Alphans cannot identify oppression for what it is.

A similar situation arises in "Paradise Towers," a serial that walks a fine line between nonsense and brilliance. So specialized is the language of this serial, in fact, that half the fun of watching it stems from decoding the jargon of those who inhabit the titular Towers. In addition to the officious, rule-book-citing Caretakers who do their best to keep the Towers clean, there are the Rezzies, whose cannibalistic tendencies are a cause of some concern for companion Melanie Bush, and Kroagnon, who turns out to be the disembodied brain of the architect who designed the Towers. Like "The Happiness Patrol," moreover, "Paradise Towers" suffers no shortage of double-speak: those who lack courage are "cowardly cutlets," hideouts are referred to as "brainquarters," and the dead are simply "unalive." Similarly, the Doctor is deemed "icehot," which is to say "cool," for his sense of fashion despite the fact that he is an "old one."

Perhaps most notable in this serial are the Red, Yellow and Blue Kangs, a trio of juvenile girl gangs whose members derive their names from the immediate environment—hence such otherwise outlandish monikers as "Bin Liner" and "Fire Escape." Upon the Doctor's first encounter with the Red Kangs, they attempt to boost their social standing in his estimation by chanting their mantra, "Who's best? Red Kangs, Red Kangs, Red Kangs are best!" What becomes clear after the Doctor encounters a gang of Blue Kangs, however, is that there is little if next to nothing, apart from hair and clothing, that differentiates the groups of Kangs. In other words, what separates the various Kang sects has less to do with ideology than sheer happenstance, which begs the question of why the Kangs are split into arbitrary yet antagonistic groups at all.

The sheer folly of the antagonism among the Kangs becomes apparent when the last of the Yellow Kangs is made "unalive" by a robotic Cleaner and, despite being faced with a mutual threat, the Red and Blue Kangs continue to snipe at each other. Because there is no real difference between the Red and Blue Kangs, the question of who's best begins to take on the nonsensical and ultimately meaningless ring of a pair of competing ad campaigns insofar as asking whether Red Kangs are better than Blue is akin to asking whether Coke is truly "it" or, conversely, Pepsi is indeed "the choice of a new generation." The insistence of Madison Avenue advertising executives notwithstanding, the majority of reasonable human beings recognizes that neither drink is all that different from the other, yet massive fortunes are spent every year promoting the so-called "cola wars."

In an echo of the split between the Sevateem and the Tesh depicted in "The Face of Evil," the split between the Red and Blue Kangs stems largely from a refusal of each group to think beyond the polarizing rhetoric that divides them. Unfortunately, for those of us here on Earth, terrestrial political parties have begun in increasing numbers to suffer from the same malady. The United States, for example, has been split by the media and politicos alike into "red" and "blue" states, and while this divide purportedly falls along ideological lines, the real differences among the denizens of those states are arguably no greater than the differences between Red and Blue Kangs. What's more, because the competing political parties use the idioms of advertising to convince us of their superiority over each other, the ads of the respective parties amount to little more than the kind of chanting that the Red Kangs use to convince the Doctor that they are, in fact, the best.

None of this, however, is to critique political parties *per se*, but instead to critique the medium by which they advance their agendas. As Barthes intimates in *The Semiotic Challenge*, the language of advertising is so simplistic that it eliminates difference and, in so doing, "entirely exhausts the intention of communication."[7] If Coke and Pepsi, for example, are both "the best," then the word "best" doesn't mean anything. Likewise, to say that one political candidate is simply "better" than the other—as political ads tend to do—is to ignore the real ideological differences between the candidates and to substitute empty rhetoric for a meaningful discussion of those differences. And, it goes without saying, the lack of any real difference between the Red and Blue Kangs means that each group's claim of being "best" is as meaningless as similar claims made by the likes of soft-drink manufacturers and politicians.

Of course, just as it's unfair to hold the Sevateem and the Tesh completely responsible for fighting each other at Xoanan's behest, it's also unfair to blame the Kangs for their own predicament. Living in a world where the majority of adults have gone off to war, the competing gangs have no real role models and, as a result, spend their days engaged in petty turf wars while Kroagnon aggressively attempts to "cleanse" his towers of all humanity. Rather than working together to deal with the threat that Kroagnon poses, then, the Kangs rejoice when their rivals are eliminated by Kroagnon's agents, the Cleaners. Horrified by this state of affairs, the Doctor beseeches the two groups to work together to defeat their mutual enemy. Upon recognizing the wisdom of the Doctor's words, the Kangs set aside their nonexistent "differences" and, as the serial concludes, make the Time Lord an honorary Kang—neither Red nor Blue but, as evidenced by the reversible sash the reconciled Kang factions give him, a healthy combination of both.

The Language of the Universe

Where serials like "The Face of Evil" and "Paradise Towers" clearly demonstrate the ways in which language can frame our perceptions and shape our social structures, the melancholy yet fascinating "Logopolis," which marks the end of Tom Baker's record-setting seven-season tenure as the Doctor, explores the potential for language to shape physical reality as well. As this adventure commences, the Doctor and Adric travel to twentieth-century Earth in order to take the measurements of a real police box. These measurements, the Doctor reveals, will allow the mathematicians who inhabit the city of Logopolis to create a precise mathematical model that will allow him to repair the chameleon circuit on his TARDIS. After this repair has been made, the TARDIS will be able to take on nearly any shape so that it might better blend into its surroundings.

From a standpoint rooted in the study of signs, the repairs the Doctor has in mind will immensely increase the capacity of the TARDIS to serve as a misleading signifier. Before he can make these repairs, however, the Doctor, like Ian Chesterton before him, must learn not to judge a police box by its cover. This is because the police box he has chosen to measure is actually the Master's TARDIS. Having materialized around another TARDIS, the Doctor and Adric find themselves temporarily trapped in a "localized gravity bubble" as they open the doors of the faux police box only to find a seemingly infinite regression of increasingly darker versions of the TARDIS control room. Meanwhile, in an echo of the mistake made by many of the Doctor's companions over the years, Tegan Jovanka stumbles into the TARDIS under the distinct impression that she's found an actual police box.

Although the opening scenes of "Logopolis" examine the power of signs such as the TARDIS exterior to mislead, the serial also introduces the notion of Block Transfer Computation, the means by which the denizens of Logopolis conjure physical objects into existence and, more importantly, maintain order in the universe. One example of the fruits of Block Transfer Computation is an exact replica of a terrestrial computer bank that the Logopolitans have "constructed" in order to help with their more menial and tedious computations. Additionally, the computations of the Logopolitans also prevent the heat death of the universe by creating so-called "Charged Vacuum Emboitments" that drain excess entropy from the cosmos. The physical complexities involved in siphoning entropy from the universe notwithstanding, what's particularly noteworthy about the *modus operandi* of the Logopolitans is that they perform their Block Transfer Computations orally, which means that the act of speaking literally shapes their universe.[8] In the words of the chief Logopolitan, the Monitor, "Structure is

the essence of matter, and the essence of structure is mathematics." By extension, the Monitor continues, his race's spoken manipulation of numbers
"alters the physical world."

In many ways, the relationship between the Logopolitans and reality
hearkens back to the Biblical book of Genesis in which God creates the universe by addressing a "formless and empty" creation and naming various phenomena to separate light from darkness, the sea from the sky, land from
water and so on.[9] Of course, one doesn't have to be particularly religious to
recognize that what God and the Logopolitans have in common is the ability to make order from disorder through the power of speech. Indeed, the
name Logopolis itself is comprised of *logos* and *polis*, Greek terms for *word*
and *city* respectively, a fact suggesting that the words spoken by the Logopolitans constitute their world. Similarly, the Gospel of John describes the Logos
and God as being one and the same.[10] In both instances, power over "the
word" amounts to the power to create something from nothing. That the
Logopolitans bring the specific language of mathematics to the equation,
moreover, echoes Albert Einstein's understanding of math and science as
the language of what, for lack of a better term, he called God, or the gen-
erative force of the universe.

Although it is well known that Einstein rejected the notion of an
anthropomorphic God, he has also frequently been quoted as saying that
God "does not play dice." In other words, Einstein believed in an orderly
universe that could be understood via scientific and mathematical observation. Explaining his "faith," Einstein once noted that scientists "are in a position of a little child entering a huge library filled with books in many
different languages. The child knows someone must have written those
books. It does not know how. The child dimly suspects a mysterious order
in the arrangement of the books but doesn't know what it is."[11] In other
words, Einstein explained, "We see a universe marvelously arranged and
obeying certain laws, but only dimly understand those laws."[12] Yet while
humanity's "limited minds" cannot, in Einstein's estimation, fully grasp "the
mysterious force that moves the constellations,"[13] the citizens of Logopolis
have an apparently unlimited capacity to both understand and manipulate
that force—until, that is, the Master begins to meddle in their affairs.

Despite the Monitor's warning that interfering with the work of the
Logopolitans will lead to dire consequences, the Master impulsively mur-
ders a small number of the city's mathematicians and silences the computations of the rest with a sonic disruptor. Since the Monitor is not prone
to bluffing, his predictions inevitably prove correct, and as soon as the Master puts his plot into action, the universe begins to deteriorate. Realizing
his mistake, the Master deactivates his sonic disruptor, but doing so proves
useless, for even the briefest of pauses in the incessant chanting of the

Logopolitans breaks the mathematical spell that holds the universe together. In order to save himself, then, the Master must return to Earth with the Doctor to broadcast a final set of Logopolitan computations into space using a massive radio telescope.

Per usual, the Doctor succeeds in saving the universe by the conclusion of "Logopolis," but not without a price: the loss of yet another of his lives. Foreshadowed by much of the dialogue throughout the serial, the somber air of the Doctor's last moments resonates strongly with the gravity of the subject matter that permeates the story. As masters of the language that holds the universe together, the Logopolitans approach their work with utmost seriousness, an attitude that proves especially warranted when the Master blithely stops their computations and all hell—in the form of entropy and disorder—breaks loose. While we humans are still mere dabblers in the language of the universe, we can certainly read the consequences of the Master's actions as an object lesson on the sensitive (if not sacred) nature of our efforts at decoding that language. Splitting the atom, for example, represents a major step forward in our collective understanding of the mathematical and scientific principles at work in our universe. Or, to borrow Einstein's terminology, unlocking the power of the atom is akin to opening one of the many books in the library that is the universe. What remains to be seen, however, is whether this is a book we are ready to open or, as with the Master in "Logopolis," our feckless experimentation with forces whose significance we don't yet fully grasp will lead to certain doom.

Faith—Shaken, Not Stirred

For those of us who love words and their meanings, the current crop of new *Doctor Who* adventures do not fail to fulfill the show's occasional mission of contributing innovative ideas on language to the series. In "New Earth," the opening story of the second series, the tenth Doctor embraces the idea of the impossible when he visits a hospital near New New York on New Earth in response to a message that appears on his psychic paper and asks him to visit Ward 26. Taking a tour of Ward 26, the Doctor finds the being who sent the imploring message: the Face of Boe, whom he previously met in "The End of the World." Novice Hame, one of the Sisters of Plentitude who run the hospital, tells the Doctor that the dying Face of Boe is, according to some sources, millions of years old, but she quickly dismisses this conjecture as impossible. The Doctor, ever the seasoned traveler, then optimistically replies, "Oh, I don't know. I like the impossible." In "The Impossible Planet," however, the Doctor contradicts this very sentiment several times.

Materializing on a space station called Sanctuary Base at the beginning of this adventure, the Doctor and Rose step out of the TARDIS to find the words "Welcome to Hell" spray-painted above writing that is so ancient that even the TARDIS's telepathic field cannot translate it for the two time travelers. Commenting upon the TARDIS's failure to interpret the writing, the Doctor says, "If that's not working, then it means that this writing is old, very old—*impossibly* old." The Doctor is thus instantly confronted with a mystery that can only challenge his confident, time-tested vision of the universe.

Shortly after discovering the indecipherable writing on the walls of the space station, the Doctor and Rose encounter the Ood, alien creatures whose menacing greeting, "We need to feed," leads directly into the program's opening credits. However, we soon discover that the Ood's translation globes are malfunctioning due to electromagnetic interference. Their correct sequence of words is then relayed: "We must feed you if you are hungry." With this language mix up, we can once again see that meaning, as is almost always the case in the Whoniverse, depends entirely upon context. Yet, even though the Doctor discovers the proper context for understanding the initial greetings of the Ood, a lack of context for a series of increasingly baffling other phenomena leaves him entirely puzzled.

Continuing to utter the word "impossible," the Doctor expresses his incredulity at the fact that the "Bitter Pill," the apt nickname for the "lump-of-rock" planet upon which Sanctuary Base stands, is suspended in perpetual geostationary orbit around a black hole. Of course, this phenomenon truly is impossible insofar as black holes, in the Doctor's experience and according to every known scientific principle, tend to have such powerful gravitational fields as to be completely inescapable, yet the Time Lord cannot deny the evidence with which he is presented. What's more, the "solution" to the Doctor's conundrum provides only a modicum of context for understanding the impossible situation in which he finds himself: the planet has not yet fallen into the black hole because it serves as a prison for the creature known throughout the universe as the Beast.

Although he can never break free from his prison without being sucked into the black hole as a consequence of his escape, the Beast does have the ability to embody himself in others. His first victim is Toby, the Sanctuary Base archaeologist who is working on translating the ancient writing his team has found on the planet's surface. As Toby analyzes the writing, the Beast announces his presence by telling the archaeologist not to turn around and look at him upon the threat of death. Unable to resist temptation, Toby turns around, and the Beast enters his body—a fact that is symbolized by the sudden appearance of the undecipherable text across the entirety of the archaeologist's skin. In this instance, the written word literally marks the inscription of the Beast's mind over Toby's matter.

As for the Ood, the other victims of the Beast's malevolent machinations, we learn that they are empaths who communicate on a low-level telepathic field connecting them to one another. When Rose asks an Ood his name, he humbly replies that the members of his race "have no titles" and that they "are as one." In this sense, language for the Ood is somewhat superfluous; though an expedient means of interacting with humans, mental telepathy coupled with a lack of distinction among individual Ood themselves obviates the need to speak or write. While this arrangement certainly contributes to Ood solidarity, however, it also leaves them open to psychic attacks from the Beast, who appropriates their minds and translation globes so that he can voice his dark intentions to the crew of Sanctuary Base.

Through the Ood, the Beast announces himself with such self-aggrandizing phrases as "He is awake, and you will worship him," "The Beast and his armies shall rise from the pit to make war against God," and "We are the Legion of the Beast. The Legion shall be many, and the Legion shall be few." Undeterred by his overbearing use of third person, the Doctor asks the Beast, who claims to have inspired all mythical depictions of the devil, how he arrived on the planet, and the Beast explains that the "disciples of the light" rose up "before time" and chained him in the pit for all eternity. Once again, however, the lack of a familiar context leaves the Doctor completely baffled, and he has great difficulty comprehending the Beast's darkly poetic and obscure meaning.

What has the Doctor most perplexed in this exchange is the Beast's reference to battling the disciples of light "before time." Pressing the Beast on the issue, the Doctor learns that "before time" means more or less what it sounds like: "Before time and light and space and matter. Before the cataclysm. Before the universe was created." Yet, as far as the Doctor knows, nothing existed before time, so he has quite a bit of trouble accepting the Beast's response. Voicing his opinion that what the Beast has just said is "impossible" because no life could have existed before time, the Doctor is taken slightly aback by the suggestion that his thoughts on the subject are very much akin to religion. And although the Doctor responds to this suggestion by substituting the term "belief" for "religion," he is clearly humbled and shaken by the exchange.

From a semantic perspective, and judging from the Doctor's somewhat weak answer to the Beast's question, the words *religion* and *belief* may be interchangeable. Religions are usually based upon belief rather than proof. Likewise, the Doctor's belief stems from his distinctly Gallifreyan vision of the universe, but it is not grounded in concrete fact since he himself knows that the Time Lords have no knowledge of the time before time. As with the Sevateem and their relationship with Xoanan, then, the context in and through which the Doctor comprehends the universe is not only incomplete but also flawed, as the very existence of the Beast demonstrates.

In order to save the crew of Sanctuary Base, the Doctor must accept the Beast's rhetoric at face value. Even as the Doctor defeats the Beast, however, he is left with the lingering uncertainty that the encounter has evoked in him. To put it plainly, the Doctor is not sure whether to believe that the Beast is, indeed, the quintessential embodiment of evil, let alone to understand how he might have existed before time. While the Time Lord certainly labeled enemies like the Master and the Daleks as "evil" in the past, the full weight of this adjective has never quite hit him, nor has the concept of hell, the name he gives to the void into which he casts the Daleks and Cybermen in "Doomsday," had so much meaning for him until his encounter with the Beast.

Although his encounter with the Beast does indeed give the Doctor a new context in which to understand terms like *evil* and *hell*, it leaves the Time Lord with far more questions than answers. Still unable to decipher the Beast's "before time" writing as "The Satan Pit" draws to a conclusion, the Doctor is faced with many unknowns, including the true identity of the Beast himself. Maintaining his trademark confidence, he claims to be glad that he doesn't know everything. On one hand, we might be tempted to accept this assertion at face value; this is, after all, the man who claimed in "New Earth" to "like the impossible." On the other hand, this particular "impossibility" is so far beyond the pale as to render it much more than a tantalizing mystery for the Time Lord to solve in the space of a single adventure. Rather, as the impenetrable language of the Beast stares back at the Doctor, we begin to get a sense of why Neeva went insane upon learning in "The Face of Evil" that his entire system of belief amounted to little more than a story designed to make sense of an indecipherable world. With his own story shaken by the Beast's rhetoric, the Doctor can never view the universe in the same way again.

8

Wrinkles in Time:
Life, Death and
Everything in Between

Appearing on the morning news program *BBC Breakfast* in 2005, Christopher Eccleston noted that *Doctor Who* is different from many other contemporary science-fiction dramas in that the show represents a celebration of life. "What a lot of the science fiction programs we're going up against don't have is the central message of *Doctor Who*, which is *love life*," the actor remarked as he promoted the newly revived series; "The Doctor's message seems to be [that] you have a short life, [so] make sure it's a happy one. Seize every moment, and accept life in all its forms."[1]

At the same time, however, one of the first things we learn in the new series is that while the mysterious man in the blue box has been seen with a myriad of associates throughout time, his only constant companion appears to be the Grim Reaper. The Doctor, it soon comes out, was present for both the assassination of John F. Kennedy and the departure of the Titanic, and the only thing Rose initially knows about him is that he witnessed the death of one of her coworkers before blowing up her place of employment. From this perspective, death certainly seems to follow the Doctor around like a meddlesome associate. Yet if this is the case, then what are we to make of Eccleston's argument that *Doctor Who* represents a celebration of life?

Without a doubt, the tension between life and death has been a major theme in *Doctor Who* since the beginning and is arguably the driving force behind all great works of literature. What, after all, would *Hamlet* be without the ghost of the melancholy Dane's father—or without poor Yorick, for that matter? And how, without first killing off the beloved Vulcan Mr. Spock in its dramatic conclusion, could *Star Trek II: The Wrath of Khan* have given birth to *Star Trek III: The Search for Spock* and *Star Trek IV: The Voyage Home?* As protagonist James Axton remarks in Don DeLillo's *The Names*, the knowledge of death is what separates humanity from the rest of creation by providing us with the "special sadness" that gives life "a richness, a sanctification."² Correspondingly, *Doctor Who* frequently addresses the tension between life and death in a way that allows death to serve as a dark backdrop against which life can shine more brightly. We bear witness to the "special sadness" DeLillo attributes to humanity each time the Doctor recounts the destruction of his home planet Gallifrey. We see it in "The Girl in the Fireplace" when successive visits to eighteenth century Paris allow the Time Lord to witness the aging and death of Madame Reinette De Pompadour. And we see a version of this sadness whenever the Doctor parts company with one of his companions—for the goodbyes are usually permanent, and the Doctor knows that while he will live on through the centuries, the companions he abandons must surely pass away without ever meeting up with him again.

Most of the time, anyway.

Good for You, Sarah Jane Smith!

It was the moment we'd been waiting for.

Sure, the Daleks and UNIT had returned in season one of the new series, and the Cybermen were slated to make a return later in season two, but for longtime fans of *Doctor Who*, nothing could compare to the thrill of seeing Sarah Jane Smith return to the small screen in "School Reunion." After all, this is the same Sarah Jane who, at the tender age of twenty-three, stumbled into the TARDIS in search of the scoop that might jumpstart her burgeoning career as a journalist only to find so much more. Initially traveling with the third Doctor, Sarah Jane faced Sontarans, dinosaurs, Daleks, Ice Warriors and giant spiders before seeing the Time Lord regenerate into his fourth incarnation. From there, she stuck with the Doctor for a little over two more seasons, adding Cybermen, Zygons, Kraals, mummies and a severed hand to the menagerie of other-worldly creatures she encountered in her travels. Even after the Doctor abandoned her upon being recalled to Gallifrey, her adventures continued when she teamed up with the Doctor's robotic dog K-9 in the short-lived spin-off *K-9 and Company* and took a trip to Gallifrey's Death Zone in "The Five Doctors."

Judging by the number of televised episodes in which she has appeared, it's no wonder that Sarah Jane is a fan-favorite: she's easily logged more hours in the TARDIS than some of the Doctors themselves. As a result, many of our fondest memories of *Doctor Who* are bound up with this erstwhile time traveler, and her appearance in "School Reunion" rightfully gives the new series a strong sense of legitimacy and true continuity with the original. When Sarah Jane appears onscreen for the first time in this adventure, we know beyond all doubt that this new iteration of *Doctor Who* is not simply using its predecessor as a blueprint but is, in fact, building upon the towering success of the original to create a shared universe with a common history. And when the tenth Doctor is rendered a speechless, giddy schoolboy at the sight of her, we who fell in love with the original series all those years ago also know that despite the changes in the program's format, advances in computer-generated imaging and a complete re-imagining of the TARDIS control room, this is still our hero, our champion, our Doctor.

At the same time, however, the return of Sarah Jane amounts to a bittersweet event for all involved. The juxtaposition of the youthful "new" Doctor as portrayed by David Tenant and the mature yet no-less-stunning Sarah Jane as portrayed by Elisabeth Sladen underlines the plain fact that time has passed—not only for the Doctor and Sarah Jane, but for fans of the original series as well. Upon their first encounter—at which point Sarah Jane has yet to discover the true identity of the slightly nerdy substitute physics teacher to whom she's being introduced—the Doctor says that his name is John Smith, an allusion to the alias adopted by the third Doctor during his exile on Earth. When Sarah Jane hears this name from her past, she grows immediately wistful as if yearning for a moment in time that she can never recapture. Yet where Sarah Jane is honest with herself regarding the passage of time, the Doctor, on the other hand, is clearly in denial with regard to his age.

Though nearly a thousand years old (give or take a few centuries), the Doctor takes great pains to prove to the youthful nineteen-year-old Rose Tyler that he's still hip and with-it: "Don't tell me I don't fit in," he declares proudly, dropping ultra-contemporary references to the "happy slapping hoodies with ASBOs and ringtones" he expects to find populating the school. Yet the Doctor's mastery of twenty-first century hip-kid slang serves less to prove to Rose that the older man with whom she's traveling is eternally young at heart than to draw attention to his own insecurities about losing touch with the younger generation. Rose recognizes this fact when she first lays eyes on K-9 and asks why the Doctor would ever design a robot dog that looks "so ... disco," and even Sarah Jane begins to play on the Doctor's insecurity when she needles him with a playful barb about his age: "You can tell you're getting older. Your assistants are getting younger."

Not that the Doctor needs these reminders—the passage of time is an underlying theme throughout the new series and is given special attention in "School Reunion." When the Doctor tells Sarah Jane that she looks incredible, she replies dismissively that she simply "got old," and when Sarah Jane tells the Doctor that she thought he was dead, he admits to her that although "everyone else died," he survives. While this last admission is clearly a reference to the fact that the Doctor is the last surviving Time Lord, it also suggests that the Doctor is well aware that he must eventually leave all of his traveling companions to wither and die.

"I don't age. I regenerate," the Doctor says when Rose demands to know why he's never mentioned Sarah Jane; "But humans decay. You wither and die. Imagine watching that happen to someone.... You can spend the rest of your life with me, but I can't spend the rest of mine with you. I have to live on. Alone. That's the curse of the Time Lords." In other words, the Doctor is doomed to a life of loneliness due to the fact that he ages much more slowly than the rest of us, an assessment that is reiterated when the Doctor confronts the Krillitanes, the latest alien race to attempt an invasion of Earth. The trouble with the Time Lords, the chief Krillitane argues, is that even while they were alive, they were a "pompous race" of "ancient, dusty senators, so frightened of change." Compared to the ever-changing Krillitanes, of course, this assessment is dead-on insofar as the Time Lords of the original series are heavily invested in maintaining the status quo on their own planet and throughout the universe: members of the High Council of Gallifrey retain the outmoded ceremonial garb of their predecessors and demonstrate intense xenophobia as evidenced by their refusal to allow Sarah Jane to return to Gallifrey with the Doctor at the conclusion of "The Hand of Fear."

On the other hand, however, the Krillitanes are anything but frightened of change. In fact, their continued survival hinges upon it. Traveling throughout the universe like a tribe of nomadic space vampires, the Krillitanes not only suck the life out of every planet they visit, but also assimilate the traits and characteristics of every race they conquer into their own physical makeup. Because they exhaust the resources of each planet so quickly, moreover, the Krillitanes take the Hegelian notion of synthesis to an extreme. Where Hegel argues that progress occurs as a result of competing forces—thesis and antithesis—working against each other to create a new force or synthesis, the Krillitanes have adopted a strategy that accelerates this process and forces history and their own evolution to march forward at an alarming rate. While this strategy clearly renders the Krillitanes infinitely adaptable, it also *ensures* the destruction of every planet in their path. More significantly—at least as far as the Krillitanes are concerned— the accelerated process of evolution that provides for their survival also hastens the race's extinction in that they have evolved to the point where the very oil that once nourished the race is now poisonous to them. Likewise, their rapid conquest of the universe threatens to exhaust all of the resources that might otherwise support the Krillitanes.

Given the extreme examples before him, the Doctor must discover a middle ground between the stodginess of the Time Lords and the malignant metastasizing of the Krillitanes. That is, the Doctor must learn to allow change to occur at its own pace—neither to deny it nor to compel it. Time must be allowed to take its natural course. The universe must be allowed to age. And, heartbreaking though it is for the Time Lord to accept, people must be allowed to die. For the Doctor, this revelation applies not only to his companions but to himself as well; he is *not* as he suggests early in the episode, immortal. Rather, he experiences the passage of time and the effects of aging at a glacial pace, a fact that becomes clear when the Doctor reveals his own change of heart since the destruction of Gallifrey: "I'm so old now. I used to have so much mercy," he says when the chief Krillitane threatens Earth; "You get one warning. That was it."

Clearly these are not the words of an unchanging individual. By admitting his old age, the Doctor signals that he is, indeed, beholden to the tides of time as are the rest of us. Yet even as the Doctor takes baby steps toward embracing his own mortality, the Krillitanes manage to tempt the Doctor with the power to control time and thus to halt the aging and death of those he holds dear. Their plot, the Doctor quickly discovers, is not to suck Earth dry but to decode the Scasis Paradigm, which is said to hold the keys to controlling the building blocks of time and space. Inviting the Doctor to join in their efforts, the Krillitanes argue that the last Time Lord will become a god once their plan comes to fruition. Theoretically, the Scasis Paradigm should allow the Doctor to restore his all-but-extinct race to life and allow Sarah Jane to remain by his side throughout eternity—young, fresh, never withering, never aging, never dying. Human lives "are so fleeting," the Krillitane observes, further tempting the Doctor, yet as Sarah Jane reasons, death is a central part of life: "The universe has to move forward. Pain and loss—they define us as much as happiness or love. Whether it's a world or a relationship, everything has its time. Everything ends."

Eloquent though it is, Sarah Jane's reflection upon the necessity of time, aging and death is nothing new. Indeed, she may have picked up the basic gist of it when she met up with the fifth Doctor and his other selves in "The Five Doctors." At the conclusion of this adventure, Time Lord President Borusa attains true immortality only to learn that life without death is a curse. His spirit becomes locked in the frontispiece of Rassilon's crypt, and he is condemned to an eternity of complete and perfect stasis as his horrified gaze looks out upon an unchanging world forever. As with Sarah Jane's observation regarding the relationship between life and death, Borusa's fate suggests that Rassilon, one of the founding fathers of Time Lord culture, sees change as an essential element of a meaningful life, and death as an essential element of change. Accordingly, Borusa's fate echoes the thoughts of the ancient Greek philosopher Lucretius, who argues that "all things that endure forever must either, through having a solid body, repel impacts and allow nothing to penetrate them which might separate their tight-fitting parts from within ... or be able to endure through all time because they are free from blows, like void, which remains untouched and is quite unaffected by impact."[3] From this perspective, a life without change—like a life without death—is no life at all.

But recognizing the centrality of death to the value of life and stopping the Krillitanes from conquering the universe are two separate issues, and Sarah Jane's eloquence is not enough to prevent the latter from occurring. Stopping the Krillitanes requires action, and the Doctor must call upon all of his companions—old and new—to foil the fiendish plot of the belligerent alien race. Poignantly, his plan of action also requires that K-9 make the ultimate sacrifice, which he does in the tradition of Adric, Katarina, Sarah Kingdom and (if the comic strip series is to be believed) Ace, all of whom died valiantly while helping the Doctor defend the universe from evil.

Though a robot and technically lifeless, K-9 is nonetheless a much-loved character from the program's past, and his destruction drives home Sarah Jane's point that death is a part of life. At the same time, the fact that K-9 "dies" while defending the universe from certain doom echoes another element of ancient Greek philosophy with regard to death. In *The Nicomachean Ethics*, Aristotle writes that because "death is the most fearful of all things ... he will be called brave who is fearless in the face of a noble death and in all emergencies that involve death; and the emergencies of war are in the highest degree of this kind."[4] The idea here is that dying in defense of one's own civilization—whether against foreign armies or in the face of natural disaster—is an innately noble gesture (even for a mechanical dog) since doing so requires facing "the most fearful of all things."

In the context of "School Reunion," however, Aristotle's argument receives a slight twist—and an update. While Aristotle theorizes that dying for one's civilization is intrinsically noble, the natural issue that arises is that of whether dying for a civilization predicated on evil is noble as well. If, for example, a Dalek self-destructs in the name of the Dalek Empire or a Cyberman dies while administering "upgrades" to the human population of Earth, can we truly say that this death is ennobling or intrinsically good? In some ways, Aristotle's answer would appear to be in the affirmative insofar as the philosopher makes no distinctions with regard to the dying warrior's national allegiance. Whether a Dalek kills a Cyberman or vice-versa within the context of war, the resulting death is intrinsically noble. Yet since both cultures are largely evil, no good can result from either spreading its reign throughout the universe, so the defense of one's civilization is not what makes death noble or good within the context of a war between the Daleks and Cybermen. In order to determine what makes such deaths somehow noble or positive, we need to return to (or fast-forward to, if we're considering these issues historically) Hegel.

As noted earlier, Hegel holds that progress results from conflicts between the opposing forces of thesis and antithesis. But what if the antithesis doesn't put up much of a fight? What if the thesis simply comes along and trounces the antithesis before the antithesis even has a chance to get out of bed? Consider the example set forth by the Krillitanes: blitzing through the universe like a cancer or a virus, they move so quickly that the inhabitants of their "host planets" can do little to defend themselves. Yet while the Krillitanes (or the thesis in this example), provoke something akin to synthesis in that they assimilate the physical traits of their victims (or their antithesis), the lack of spirited or significant resistance on the part of the victims casts suspicion on the nature of said synthesis. To wit: does a Krillitane invasion present a true opportunity for synthesis? Or is the result of such an invasion something more akin to bricolage, the act of assembling an end product from bits and pieces of available material? Clearly, the Krillitanes are engaged in the latter as they move from planet to planet, picking up useful pieces of genetic information the way tourists might purchase artifacts, trinkets and handicrafts from seaside vendors on foreign shores.

Until, that is, the Doctor intervenes. Called to Earth by Mickey Smith (no relation to Sarah Jane, and certainly no relation to the Doctor's alterego John Smith),[5] the Doctor, as he is frequently inclined to do, helps the denizens of his favorite planet put up a good fight and gives the Krillitanes the butt-whooping they have coming to them. As a result, the Krillitanes receive their first real challenge in ages and must put up a fight in order to get what they want. That they lose the battle as a result of K-9's self-sacrifice, moreover, makes the robotic dog the hero of the episode and also recasts Aristotle's dictum on the nobility of the warrior's death in Hegelian terms: death in battle is not intrinsically noble simply because defending one's civilization or advancing one's empire is intrinsically good, but because death in this context ensures the rigor of Hegelian dialectic. If not for K-9's readiness to die in defense of the Earth, the Krillitanes would once again be in a position to cherry-pick elements of the planet's biological and cultural DNA as they see fit, but because K-9 and company are willing to sacrifice everything in order to save their civilization, the Krillitanes must truly strive for conquest—or die trying. And when they do, in fact, die trying, they die the noble deaths that Aristotle describes in *The Nicomachean Ethics* not because their own culture is good but because they have, perhaps for the first time, truly participated in the cross-cultural dialectic of battle.

And time marches on.

With the Krillitanes defeated, the Doctor must face the ghosts of his own past—or at least bring a sense of closure to his relationship with Sarah Jane. When the Doctor's former companion re-enters the redesigned TARDIS for the first time, she notes that the Doctor has redecorated since her days of traveling in time and space, and that while she prefers the old TARDIS interior, she's also happy with the new. But what else can she say? The Doctor's beloved Sarah Jane has already argued that change and loss are essential to life, so in order to embrace life, she must also embrace the new version of the TARDIS as well as the sense of change and consequent loss it implies. Along similar lines, longtime fans are also free to prefer the camp of the original series to the slick production values of the new, but we must also accept that the new series is a product of its time and that a reiteration of the old would seem entirely out of place on the present-day airwaves. Thus, when Rose asks Sarah Jane if she should continue on with the Doctor, we get the sense that the new generation of fandom may well be asking the old if the show is worth following—and if Sarah Jane's response is any indication, then the answer is a resounding *yes*. Even if *Doctor Who* disappoints us from time to time, even if some of the scripts or special effects leave something to be desired, and even if the show is canceled once again and leaves us alone in the universe without so much as a long scarf and a floppy hat to keep us warm, some things are, indeed, worth a broken heart.

Forever Young?

Despite their apparent reconciliation at the conclusion of "School Reunion," a major source of dramatic tension throughout the adventure is the difference in age between Sarah Jane and Rose. When the adventurers stumble upon a stash of dehydrated rats, the cleft that emerges between the Doctor and Mickey when the latter lets out a "girly" scream divides the males along the lines of machismo and perceived courage (or lack thereof), but the rift between Sarah Jane and Rose takes a decidedly different turn. Opining that students most likely use the rats for dissection purposes in high school biology classes, Sarah Jane finds her theory immediately shot down when Rose points out that students haven't dissected real animals in years and suggests that Sarah Jane must have gone to school sometime in the dark ages. By drawing attention to Sarah Jane's age in this fashion, Rose also draws attention to the fact that while the men in her world are frequently evaluated in terms of intangibles like character, skill and courage, women are judged according to the more superficial yardsticks of age and beauty. Hence where age, wisdom and experience give the Doctor an edge over Mickey, these same characteristics are (at first glance, anyway) liabilities in the apparent competition between Sarah Jane and Rose.

In short, when Rose points out that Sarah Jane is old, she's also saying, by way of contrast, that she is decidedly younger than the former time traveler and that, as a result, the Doctor should naturally like her better because, in the context of twenty-first century Western Eurocentric culture (and particularly with regard to women), younger simply *is* better. Shallow though this formulation may be, it is a conceit that is not only endemic to the youth-oriented, consumer-driven mindset of twenty-first century Earth but also permeates the seemingly sacrosanct world of *Doctor Who* as well. When Sara Kingdom dies in "The Daleks' Master Plan," the insult that is added to the injury of her demise is that she is not simply gunned down by the Daleks but "aged to death" when the first Doctor sets in motion a device called the Time Destructor. Additionally, when the evil Axons want to torture the third Doctor in "The Claws of Axos," they plague him with images of his young companion Jo Grant growing old and decrepit. And while the accelerated aging, death and decomposition of the dithering Professor Kerensky in "City of Death" barely warrants a gasp, the Doctor's rapid aging in "The Leisure Hive" causes Romana to recoil in horror at the thought of tooling around the universe with a wizened old coot and a malfunctioning metal dog for the rest of her life. Yet while the specter of old age does, in many instances, represent a terrible fate even in the context of the Whoniverse, *Doctor Who* has, in other instances, managed to critique the cultural assumptions that place a premium on youth at the expense of maturity.

It isn't for nothing that the rare chemical Spectrox is described in the fifth-Doctor serial "The Caves of Androzani" as "the most valuable substance in the universe," a "wonderful restorative," and "the greatest boon ever bestowed on humanity." Offering humans "at least twice normal lifespan," Spectrox is the stuff of legends, akin to the mythical fountain of youth that led early Spanish explorers like Juan Ponce de Leon to explore the Americas in a fruitless effort to cheat death and sidestep the ravages of time. In more recent times, Spectrox finds many corollaries in the modern beauty industry where companies like Revlon, Nivea, St. Ives and Olay slap the "age-defying" prefix on a wide selection of creams, oils and lotions in order to boost sales. As with Rose's critique of Sarah Jane in "School Reunion," the general message that these products convey is that aging is bad. This message is reinforced by the fact that marketers focus the majority of their efforts on capturing the $175 billion-a-year youth market by depicting in ads, films and television programs a universe where children rule and adults are rendered irrelevant, incompetent or completely nonexistent. To age in this context is to either fade away or become a monstrosity, so adults in increasing numbers are shelling out small fortunes to hold the signs of aging at bay in order to maintain the illusion of youth.

Yet as the subtext of "The Caves of Androzani" suggests, youth is not the be-all and end-all of life. Lurking in the caves of Androzani Minor is the mad genius Sharaz Jek, whose physical deformity precludes any chance that you'll ever catch him frolicking on the beach with the cast of *Beverly Hills*

90210, Dawson's Creek, The OC or whichever youth-oriented teen-drama is currently being broadcast in your corner of the universe this evening. Beyond his lack of youthful good looks, moreover, what separates Jek from those who would risk life and limb for the opportunity to get their hands on even the smallest quantity of Spectrox is his cunning will to survive. To borrow a phrase from the journalist P.J. O'Rourke, Jek demonstrates that age and guile beat youth, innocence and a bad haircut any day of the week, and as his enemies fall prey to their own cupidity, the mad genius of the caves clings to life with unparalleled tenacity throughout much of the serial— until, that is, his infatuation with Peri, the Doctor's latest young companion, leads to his undoing.

Young, attractive and full of life, Peri becomes Jek's object of desire largely because she possesses traits that are completely alien to him. Faced with Peri's youth and apparent *joie de vivre*, Jek recognizes that although he can't be young and beautiful himself, he can at least imprison someone who possesses those traits. Caught up in his infatuation, however, Jek becomes distracted from the business of survival. Subsequently, when the mad genius learns that Peri is dying of "Spectrox toxemia," the news proves too much for him to bear, and he is so driven to despair that he allows a pair of gun-runners to infiltrate his secret lair. In the ensuing battle, Jek's lab catches fire, and Jek himself dies in the arms of a young-looking android—a poetic ending for the mad genius, perhaps, insofar as the apparent youth and beauty denied Jek throughout the serial offers him comfort in his time of dying. At the same time, however, the comfort offered by the android is cold at best, and its youth, like everything else in Jek's world, is entirely artificial. Jek's death, then, offers partial resolution to the tension that drives "The Caves of Androzani." In effect marrying the cold and artificial youth of the android with the natural decrepitude of the mad scientist, Jek's final scene suggests that while the quest for eternal youth may indeed serve to postpone death, the "life" promised by that quest is a far cry from truly being alive.

The folly of seeking eternal life, however, is only half of the equation that marks "The Caves of Androzani." The other half is the value of self-sacrifice. While Jek and the greedy industrialist Morgus struggle for survival, the Doctor freely sacrifices one of his own lives in order to save Peri. As the serial concludes, the Doctor, who is also suffering from Spectrox toxemia, gives the only available dose of the cure to his young companion and, in so doing, is forced to regenerate. Reinforcing our sense of the Doctor's hero-ism, this gesture indicates that a life lived to the fullest is one lived not in fear of death but with a respect for its undeniable preeminence. In other words, the knowledge of death's inevitability has the potential to make every life meaningful, and the nearness of what Aristotle calls the "most fearful of all things" is what, in the end, makes heroes truly heroic. As with his other regenerations, the Doctor's "death" at the conclusion of "The Caves of Androzani" clearly signals the passage of time and serves as a reminder that even Time Lords are not immortal. More significantly, his willingness to "die" not as part of a quest for power or riches but in order to save the life of another poses a challenge to the rest of us: given similar (admittedly far-fetched) circumstances, would we be willing to do the same?

Perhaps, perhaps not.

But then again, the Doctor himself might be plagued with doubts as to whether sacrificing his lives time and again for the sake of humanity is a worthwhile endeavor. If the form the Time Lord takes just before the curtain closes on "The Caves of Androzani" is any indication of his position on this issue, in fact, it's safe to say that the Doctor does indeed harbor some degree of regret at his own self-sacrificing nature and wishes, at least on a subconscious level, to take steps to ensure his own survival. Echoing O'Rourke's sentiment on the issue, youth gives way to guile when the youthful fifth Doctor played by Peter Davison regenerates into the less youthful sixth Doctor portrayed by Colin Baker. Perhaps ironically, the Doctor clings to life not by becoming younger (as was the case in his two previous regenerations) but by growing older and perhaps slightly wiser—or, at the very least, more wily.

Despite his poor fashion sense and a tendency to ramble, the apparently older sixth Doctor lacks the trusting nature of the fifth. For example, where the fifth Doctor practically welcomes the murderous Turlough into the TARDIS with open arms, the sixth Doctor has trouble warming up to the relatively innocent Peri. In addition to trying to strangle the hapless young companion in "The Twin Dilemma," the Doctor also remains unmoved by the prospect of her likely death of old age within the walls of a stalled TARDIS in "Vengeance on Varos." Though softening somewhat in relation to his companions, the Doctor becomes older and wiser still when he regenerates into his seventh incarnation. His relationship with Ace is akin to that of a sensible yet kind-hearted uncle to a rebellious yet eager-to-please niece, and his apparent prescience may be less a matter of having already seen the future than of having been around the block enough times to find the actions of his enemies and the motions of the universe fairly predictable. For the Doctor, then, regeneration can serve not simply as a means of evading death or achieving eternal youth but as a process that allows certain aspects of his personality to die so that those more suited to survival might live. All of this is to say that regeneration doesn't stunt the Doctor's development. On the contrary, it forces the Time Lord to "grow up" by putting him in touch with his own mortality.

States of Decay

Of course, not every Time Lord is as accepting of his or her own mortality as the Doctor. As noted, Gallifrey's Lord President Borusa seeks to extend his life throughout all of eternity in "The Five Doctors," and the Doctor's longtime foe, the Master, manages to survive well beyond his allotted twelve regenerations by assuming the bodies of innocent bystanders in "The Keeper of Traken" and *Doctor Who: The Movie*. And then there's Morbius, whose brain appears in the aptly titled fourth-Doctor serial "The Brain of Morbius." In this serial, we learn that despite having been atomized by his fellow Time Lords for crimes against the universe, the rogue Morbius has managed to cling to life for the sole purpose of exacting revenge upon those who punished him. As with Borusa and the Master, then, conquering death via any means possible is a key element of the vengeful Time Lord's *modus operandi*.

Borrowing heavily from Mary Wollstonecraft Shelley's *Frankenstein*, "The Brain of Morbius" provides an extended critique of the quest for eternal life, a critique that is accentuated by the juxtaposition of two opposing forces who are equally interested in deferring death for as long as possible. On one hand, there's Morbius, whose brain remains preserved in a vat of bubbling chemicals while his servant, the mad scientist Solon, attempts to cobble together a body suited to the rigors of conquering the universe. On the other hand, there's the Sisterhood of Karn, the members of which have managed to halt the aging process throughout much of eternity not (as one might guess) by stocking up on Oil of Olay but by periodically imbibing an elixir which, it turns out, is available for a limited time only. Per usual, the Doctor is caught in the middle of these forces, and as the serial unfolds, he renders the folly of pursuing eternal life increasingly clear.

In the opening shots of "Brain of Morbius," an insectoid astronaut struggles for survival on the barren surface of an alien planet. Dragging itself from the wreck of a spacecraft, the creature has little hope of survival, yet some instinct propels it forward. Fate, however, rears its ugly head when a mysterious figure emerges from the shadows and decapitates the bug-eyed alien. Foreshadowing the theme that pervades the adventure, this murder suggests that, try as we might, we can never elude death completely. Yet while the aforementioned alien is certainly doomed, the image of its death is juxtaposed with the immediate arrival of the TARDIS and the emergence of a childishly sulking Doctor from its interior, followed by a somewhat maternal Sarah Jane. As the Doctor complains about the "meddlesome interfering idiots" from Gallifrey who forced his TARDIS to materialize on the barren surface of the planet, Sarah Jane leaves him to sulk and play with his yo-yo while she goes off to explore the mysterious planet. Further establishing the theme of the adventure, these opening scenes present the audience with the cycle of life, death and rebirth, with the TARDIS serving as the womb-like interior from which the temporarily infantile Doctor emerges. Yet as the Doctor and Sarah Jane soon discover, the cycle of life on this planet has been halted with disastrous consequences.

Like the eponymous doctor of *Frankenstein*, the mad scientist Solon seeks to conquer death via scientific means, but his efforts at preserving life have left his world in a state of absolute stagnation. Accompanied only by an Igor-like "chicken-brained biological disaster" named Condo, Solon leads a fairly solitary life on an isolated planet where time seems to have come to a grinding halt. His efforts at finding a suitable head in which to encase the brain of Morbius have reached an impasse, as has any progress Solon has made in the field of scientific inquiry. Accordingly, his castle is a throwback to a once-prosperous age, and his equipment bears greater resemblance to the contents of a yard sale than that of a working laboratory. Beyond the castle walls, moreover, the remainder of the planet is barren and lifeless as well. As Sarah Jane remarks, the planet's surface is very much like the Sargasso Sea—renowned for its sunken ships and apparent stillness—and although Solon claims to have discovered the secret of creating life, his environment is marked by nothing but a torpid sense of inertia.[6]

Furthering the sense of stagnation inherent in "The Brain of Morbius" is the Sisterhood of Karn, a coven of witches who, like Solon, are so hell-bent on conquering death that they fail to recognize the utter lifelessness that results from their efforts. Unlike Morbius, however, the Sisterhood relies not on science but upon magic to ensure eternal youth. Worshipping a Sacred Flame and imbibing the so-called Elixir of Life that flame produces, the members of the Sisterhood have managed to postpone death for centuries. As the adventure unfolds, however, we learn that the supply of elixir is dwindling, and while the Doctor observes that "one could possibly synthesize the stuff by the gallon" (and conceivably make a killing in a head-to-head marketing war against the purveyors of Spectrox), he refuses to do so because "the consequences would be appalling." Death, the Doctor observes, "is the price we pay for progress," a point that becomes especially clear when the leader of the Sisterhood notes that nothing on her isolated world ever changes. And while the Sisterhood takes great pride in maintaining the status quo, an existence without change is, from the Doctor's perspective, a fate worse than death.

In order to progress, in order to evolve, in order to *live*, the Doctor argues, we must allow death to occur, yet everyone on Karn remains fixated upon holding the Grim Reaper at bay. That doing so is unnatural is made clear by the grotesquery of both factions that inhabit the planet: the body Morbius eventually adopts consists of a bizarre and generally impractical hodgepodge of alien limbs and organs, and the members of the Sisterhood are so beholden to tradition that their days amount to little more than endless exercises in dreary pomp and circumstance. Yet the unexpected death of one of their own forces a change in the Sisterhood's outlook, and upon recognizing the threat that Morbius poses not only to their own world but to the universe at large, the heretofore socially inert witches venture into the wilds of Karn to confront the murderous Time Lord and their own mortality as well. This confrontation with mortality, moreover, signals a sea-change in the Sisterhood's worldview; after seeing to the death of Morbius, Maren, the leader of the Sisterhood, sacrifices her own life in order to save the Doctor's. By allowing the Doctor to imbibe the only available dose of the Elixir of Life after he has been mortally wounded, Maren not only serves as the model of self-sacrifice that may well inspire the Doctor's fifth incarnation to give up his own life to save that of a companion in "The Caves of Androzani" but also, and perhaps more importantly, breaches the taboo that her own Sisterhood has placed upon death.

As the Sisterhood moves on with a youthful and comparatively progressive Sister named Ohica at the helm, a new day dawns on Karn, and for the first time in ages, the planet's previously stagnant culture returns to the land of the living. Yet while the Doctor has managed to reintroduce death to the cycle of life on Karn, the temptation offered by the promise of eternal life continues to be too great for other civilizations to resist. Long after unceremoniously ditching Sarah Jane, the Doctor and his newer, perhaps younger, and definitely more-scantily clad companion Leela encounter the Minyans of Minyos, whose former intimacy with the Time Lords has resulted in a prolonged and dreary life without death.

In "Underworld," the Doctor reveals that before adopting a strict non-intervention policy, his fellow Time Lords once took an interest in the people of Minyos. After learning all they could from the Time Lords, however, the Minyans found themselves caught up in a civil war that ultimately resulted in the destruction of their planet. Yet as the action of "Underworld" gets underway, the Doctor learns that a small contingent of Minyans survived the war only to wander through space, seemingly for all of eternity.

Using Time Lord technology, the surviving Minyans have managed to prolong their lives for over a thousand generations as they travel the galaxies in their ship, the R1C. Trapped in a long-term quest for the P7E, a ship containing their planet's "race bank," however, these survivors have become little more than "a ship of ghosts ... going on and on and unable to remember why." "The quest is the quest," the survivors repeat *ad infinitum*, but the solipsistic nature of this mantra belies the hopelessness of their cause: with no true faith in the likelihood of ever reaching their goal, the Minyans have only the quest itself to believe in. So disheartened are they, in fact, that their only solace is that their ship will likely break down and die before they do, thereby ending their otherwise interminable journey.

What the surviving Minyans seek, of course, is a form of death: they want to reach their goal so that they might, in a phrase, rest in peace. Yet their goal, ironically, represents everything the crewmembers of the R1C detest about the situation in which they find themselves. Described alternately as "the future of the Minyan race" and the "genetic inheritance" of the Minyan people, the so-called race bank is, in reality, less a means of providing the Minyans with a future than of perpetuating their past. Containing what is thought to be the pure genetic code of the Minyan people, the race bank can only preserve the Minyans in amber, as it were, and does not allow for evolution or change. Like the ship of ghosts, then, the race bank represents not life, but lifelessness, and though the crew is armed with the best of intentions, their goal of providing a future for their culture is confounded by their desire to preserve the past.

The conundrum at the heart of "the quest" is brought to life when, against all odds, the surviving Minyans discover the P7E and almost immediately begin to battle the descendants of the ship's crew. Clearly, these people are the true "future" of Minyos, but the crew of the R1C is so fixated with rescuing the race *bank* that attacking actual members of the race itself becomes a matter of little or no consequence. That the survivors of Minyos are misguided in their veneration of the race bank is further emphasized by the fact that the megalomaniac computer at the heart of the P7E (a.k.a. the Oracle) is itself more interested in protecting the genetic information contained therein than in providing for the well-being of the living manifestation of that information in the physical world. To this end, the Oracle has enslaved the descendants of the P7E crew and has created a separate, hyper-evolved race of "Seers" to govern the enslaved masses. Thus while the Minyan survivors have grown stagnant and lifeless over the course of their hundred-thousand year journey, some of their descendants have evolved so far as to become utterly alien and unrecognizable, suggesting that the actual future of the Minyan race is not necessarily the future envisioned by the crew of the R1C.

As with the Sisterhood of Karn in "The Brain of Morbius," true life for the Minyans hinges not on clinging to the past but upon allowing for change. Yet if the Seers are any indication of what's to come, then the future of the Minyan race is grim at best. Their dome-shaped, golden, phallic heads reflect the spirit of patriarchal despotism at the root of their power, and their belief in their own genetic superiority carries unpleasant overtones of Nazi rhetoric. Nonetheless, what must be remembered about the Seers is that they are more than likely the creation of the Oracle, a mere extrapolation based upon the information contained in the Minyans' race bank and not the result of a truly organic evolutionary process. In fact, the apparently asexual nature of the Seers suggests that they've reached the end of their evolutionary line. Because each is a clone of the others—in essence, a walking, talking phallus—there is no hope of any of the Seers finding a mate suited to sexual reproduction. As a result, no new genetic information can enter the Seers' gene pool, and the Seers can therefore no longer evolve.

By way of contrast, the slave classes still reproduce via traditional means as suggested by the presence of parents and children throughout the adventure. Although the crew of the R1C has apparently given up on passing along genetic information the old-fashioned way, their rescue of the Oracle's slaves (at the Doctor's insistence) allows the race to continue on its natural course of evolution. Liberated from the Oracle's influence, the former slaves might well discover a genetic trajectory that is distinct from that of their former masters. As a result, while the crew of the R1C does, in due course, retrieve their treasured race bank from the Oracle, they eventually come to realize that the true future of Minyos lies in the hands of the living, dying, loving, breeding and evolving slaves they initially held in contempt. Indeed, one of the more evocative scenes of "Underworld" suggests that the adventure is a metaphor for sexual reproduction writ large: as the R1C penetrates the surface of the planetoid surrounding the P7E, one gets the distinct impression that (apologies to Sigmund Freud) sometimes a spaceship is *not* just a spaceship. What's more, this imagery reveals the sexual nature not only of conflict between the crews of the R1C and the P7E, but of Hegelian dialectic itself.

Sex derives from the Latin *secare*, meaning *to divide or cut.* In modern terms, of course, the sexual divide falls along gender lines, and for reproductive purposes, sexual intercourse involves the commingling of a couple's genetic information. But what is this commingling of genetic information if not a from of synthesis, the opposition of one parent's genes against those of the other for the purposes of creating a third, unique set of genes? And by way of analogy, what is war but synthesis as well, an opposition of cultures which gives rise to a new culture that is neither entirely one nor the other but a third, unique culture with its own mores and values? Perhaps all is fair in love *and* war precisely because love *is* war, and vice-versa. As the underlying logic of "Underworld" suggests, acts of war and acts of lovemaking perform roughly the same function by providing a forum for the union of disparate elements, a union which results in something new and distinct from either of the elements that contributed to its creation. This is not, of course, to justify or romanticize war but to suggest that war is one mode of encounter that allows for the temporary union of differing cultures and thus allows those cultures to give birth, metaphorically speaking, to something new. Yet with birth comes death, and as the encounter between the R1C and the P7E gives rise to a new iteration of Minyan culture, the Oracle is consumed in an explosion while the crew of the R1C, having finally reached the end of their quest, can arguably rest in peace.

Which is more than can be said for a certain triumvirate of vampires across whom the Doctor stumbles in "State of Decay." Before the TARDIS materializes on the socially and technologically underdeveloped planet in this adventure, we meet Zargo and Camilla, the planet's pasty sovereigns, as well as their counselor, Aukon. Ostensibly a family of vampires, "the Three Who Rule" (as they are known to their primitive constituents) were once the human officers of the starship Hydrax. Tempted by the promise of eternal life, they threw in their lot with an intergalactic parasite known as the Great Vampire, moored their ship on an uncharted planet and enslaved the ship's crew. Over a period of twenty generations, "the three" bred "dullness, obedience [and] conformity" into the descendants of the crewmembers and also wiped out any memory of the their true origins. Thus, having remodeled the Hydrax to resemble a towering medieval castle, Zargo, Camilla and Aukon now rule over a world whose culture is locked in a state of permanent arrested development. Moreover, as if stunting the intellectual and cultural progress of an entire village weren't cause enough for concern, the Three Who Rule gain their only sustenance by feasting on the blood of their constituents.

Needless to say, the Doctor is not amused when he learns of the events transpiring in the tiny, isolated village. A traveler, a scientist, a philosopher, a man of learning, the Doctor cannot tolerate a world where "all science, all knowledge is forbidden," yet when Aukon offers the Time Lord an opportunity to become a vampire himself, one senses—as in "School Reunion"— a moment of trepidation as the Doctor contemplates the promise of eternal life. This, after all, is season eighteen of the series, and the fourth Doctor is beginning to betray a touch of gray. Earlier in the season, we were introduced to the "dance-floor-friendly," upbeat version of the program's theme song along with a new title sequence complete with a moving star field and a trendy (for the time, anyway) neon logo—all signs, perhaps, of a Time Lord and television icon going through a midlife crisis. Likewise, the Doctor's new burgundy ensemble suggests that he is growing more somber and contemplative as the years take their toll. As if to call attention to this passage of time, the Doctor's old jacket and scarf hang on the TARDIS coat rack throughout much of season eighteen—a throwback, perhaps, to happier, more innocent times, and a sign that the Time Lord, like the rest of us, is changing, maturing and growing older.

Why shouldn't the Doctor be tempted?

Why shouldn't he accept Aukon's offer?

Why shouldn't he be granted eternal life?

He is the Doctor, isn't he? Surely if he became a vampire, he would be some kind of "good-guy" vampire *à la* Angel of *Buffy the Vampire Slayer* and *Angel* fame!

For the Doctor, however, there can be no "good-guy" vampires because the vampire lifestyle is no life at all. Bloodsucking and terrible fashion sense aside, the Three Who Rule represent everything the Doctor detests. Torpor, stasis, boredom, repression, apathy, inaction, indifference and complacency are all traits of the Three Who Rule as well as characteristics of the Time Lord culture against which the Doctor has rebelled throughout much of his career as a renegade. Without death as a limit upon life, the Three Who Rule have no true sense of urgency, no real reason to accomplish anything and, as a result, have no real raison d'être beyond holding back death. And because the Three Who Rule have no grand vision, no true sense of their duties or identities as leaders, no desire whatsoever to advance the culture of their followers, the tiny village that surrounds their castle can never progress.

One way to examine the relationship between the Three Who Rule and the villagers who serve them is in terms laid out by the Slovenian sociologist, philosopher and cultural critic Slavoj Zizek. Culture, Zizek argues in *The Sublime Object of Ideology*, represents an attempt to cultivate the death drive.[7] In other words, since we all know that we're inexorably moving toward death and that death is everyone's inevitable end, we engage in this thing called "culture" not simply to pass the time between birth and death but also to make that time seem more meaningful to ourselves. Culture makes us feel like we're part of something bigger than ourselves, and contributing to culture makes us feel like we matter. At the same time, however, Zizek also observes that fascism, which demands uniformity and forbids true progress, is culture carried to an extreme, and that the aspiration to completely abolish the death drive is "the source of the totalitarian temptation."[8] That is, fascism attempts to create a single, unchanging definition of the "perfect" culture and, in so doing, freezes progress in its tracks. To put it bluntly, fascism is about maintaining the status quo at all costs, even if doing so results (as it inevitably must), in a state of perpetual decay.

Yet as the Doctor observes early in the serial, "Night must fall ... even in E-Space." It comes as no surprise, then, when the formerly hopeless and downtrodden villagers rise up against their oppressors and put an end to the repressive regime under which they've lived for so long. The full import of this revolution is seen when the Great Vampire dies and, as a result, the Three Who Rule wither and die along with it. In this scene, the graphic nature of the vampires' demise indicates the degree to which they've outlived their usefulness; having held back progress for so long in the name of a (literally) fruitless eternal youth, the Three Who Rule can do nothing but turn to dust with the dawning of a new age.

And so the Doctor moves on.

Over the course of the next three episodes, our favorite Time Lord loses two companions, picks up two more, and regenerates at the conclusion of the somber and melancholy "Logopolis." And while the passing of this longtime and much-loved incarnation of the Doctor is in many ways traumatic and painful for those of us who grew up thinking of Tom Baker as the Doctor, it is also, in the final analysis, part of the natural order of things—for in the fifth-Doctor serial "Mawdryn Undead," we catch a brief but horrifying glimpse of a world that might have been, a world in which the fourth Doctor never left but, instead, stayed long past his welcome.

As in "Underworld," the presence of Time Lord regeneration technology in "Mawdryn Undead" gives the Doctor a chance to consider the complications inherent in the promise of eternal life. As the serial gets under way, we are introduced to Mawdryn, the leader of a team of scientists who, in the distant past, stole a "metamorphic symbiosis regenerator" from Gallifrey in an effort to conquer death. Normally reserved for cases of "acute regenerative crisis" among Time Lords, the regenerator has been modified by Mawdryn and company with predictably horrendous results. Rather than providing the scientists with the ability to regenerate as the Time Lords do, the modified regenerator has simply trapped Mawdryn and his followers in a "life without form," a perpetual state of "endless torment." Like the Energizer Bunny, they just keep going and going and going and going with no end in sight. In their botched attempt to gain the ability to regenerate, then, Mawdryn and his associates have instead become undying (yet, curiously, unliving) shadows of their former selves.

Against this backdrop, "Mawdryn Undead" also presents the return of many familiar faces. The Brigadier, for one, is back in action, and as the Doctor attempts to restore his old friend's addled memory, the audience is treated to a series of flashbacks depicting the Time Lord's former incarnations. Furthering his efforts to jog the Brigadier's memory, the Doctor speaks the names of Liz Shaw, Jo Grant and Sarah Jane Smith. As in "School Reunion," then, the return of an old friend gives the Doctor an opportunity to look back upon his past and appreciate the bittersweet character of time's natural passage. Along more sinister lines, however, Mawdryn's experiments with the metamorphic symbiosis regenerator forces the Doctor to consider once again the dangers inherent in interfering with the natural flow of time.

Inexplicably "infected" with Mawdryn's "disease," the Doctor's young companions Nyssa and Tegan find that they can no longer travel in time without suffering undesirable side effects. Echoing Jo Grant's fate in "The Claws of Axos," Nyssa and Tegan begin to wither away before the Doctor's eyes as the TARDIS moves forward in time. In this instance, as in "The Claws of Axos," growing prematurely gray and wrinkled represents what may well be the worst of all possible fates in the Whoniverse. By way of contrast, however, the "infection" also causes Nyssa and Tegan to grow exceedingly youthful when the Doctor attempts to travel backwards in time. Although this twist certainly serves as a countermeasure against the usual biases that posit old age as a curse, the bottom line remains the same: tampering with the natural flow of time is never a good idea—a fact that becomes particularly apparent when two manifestations of the Brigadier, each from a distinct period in history, come into contact with each other and trigger a massive explosion.

Visually, the most striking warning against tampering with time and the aging process is the ghastly figure of Mawdryn himself. Caught in his own personal state of decay, Mawdryn is pale and gaunt, and his brain protrudes disturbingly from under his scalp. This, it would seem, is the punishment for seeking immortality, the penalty for daring to cheat death. And when the badly injured Mawdryn is mistaken for the Doctor, we also come to understand the necessity of change. For in their efforts to comfort the creature whom they believe to be their friend and fellow traveler, Nyssa and Tegan dress Mawdryn in the fourth Doctor's burgundy jacket, effectively bringing a grotesque version of the Time Lord's previous incarnation to life again. Thus, as Mawdryn rambles about the TARDIS control room in the fourth Doctor's clothing, it becomes increasingly difficult not to draw a parallel between the two figures and to view the Doctor's frightfully cranky and emaciated doppelganger as the Doctor himself or, more accurately, as a vision of what might have been, a ghost image from an alternate reality where the fourth Doctor never met his end but instead continued to roam through time and space in increasingly ill spirits and failing health. In many ways, then, the image of Mawdryn ensconced in the Doctor's old overcoat serves as a visual cue suggesting that change is a good thing and that clinging too tenaciously to the past amounts to an exercise in futility.

Spared "the endurance of endless time, the agony of perpetuity," Mawdryn receives what the Doctor describes as the "reward" of death at the conclusion of "Mawdryn Undead." Accordingly, the serial is clearly in line with "The Brain of Morbius," "Underworld" and "State of Decay" in that it drives home the notion that the substance of life hinges upon the imminence of death. Death, in the final analysis, gives life form by placing a limit upon it, and by placing a limit upon life, death also forces each of us to make the most of the time we have. More importantly, death also ensures change, for without death, we would become—like Mawdryn and Morbius, like the Three Who Rule and the crew of the P7E—tired, world-weary ghosts of the past. From this perspective, death serves as a positive force, because only through death—whether on an individual or cultural scale—does change emerge, and only through change do we truly find life. For life, like progress, lies not in clinging to static, idealized models of who we are but in allowing for such models to fall so that we might grow into our future selves and so future generations might, in their own time, come into their own.

New Life?

In December of 1989, the curtain closed on the original *Doctor Who* series—a passing which, while initially and justifiably deemed lamentable by longtime fans of the program, ultimately saved the Time Lord from the agony of perpetuity and what the sixth Doctor once described in a moment of post-regeneration terror as "the crushing boredom of eternity."[9] The previous season had seen the return of the Daleks as well as the Cybermen, and nothing new had been added to either race's collective mythology: the Daleks were still engaged in a protracted civil war, and the Cybermen were yet again trying to colonize Earth. Likewise, the final season of the original series also included the return of a pair of familiar faces, and although the Brigadier and the Master were both older and presumably wiser, their respective appearances on the program served less to develop the subtleties of either character than to serve as a wistful nod to a time when *Doctor Who* was perhaps more magical and full of life. This is not, of course, to denigrate the performances of any actors in the grand drama behind the scenes of the final seasons of *Doctor Who*, but to reiterate the well-documented fact that higher-ups in the BBC were not particularly enamored with the program and therefore offered it little support—financial or otherwise. Most notably, former BBC Controller Michael Grade has admitted publicly to his distaste for everyone else's favorite time traveler, and even longtime *Doctor Who* producer and champion John Nathan-Turner was beginning to see the program as somewhat of an albatross at the time of its cancellation.[10] And so it was that in 1989 the Doctor bid his fans adieu with the optimistic observation that he still had worlds to visit, injustices to correct and other work to do. The only problem was that we weren't going to be seeing any of it on television.

Or so we thought.

But then along came producer Philip Segal and talk of a made-for-TV movie (along with the possibility of a new series) in the mid 1990s. A joint venture between BBC Worldwide and Universal Television, the movie, simply titled *Doctor Who*, appeared in the United States on Fox television in May of 1996. Despite much fanfare in the pages of *Doctor Who Magazine* and elsewhere, however, the movie failed to capture much of an audience. Pit-ted against the popular situation comedies *Frasier*, *Home Improvement* and *Roseanne*, the world premiere of *Doctor Who* went largely unnoticed by mainstream American audiences, and while the show performed fairly well in the UK, the numbers did not justify (in Fox's eyes, anyway) a full revival of the series. Nonetheless, Segal's vision of *Doctor Who* accomplished the Herculean task of both bringing the Doctor back to the small screen and demonstrating that the seemingly established mythology of the program was not entirely sacred. More importantly, by playing with elements of the show's established "formula," the television movie breathed new life into the *Doctor Who* franchise and paved the way for the innovative and radical retooling that marked the successful revival of the series nearly a decade later.

In a clear nod to the past, *Doctor Who* opens with the return of a familiar face—that of Sylvester McCoy, reprising his role as the itinerant Time Lord. The film also provides glimpses of several icons from the television program's past—the sonic screwdriver, the Doctor's toolkit and a multi-colored scarf among them. Yet just as the newly regenerated Doctor spurns the curiously decontextualized scarf early in the film, the film itself also abandons or revises many central pieces of *Doctor Who* mythology from the outset. On a largely superficial level, the TARDIS control room has been remodeled, but (despite the much-rumored exorbitant cost of the set) this fact is barely remarkable, as the TARDIS interior has been known to change. Nor is it especially remarkable that the sonic screwdriver is back after having been destroyed by the Terileptils in "The Visitation;" it's entirely conceivable that the Doctor built a new one or that he had a spare lying around somewhere.

What *is* remarkable, however, is that the Daleks (of all people) have apparently set up an intergalactic court of law on Skaro (despite the planet's destruction in "Remembrance of the Daleks") and have subsequently tried, convicted and executed the Master for his "evil crimes." Moreover, the Daleks and the Time Lords have apparently entered a period of *détente* that allows the Doctor to collect the Master's remains for the purposes of returning him to Gallifrey for proper interment. Similarly, in what may be a reference to *Star Trek*'s Mr. Spock, the Doctor is revealed to be half-human. And in a move that continues to be a sore spot for many fans to this day, the Doctor does the unspeakable when, as noted elsewhere in this volume, he kisses his companion Dr. Grace Holloway onscreen. Without a doubt, the precise meaning of each of these changes is debatable and far beyond the scope of this discussion. Taken as a whole, however, they demonstrate that *Doctor Who* is not a static monolith but a changing, growing, evolving and almost organic phenomenon, a notion that is mirrored in the themes and images that pervade much of the made-for-TV movie.

Like the program itself, the Doctor is pronounced "dead" early in the film, but while he's in cold storage, the Time Lord undergoes the most visually stimulating regeneration to date as the seventh Doctor's face twitches and contorts until eighth Doctor's face emerges from the dermal chaos. Shortly thereafter, the new Doctor takes what may not only be his own first breath, but the first breath for a completely new version of *Doctor Who*. In other words, the Time Lord is not the only one regenerating in this scene; the entire body of the *Doctor Who* legend is regenerating as well. Given the relative enormity of this regeneration, it isn't surprising that the Doctor suffers somewhat of an identity crisis as he emerges from his tomb to face his new life. After wandering past a television broadcast of *Frankenstein* and scaring the hell out of an unfortunate hospital attendant, the Doctor finds himself in a leaky, abandoned room full of mirrors. With lightning flashing and thunder cracking overhead, the Doctor is naturally frightened, much like a young child might be. And what could be a more natural or fitting response to the situation in which the Doctor finds himself? In many ways, he *is* a child, newly born into a chaotic world—a fact that is reinforced by the appearance of a plastic baby doll leaning against one of the many mirrors in which the Time Lord's image appears. Alone and frightened in this confusing environment, the Doctor (for the time being, anyway) has no point of reference, no link to the past, and can therefore only cry out to the heavens the one question that so many have asked but to which, in the end, there can be no satisfying answer: *Who am I?*

That the Doctor can ask such a question after so many years bespeaks the malleable nature of both his character and the overall phenomenon of *Doctor Who* as well. In fact, to speak of *Doctor Who* as a television program is only to get part of the picture, and fans who need a greater *Who*–fix than the program can give have the luxury of turning to many other media for the purposes of reveling in the further adventures of their favorite Time Lord. In print, there is an abundance of comic strips, novels and annuals. Fans have also been able to listen to *Doctor Who* audio adventures since as far back as the 1976 release of *Doctor Who and the Pescatons*, starring Tom Baker and Elisabeth Sladen. *Doctor Who* webcasts have gone online courtesy of the BBC, and the BBV production company has released a number of *Doctor Who* spin-offs in video and audio formats featuring such *Who* regulars (and irregulars) as K-9, the Rani, the Sontarans, the Rutans, the Autons and the Zygons. Along similar lines, the *Torchwood* series presents a healthy riff on the *Doctor Who* mythos, and it goes without saying that the catalogue of officially licensed tales of the Time Lord very likely pales in comparison to the amount of unlicensed fan fiction circulating on the internet and beyond in various media.

For continuity buffs, this cornucopia of *Doctor Who*–related storylines represents nothing more than a massive headache given the tendency of the comic strips and audio adventures to feature characters and events that stand in stark contrast to those appearing in the television program. To the rest of us, however, the frequently conflicting details of these "non-canonical" stories (and, to be completely accurate, within the accepted canon of the series itself) point to the complexity and lack of restriction that make the Whoniverse so fascinating. This isn't the monolithic *Star Wars* universe we're dealing with, a realm where every last breath of every walk-on character who appears in any form of licensed media must be reconciled with the dictates of the Lucasfilm bible in order to prevent the fictive world of the franchise from becoming anything other than orderly. This is a thick tangle of paradoxes, ambiguities and contradictions. This is a realm of uncertainty with an ever-shifting topography of conjectures, hypotheses, theories, presuppositions, speculations and ideals. There is no single or singular vision of *Doctor Who* because *Doctor Who* is an organic phenomenon, akin to a jazz composition, with many voices and talents—not the least of which are those of the fans—contributing to an infinitely complex whole.

At its best, *Doctor Who* is not fixed or static, but unpredictable, erratic, imperfect, inconsistent, mind-bending and, most of all, *alive*. It is only fitting, then, that the made-for-television film played with the "established" mythology of *Doctor Who* yet also managed to maintain the show's sense of wonder. Indeed, if the pages of *Doctor Who Magazine* are any indication, Paul McGann's embodiment of this sense of wonder helped to buoy the *Doctor Who* franchise among the show's established fan base and also to draw new fans into the fold long after the original series had run its course: in the months leading up to the broadcast of the made-for-TV movie, the magazine was abuzz with news of the film's progress, and shortly after its premiere, the magazine featured commentary from a group of ten and eleven-year-old children who found the latest incarnation of *Doctor Who* to be, among other things, "really funky."[11] Shortly thereafter, the magazine started featuring the eighth Doctor in its monthly installment of comic-strip action, and from there, it wasn't long before the eighth Doctor came into his own not on the small screen but in the multi-media realm of *Doctor Who* spin-offs.

Despite (or perhaps *because* of) the fact that a new series did not materialize subsequent to the broadcast of the made-for-TV movie, the Doctor not only survived but thrived in the collective imagination of his fans. By "going underground," as it were, the Doctor and his legacy came increasingly under the jurisdiction of those who had grown up with the program, recognized its inherent magic and potential for wonder, and were not afraid to experiment. Liberated from the massive expenses involved in producing the television program, the eighth Doctor was free to explore new worlds at little or no cost to the BBC over the course of seventy-five novels and novellas, two-dozen Big Finish audio adventures, an assortment of comic strips and a BBCi webcast. During this period, the Doctor became reacquainted with his former companion Romana, engaged in the obligatory battle against the Daleks, met up with all of his former selves, befriended a Cyberman and was asked to serve as the best man at an Ice Warrior's wedding—most of which could never have happened on television given the technical and economic limitations of the medium.

As with previous forays beyond the limits of television, the eighth Doctor's reign was marked by a lack of consistency from one medium to the next—a lack of consistency that should, once again, be read as a sign of the infinitely complex and open-ended nature of *Doctor Who* rather than a symptom of flawed storytelling. Growing, changing, shifting, metastasizing, the *Doctor Who* legend continued to take on a life of its own in the absence of regularly televised adventures, thus paving the way for the imaginative approach a new generation of writers, directors, actors and designers would take when the series finally returned to the airwaves in 2005.

Moving On...

In many respects, the 1996 television movie represents the ultimate expression of *Doctor Who* fan fiction: shortly after the film's debut in the United States, Segal noted that he had to "fight and fight and fight" in order to bring the Doctor back to life, and added that any *Who*–related project "must be a labour of love" in order to be successful.[12] Perhaps mindful of Segal's advice on some level, BBC Controller Lorraine Heggessey appointed longtime *Doctor Who* fan Russell T. Davies to oversee the legendary program's revival. In turn, the writers whom Davies selected to script the new series were also fans of the show. Case in point: Mark Gatiss, who admits in *Doctor Who: The Shooting Scripts* to having, in his childhood, penned tales of the third Doctor battling the Yeti and of the Autons appearing on Earth in the 1930s only to discover an affinity for bakelite products. Likewise, the eventual casting of David Tennant—who had purportedly aspired to playing the Doctor since the tender age of three—to replace Christopher Eccleston in the second season of the newly revived series suggested that the inmates were indeed taking over the asylum. That is, one-time fans were now producing the program, and their enduring love for the show inspired them to reinvent the myth in a way that brought new life to the series yet, at the same time, remained faithful to the animating spirit behind *Doctor Who*.

Apropos of any "re-imagined" version of a classic series, the theme of change is central to the more recent episodes of *Doctor Who*, and a good deal of the first season's subtext serves to address (if not entirely assuage) the concerns of those fans of the original series who might take umbrage at the fact that the show is not the same as it used to be. *Okay*, the new series seems to be saying, so the Doctor happens to be wearing a leather jacket and close-cropped hair, and he's a bit of a bastard sometimes, and the sonic screwdriver is back (but not quite the same), and Gallifrey is gone, and the TARDIS control room looks a little different than it used to, and the show is no longer serialized, and we're using CGI graphics instead of costumes made of trash bags, and there's a drum track on the theme song, but this is still the Doctor, and the TARDIS is still stuck in the form of a police box, and it's still the show you've always loved—so GET OVER IT! Yes, the show has changed, these episodes seem to say—but it's not the end of the world. On the contrary—it's a new beginning.

In fact, even "The End of the World"—the second episode of the new series—isn't the end of the world. Set largely in the year five billion, this adventure sees the Doctor and Rose bearing witness to Earth's last hours, a conceit that all but forces the viewer to consider the transitory nature of life as well as the inevitability of change. "You think it's all going to last forever—people, cars and concrete," the Doctor tells Rose when he returns her to present-day Earth at the conclusion of the episode; "But it won't. One day it's gone. Even the sky." That the Doctor is speaking in the present tense when he comments upon the ultimate fate of the planet is telling: both he and Rose have already witnessed Earth's destruction, so it's a *fait accompli*. Moreover, because the Earth's future is in Rose's past (and vice-versa), it's reasonable to argue that the distinction between the two is negligible wherever the Doctor is concerned, and five-billion years might just as well be the blink of an eye. Traveling from twenty-first century Earth to the year five billion and back again allows Rose to see that we're all, quite literally, here one moment and gone the next.

Heightening the audience's appreciation for the transience of life in "The End of the World" is a brief exchange between Rose and her mother, Jackie, conducted via supercharged cell phone across a distance of nearly five billion years. Given the amount of time that separates mother and child, Rose can only assume that her mother is, in fact, dead even as their conversation is taking place. That Jackie is rambling on about her malfunctioning refrigerator throughout the discussion further highlights the fact that we don't have as much time on this Earth as we might believe: just as her refrigerator is defrosting and thus forcing Jackie to enjoy all that it holds in its heretofore frosty storage compartment as quickly as possible, so too is the clock ticking on all of our lives and reminding us, if we heed the call, to enjoy all that life has to offer while we can. Upon ending the phone call, Rose sees perhaps for the first time in her life that time spent with her mother, or with anyone for that matter, is a gift, and that while our knowledge of the passage of time and the inevitability of death are in many ways tragic facets of human nature, this knowledge is also what allows us all to appreciate being alive.

Which isn't to say that, as a race, we humans are particularly adept at accepting the passage of time and growing old gracefully. Look at Lady Cassandra O'Brien, for example. A thin layer of skin stretched across a frame like a painter's canvas, Lady Cassandra is the last "pure" human in existence. The only problem is that she's gone under the knife for a nip and tuck so many times that she looks anything but human. Even the free-floating Face of Boe and the tree-people from the Forest of Cheem, who are also on hand to witness the end of the world, bear closer resemblance to what we in the twenty-first century might consider human than does Cassandra. Meanwhile, the last human's servants must moisten her face at regular intervals not only to maintain Cassandra's "youthful" complexion but also to prevent her from withering away completely.

In essence, her quest for eternal youth defines Cassandra as much as her pride in being the last pure human, and one can only wonder how much of a fortune she might lay out for a few doses of Spectrox or a visit to Karn for a sip of the Elixir of Life. Yet, as with "The Caves of Androzani" and "The Brain of Morbius," the vanity associated with seeking immortality is revealed to be pure folly in "The End of the World" and its sequel (of sorts) "New Earth" when Cassandra realizes that all of her anxiety over youth and beauty has been for naught. Without the constant attention of her servants, Cassandra apparently withers and dies in the former episode only to be returned to life and to appropriate several bodies (including those of the Doctor and Rose) in the latter. Consequently, Cassandra learns that being human involves much more than amassing wealth, clinging desperately to one's youth or even one's so-called genetic purity. Rather, when Cassandra is forced to project her animating spirit into the body of a diseased individual towards the conclusion of "New Earth," she finally comes to understand that being human is a matter of recognizing the shared frailty of all who inhabit the universe.

Of course, simply appreciating our shared frailty is often easier said than done, particularly when one has the power to travel in time and the potential to do more than just empathize with fellow frail travelers on the road of life. With a TARDIS at one's beck and call, there's always the possibility of changing the past, of championing the underdog or, as Rose soon discovers, of saving loved ones from early graves. In "Father's Day," the TARDIS materializes in the exact time and place where Rose's father, Pete Tyler, suffered a fatal run-in with a moving vehicle—or should have done so, in any case. Despite the Doctor's sternest warnings, Rose interferes with the natural course of events by pushing her father from harm's way and thereby saving his life. Unfortunately, the effect of Rose's brash actions is to rupture the very fabric of time and space. On a more personal level, Rose soon discovers that the stories she's heard with regard to her father present a largely romanticized version of the man. Where her mother painted a relatively rosy (pardon the pun) picture of her father throughout her childhood, a nearly adult Rose is disappointed to find that Pete is far from perfect and that her parents were on the verge of divorce at the time of his death.

If his passing and the passage of time have built Rose's father up to heroic proportions in his daughter's eyes, then his rescue from the clutches of death can only blemish her perception of him, consequently demonstrating that while absence may well make the heart grow fonder, presence can be somewhat of a letdown. Nonetheless, Rose's rescue of Pete and the attendant sense of disappointment that results from it ironically give him the opportunity to prove himself worthy of his daughter's long-held belief that he is, indeed, capable of heroism. Upon realizing that the only way to prevent time and space from unraveling completely is to die the death that was meant for him, Pete hurls himself into the path of an oncoming car while dragon-like Reapers circle overhead, thus sacrificing his own life to save not only his wife and child but the universe at large as well. Once again, then, we see shades of Aristotle's *Nicomachean Ethics* as Rose's father faces "the most fearful of all things" in order to save the world as he knows it from destruction.

Following her father's example at the conclusion of "The Parting of the Ways," Rose sacrifices her own well-being in order to save both the Doctor and the universe from destruction at the hands (or toilet plungers, as the case may be) of the Daleks. After gazing into the heart of the TARDIS and absorbing the energy of the time vortex, Rose gains the power to rid the universe of the Daleks once and for all but also comes dangerously close dying herself.[13] Keeping his promise to ensure Rose's safety, the Doctor, in turn, sacrifices his own well-being in order to save his young traveling companion. Before the vortex can overwhelm Rose's body and mind completely, the Doctor kisses her on the lips and absorbs the brunt of the vortex's energy himself—a course of action that causes the last surviving Time Lord to lose yet one more of his dwindling supply of lives.

From the perspective of *Doctor Who* fans, the passing of the ninth Doctor can be read as a mildly scandalous and even insulting event: no sooner have we gotten used to this somewhat humorless and angry incarnation of Gallifrey's favorite son than he's riding off into the metaphorical sunset never to be seen again. Excepting the all-too brief tenure of Paul McGann as the Doctor, Christopher Eccleston's portrayal of the Time Lord represents the briefest span of time any actor has spent embodying the role. This brevity, however, is certainly in keeping with the hedonistic theme that pervades much of the first season of the re-imagined *Doctor Who*: life, it turns out, is short for this Doctor, so it's only fitting that he has learned not only to enjoy it but, in Eccleston's words, to *love* it again over the course of his travels with Rose. At the beginning of the season, this Doctor seems to have turned himself off to life—an understandable reaction to having witnessed the destruction of his home planet. Yet as the season progresses, his vivacious young companion reawakens the Doctor's *joie de vivre*—a reawakening that is perhaps best exemplified at the conclusion of "The Doctor Dances" when, after saving blitz-era London from an accidental run-in with alien technology, the Doctor does, in fact, dance.

In addition to pointing up the hedonistic overtones of the new series, the seemingly "premature" regeneration that caps off the season serves a practical purpose as well in that it demonstrates fairly early in the proceedings that the series can survive even after its lead actor moves on. *Doctor Who*, this early regeneration seems to say, is not about a particular actor's portrayal of the Doctor or the quirks and costumery of a particular incarnation. *Doctor Who* is an attitude, a spirit, a philosophy, a way of looking at and appreciating life in all of its wonderful intricacies. Perhaps this is why Eccelston's Doctor is replaced in season two of the new series by that of the more youthful David Tennant—the very Doctor who gushes over *The Muppet Movie* before rushing off to meet a genuine werewolf in "Tooth and Claw." If anyone can "love life" (to once again use Eccleston's phrase) despite all of the tragedy and destruction in the universe, it's the Doctor, as this particular incarnation proves throughout his first season.

There's "School Reunion," of course, in which the Doctor is overjoyed and partially dumb-struck at the prospect of meeting former companions Sarah Jane and K-9. There's "The Girl in the Fireplace" in which the Doctor saves the day, knight-in-shining-armor style, on a white horse. There's "The Idiot's Lantern" where he and Rose set out on a 1950s-vintage motor scooter to see Elvis Presley (only to learn that they're on the wrong continent). Then there's "Love and Monsters," with its Benny Hill-style opening montage and the wink-wink, nudge-nudge tribute to the *Doctor Who* fanatics who kept the show alive long after the original series was canceled. And who can forget the Doctor's wide grin upon lighting the Olympic Pyre for the London games in "Fear Her"? Clearly this is a man who loves the life he lives. Yet at the same time, like Andrew Marvell's passionate shepherd, the Doctor is forever aware of time's winged chariot drawing near.

If "School Reunion" reminds the Doctor that his human companions will all grow old and die long before he does, then "The Girl in the Fireplace" brings this fact into sharp focus by telescoping the entire life of Reinette De Pompadour into a series of painfully brief visits. Similarly, nearly all of the Doctor's "real-world" devotees meet early ends at the hands (and in the guts) of the aptly named Absorbaloff in "Love and Monsters." More dramatically, Rose's departure and apparent "death" at the conclusion of "Doomsday" serve as reminders of the Doctor's inherent loneliness: as one who walks in eternity, he has no choice but to outlive the humans he comes to love. But even as the Doctor sheds a tear at Rose's departure, he catches a glimpse of the madness and wonder his future will hold when he turns to find a mysterious woman in a bridal gown gazing at him from across the TARDIS control room—lightening the gloom of the moment by suggesting that as solitary as his road may be, at the end of the day, the Doctor will always have new discoveries to make and new adventures to look forward to.

To borrow an ancient phrase, time and tide wait for no man—not even the Doctor—and because of this, Eccleston is absolutely on the mark. What separates *Doctor Who* from many contemporary science-fiction dramas—and, in point of fact, many mainstream dramas as well—is the zest for life the program encourages. Yes, the Doctor's unique position as the last of the Time Lords puts him in greater touch with the special sadness that marks us all, the knowledge of time's passage and the realization that death awaits everyone at some point. But this special sadness is also what allows us not only to realize that life is precious but also to appreciate all of the wonder our universe has to offer. And as the Doctor moves on, so too do we—witnessing life, death and everything in between, gaining a sense of the constant state of flux that is the universe, and, when we get a moment to take it all in, catching the occasional glimpse of the big picture. In the words of Time Lord-tracker Elton Pope of "Love and Monsters" fame, *Doctor Who* shows us that the world is so much stranger, so much darker, so much madder than we might usually guess, but at the same time, it's also so much better.

Despite the sixth Doctor's fondness for cats, the tenth Doctor proves that, unlike his feline friends, he indeed possesses more than nine lives. This is his tenth persona after all, but he seems younger and more vibrant than ever, especially as he recovers from the loss of Rose's exuberant companionship and undertakes a new set of awe-inspiring adventures in time and space with medical student Martha Jones. His former companion Sarah Jane herself embraces a new beginning, as she more or less spiritually "regenerates" in her middle age by finally freeing herself from the Doctor's shadow and becoming the "lead character" of her own life. Furthermore, in her own "Doctorish" way, and in a manner similar to Romana before her, she now pursues her own destiny in the spin-off series *The Sarah Jane Adventures*, complete with a newly adopted son, young companions, and sonic lipstick—her whimsical, yet effective, version of the Doctor's sonic screwdriver. In the end, if we can follow the fine examples set by the Doctor and Sarah Jane, we too can hold back the dreary, cold winds of aging and decay, by regenerating and reinventing ourselves at any point in life, regardless of age.

What more could one ask of a TV show?

Chapter Notes

Chapter 1

1. Leslie Fiedler, *Freaks: Myths and Images of the Secret Self* (New York: Simon and Schuster, 1978), 16.

2. *Ibid.*, 17.

3. David J. Howe and Stephen James Walker, *The Television Companion: The Unofficial and Unauthorized Guide to Doctor Who* (Surrey, England: Telos, 1998), 610.

4. While the notion of the fourth wall is rooted in theater, the concept applies to television and film as well. Where the average room in the average house is composed of four solid walls, the average movie set is composed of only three—the fourth having been "removed" for the benefit of the cameras. For the sake of realism, characters usually tend to behave as if this fourth wall actually exists: they neither step beyond it nor address the camera directly. From time to time, however, characters will violate the fourth wall in order to remind an audience that what they're watching is not real and thus force the audience to take a more critical stance toward the material being presented.

5. Kathryn Perry, "Unpicking the Seam: Talking Animals and Reader Pleasure in Early Modern Satire," in *Renaissance Beasts: Of Animals, Humans, and Other Wonderful Creatures*, ed. Erica Fudge (Champaign, IL: University of Illinois, 2004), 33.

6. Robert Bogdan, "The Social Construction of Freaks," in *Freakery*, ed. Rosemarie Garland Thomson (New York: New York University, 1996), 27.

7. *Ibid.*

Chapter 2

1. Laura Lee, *The Pocket Encyclopedia of Aggravation* (New York: Black Dog & Leventhal, 2001), 52.

2. J. Hillis Miller, "Narrative," in *Critical Terms for Literary Study*, ed. Frank Lentricchia and Thomas McLaughlin (Chicago: University of Chicago, 1990), 70.

3. Before we go on, we (the authors) would like to take a moment to violate the fourth-wall on you (the faithful reader) to say that even though this chapter applies psychological theories to the Doctor, we are by no means trying to overload you with psychobabble. We realize that psychology is frequently viewed as a "soft science" that is often incomprehensible and, like *Doctor Who* continuity, contradictory. Forgive us, then, if we lay on the psych theories too thick in spots; we're only trying to point out that the Doctor, in the end, is as crazy (or sane) as the rest of us.

4. Qtd. in Samuel S. Wood & Ellen Green Wood, *The Essential World of Psychology* (Boston: Allyn and Bacon, 2000), 410.

5. Wendy Ide Williams, "Complex Trauma: Approaches to Theory and Treatment," *Journal of Loss and Trauma* 11 (2006): 321–355.

6. *Ibid.*

Chapter 3

1. It should be noted that even the term *companion* itself is contestable and that many observers have noted that the Doctor rarely, if ever, uses this term to describe those he's taken aboard his TARDIS. The issue of what to call his fellow travelers, moreover, is one that has, on occasion, stymied the Doctor as

well. In "School Reunion," for example, the tenth Doctor initially refers to Rose and Mickey as his "team" but immediately backpedals by muttering that he "can't believe" he "just said *team*." He then goes through two more options before giving up altogether on pigeonholing his companions: *gang* and *comrades*. None of these terms do justice to the relationship the Doctor shares with either Rose or Mickey, nor does the frequently bandied-about "assistant." In fact, Rose later bristles when Sarah Jane Smith uses "the A-word" to describe her. Given this perplexing state of affairs, *companion* serves as convenient shorthand for describing a relationship the Doctor himself can't even bring himself to pin a name upon.

2. As "School Reunion" suggests, the tenth Doctor is on equal footing with Rose—except, that is, when Rose gains the upper hand. In one particularly telling scene, the Doctor stumbles upon Rose and Sarah Jane to find them giggling at his expense. Helplessly watching as the "new girlfriend" and the "ex-wife" (as Mickey describes them) swap tales of the Doctor's foibles, the Time Lord sees that Rose is holding his sonic screwdriver—a phallic symbol if ever one existed! Firmly grasping the Doctor's phallus (that is, as social theorist Jacques Lacan might assert, the symbol of his power to signify or rule), Rose holds all of the power in the relationship, which she demonstrates by pointing the sonic screwdriver directly at the Doctor as she and Sarah Jane continue to laugh at him.

3. Chuck Palahniuk, *Choke* (New York: Anchor Books, 2001), 49.

4. Malcolm Gladwell, *Blink: The Power of Thinking Without Thinking* (New York: Little, Brown, 2005), 23.

Chapter 4

1. Michael Benson, *Inside Secret Societies* (New York: Citadel, 2005), 106.

2. *Quis custodiet ipsos custodes?* from Juvenal's *Satire VI* (circa A.D. 60–127) is often translated as "Who watches the watchmen?"

3. Grant Morrison, *Seven Soldiers: Shining Knight*, Issue 3 (New York: DC Comics, 2006), 7–8.

4. The Amplified Panatropic Computation (or APC) Net is a massive computer in which the combined wisdom of all Time Lords is stored.

5. Needless to say, Omega is revealed to have survived his defeat at the hands of the Doctor in "The Three Doctors" when he returns in the fifth-Doctor serial "Arc of Infinity." Predictably, since Omega is crafted in the model of the tragic villain who can only receive his (arguably) unjust desserts, his plan for exacting revenge on the Time Lords is thwarted by the Doctor, who once again condemns the fallen icon to a grim exile in the antimatter universe at the conclusion of the serial.

6. Michel Foucault, *The History of Sexuality: Volume I: An Introduction* (New York: Vintage, 1990), 45.

7. Granted, some debate exists among *Doctor Who* pundits as to whether the Shabogans described in "The Deadly Assassin" are, in fact, the tribe of outliers depicted in "The Invasion of Time." In volume two of *The Doctor Who Programme Guide*, Jean-Marc Lofficier indicates that both groups are one and the same, but in *The Television Companion*, David J. Howe and Stephen James Walker take the contrary position. Additionally, the word has alternately been spelled *Shabogans* and *Shobogans* by various authors.

8. George Orwell, "Shooting an Elephant," in *Shooting an Elephant and Other Essays* (New York: Harcourt, 1984).

Chapter 5

1. Jeremy Bentham, *Doctor Who: The Early Years* (London, WH Allen, 1986), 120.

2. Jack Katz, *How Emotions Work* (Chicago: University of Chicago, 2001), 21.

3. Bill Good, "Out of Control," *BC Business* (33:7), 255.

4. Don DeLillo, *Underworld* (New York: Simon and Schuster, 1997), 269.

5. *Ibid.*, 216.

6. *Ibid.*, 217.

7. Eric Tegler, "Loaded for Bear," *AutoWeek* (55:19).

8. Peter Dunn, "Beware of Hell's Grannies" *New Statesman* (134:4720), 14.

9. *Ibid.*

10. Jeffrey Scheuer, *The Sound Bite Society: Television and the American Mind* (New York: Four Walls Eight Windows, 1999), 10.

11. *Ibid.*, 62.

12. *Ibid.*, 82.
13. Al Franken, *Lies and the Lying Liars Who Tell Them* (New York, Dutton, 2003), 74.
14. *Ibid.*, 78.
15. *Ibid*, 79.
16. Neil Postman, *Amusing Ourselves to Death: Public Discourse in the Age of Show Business* (New York: Penguin, 1985).
17. *Ibid.*, 45.
18. *Ibid.*, 121.
19. For example: "In the holovid series *Jupiter Rising*, the Grexnik is married to whom?"
20. T.S. Eliot, "Burnt Norton."
21. Russell T. Davies, *Doctor Who: The Shooting Scripts* (London: BBC, 2005), 48.
22. For more on this topic, see the "Wrinkles in Time" chapter of this volume.
23. *Doctor Who: The Audio Scripts, Volume Three* (Maidenhead: Big Finish, 2003), 50, 62.
24. *Ibid.*, 59.
25. *Ibid.*, 37.
26. *Ibid.*, 38.
27. *Ibid.*, 45.
28. *The Office*, Season One, Episode Four. (BBC Video, 2003).
29. "The Cybermen" *Doctor Who Magazine* (238), May 1996, inside front cover.

Chapter 6

1. Erik Assadourian, "Corporate Culture Must Evolve," *Adbusters* (14:1), January/February 2006.
2. *Ibid.*
3. Naomi Klein, *No Logo* (New York: Picador, 2002), 281–282.
4. Jean Baudrillard, *The Consumer Society: Myths and Structures.* (London: Sage, 1998, 1970), 25.
5. *Ibid.*
6. *Enron: The Smartest Guys in the Room*, DVD. (Magnolia, 2006).
7. www.cybuscorporation.com/main.html
8. Joel Bakan, *The Corporation: The Pathological Pursuit of Profit and Power* (New York: Free Press, 2004), 72.
9. Grant Morrison, "Pop Magic," in *Book of Lies*, ed. Richard Metzger (New York: Disinformation, 2003).
10. George Gerbner, "Reclaiming Our Cultural Mythology," *Ecology of Justice* (Spring 1994), 40.
11. *Ibid.*
12. This sentiment is echoed in the televised version of the adventure as well when the Collector's computer notes that the Doctor's home planet has a low potential for commercial development and when the Collector himself informs an underling that the Doctor "has a long history of violence and economic subversion" and will not, therefore, be sympathetic to the Company's business methods.
13. In this exchange, a guard asks the Doctor, "What do you think of the assertion that the semiotic thickness of a performed text varies according to the redundancy of its auxiliary performance codes?" The Doctor, in turn, is rendered speechless.

Chapter 7

1. S.I. Hayakawa and Alan R. Hayakawa, *Language in Thought and Action* (New York: Harcourt, 1990), 86.
2. Ferdinand de Saussure, "Nature of the Linguistic Sign," in *The Critical Tradition*, ed. David H. Richter (Boston: Bedford, 1998), 832.
3. Roland Barthes, *S/Z*, trans. Richard Miller (New York: Noonday, 1974), 4.
4. From our own perspective, of course, we can certainly agree that Jamie and Zoe, like the Doctor himself, truly are fictional characters who lack any free will whatsoever, but from the Doctor's perspective—that is, within the parameters of *Doctor Who*—they are, nonetheless, ideally free-thinking subjects.
5. Stanley I. Greenspan and Stuart G. Shanker, *The First Idea: How Symbols, Language, and Intelligence Evolved from Our Primate Ancestors to Modern Humans* (New York: Da Capo, 2004), 337.
6. "Kinda" itself is subject to multiple religious readings, and some fans have analyzed its parallels with Buddhism while others have drawn connections to Judaism and Christianity. Moreover, a myriad of interpretations can arise from the story's overt commentary on imperialism and its reflections on time and the cycle of life. For the sake of this chapter's emphasis on language in the Whoniverse, and in the desire to offer a new

reading of the story, this passage explores the dynamics of speech occurring within the Kinda tribe.

7. Roland Barthes, *The Semiotic Challenge*, trans. Richard Howard (Berkeley: University of California, 1994), 175.

8. After receiving the dimensions of the TARDIS, the Monitor intones a series of calculations, which he broadcasts to his fellow mathematicians from the city's Central Registry. The intoning itself is a songlike chant, one that the Logopolitan choir reverently receives before proceeding to their computations. The sight of the grey-haired Logopolitans chanting in their cubicles, however, serves as a mildly disturbing analogy for corporate culture—a fact that becomes apparent when Tegan equates the working conditions of the mathematicians of Logopolis with people who work in sweatshops back on Earth. Although the Monitor insists that his fellow Logopolitans are "driven not by individual need, but by mathematical necessity," Tegan's criticism holds some validity. As far as corporations and the officers charged with directing them are concerned, the language of numbers—i.e., profit—structures reality. Yet as Tegan's remarks suggest, it is not just the corporate overseers who are defined by the profits they generate; the workers are also defined by the value they provide to the corporation. And just as the Logopolitans are so entranced by their work that the Master is able to walk in their very midst and commit sabotage, we, too, have the capacity to be so distracted by the work demanded of us that life can pass us by. Although our occupations grant us a means of support and give us a sense of purpose, the fate of the Logopolitans reminds us that if we fail to temper work with play and meaningful interaction with our friends and loved ones, the entropy of stress and depression may threaten to consume our lives.

9. Genesis 1:1–10.

10. John 1:1–3.

11. Quoted in Denis Brian, *Einstein: A Life* (New York: John Wiley and Sons, 1996), 186.

12. *Ibid.*

13. *Ibid.*

Chapter 8

1. *Doctor Who: The Complete First Series* (BBC Warner, 2006).

2. Don DeLillo, *The Names* (New York: Knopf, 1982), 175.

3. A.A. Long and D.N. Sedley, *The Hellenistic Philosophers* (Cambridge: Cambridge University, 1987), 70.

4. Aristotle, *The Nicomachean Ethics* (Oxford: Oxford University, 1925, 1990), 64.

5. Or is he?

6. Sarah Jane's remark that the planet's surface reminds her of the Sargasso Sea all but begs even the most casual viewer to compare "The Brain of Morbius" to Ezra Pound's "*Portrait D'une Femme.*" Opening with the immortal line, "Your mind and you are our Sargasso Sea," Pound's poem immediately suggests a kinship with "The Brain of Morbius" insofar as the mad scientist Solon, who keeps the evil Time Lord's brain—or, loosely speaking, mind—in a jar, frequently addresses Morbius in much the same way the narrator of the poem addresses his unnamed "*femme,*" or woman. As the poem continues, we learn that London has "swept about" the woman for many years, and that "bright ships" have given her "Ideas, old gossip, oddments of all things" as well as "Strange spars of knowledge" and "dim wares of price." Similarly, the wrecked starships on the surface of Karn have brought their own oddments to Morbius in the form of the limbs Solon has scavenged from dying aliens in order to build a body for the renegade Time Lord. "Great minds have sought" the subject of the poem, or so we are told, and the woman waits patiently for something significant to "float up" from the dull flotsam and jetsam of her life; likewise, the mad genius Solon has sought and found Morbius (as has the Doctor), and Morbius has presumably waited centuries to take his revenge upon the Time Lords. Yet just as the renegade Time Lord's plot never comes to fruition, the woman of the poem never finds true love, and her relationships remain "pregnant with mandrakes." Subsequently, as the subject of the poem lives out her days in "the slow float of differing light and deep," the brain of Morbius floats alone and lonely in a vat of life-preserving chemicals. And like the woman whose life

amounts to little more than a collection of oddments, trophies and tarnished, gaudy idols that are not quite her own but, nonetheless, constitute her entire being, poor Morbius ultimately amounts to a hideous conglomeration of alien body parts that are not his own but are, in the end, all that he is.

7. Slavoj Zizek, *The Sublime Object of Ideology* (New York: Verso, 1989), 5)

8. *Ibid.*

9. *Doctor Who: The Twin Dilemma.* VHS. (BBC Warner, 2000).

10. David J. Howe and Stephen James Walker, *The Television Companion* (Surrey, England: Telos, 2003), 640.

11. *Doctor Who Magazine*, Issue 242 (September 1996), 6–11.

12. *Doctor Who Magazine*, Issue 240 (July 1996), 9–10.

13. Or as close to "once and for all" as the Daleks ever come to being erased from the universe.

Bibliography

Adams, Douglas. *The Hitchhiker's Guide to the Galaxy*. New York: Harmony Books, 1980.

"The Age of Steel." *Doctor Who: The Complete Second Series*. DVD. BBC Video, 2006.

Aldred, Sophie and Mike Tucker. *Ace! The Inside Story of the End of an Era*. London: Doctor Who Books, 1996.

Alvarado, Manuel and John Tulloch. *The Unfolding Text*. New York: St. Martin's Press, 1984.

The Amazing Spider-Man Annual. Vol. 21. New York: Marvel Comics, 1987.

Angel: Season One. DVD. 20th Century Fox, 2003.

Aristotle. *The Nicomachean Ethics*. Oxford: Oxford UP, 1925 (1990).

"Army of Ghosts." *Doctor Who: The Complete Second Series*. DVD. BBC Warner, 2006.

Assadourian, Erik. "Corporate Culture Must Evolve." *Adbusters*. 14:1 (Jan./Feb. 2006).

"Bad Wolf." *Doctor Who: The Complete First Series*. DVD. BBC Warner, 2006.

Bakan, Joel. *The Corporation: The Pathological Pursuit of Profit and Power*. New York: Free Press, 2004.

Banks, David. *Doctor Who: Cybermen*. London: W.H. Allen, 1990.

Barthes, Roland. *S/Z*. Trans. Richard Miller. New York: Noonday Press, 1974.

_____. *The Semiotic Challenge*. Trans. Richard Howard. Berkeley: University of California Press, 1994. (1985).

Baudrillard, Jean. *The Consumer Society: Myths and Structures*. London: Sage, 1998 (1970).

_____. *The System of Objects*. Trans. James Benedict. New York: Verso, 1997 (1968).

Behrendt, Greg and Liz Tuccillo. *He's Just Not That Into You*. New York: Simon Spotlight Entertainment, 2004.

Benson, Michael. *Inside Secret Societies*. New York: Citadel Press Books, 2005.

Bentham, Jeremy. *Doctor Who: The Early Years*. London: WH Allen, 1986.

The Bible: Authorized King James Version With Apocrypha. New York: Oxford UP, 1998.

Bill and Ted's Bogus Journey. DVD. MGM, 2001.

Bogdan, Robert. "The Social Construction of Freaks." *Freakery*. Rosemarie Garland Thomson, ed. New York: NYUP, 1996.

The Boondock Saints. DVD. 20th Century Fox, 2000.

Brian, Denis. *Einstein: A Life*. New York: John Wiley and Sons, 1996.

Buffy the Vampire Slayer Collector's Set. DVD. 20th Century Fox, 2006.

Cartmel, Andrew. *Through Time*. London: Continuum, 2005.

"Castrovalva." *Doctor Who: New Beginnings*. DVD. BBC Video, 2006.

Chapman, James. *Inside the TARDIS*. London: I.B. Tauris and Company, 2006.

"The Christmas Invasion," *Doctor Who: The Complete Second Series*. DVD. BBC Video, 2006.

Cornell, Paul (Ed.). *Licence Denied: Rumblings from the Doctor Who Underground*. London: Virgin, 1997.

Cornel, Paul, Martin Day and Keith Topping. *The Discontinuity Guide*. London: London Bridge, 1995.

Couch, Steven, Tony Watkins and Peter S. Williams. *Back in Time: A Thinking Fan's Guide to Doctor Who*. London: Damaris Publishing, 2005.

"The Cybermen." *Doctor Who Magazine* 238, May 1996. (Inside Front Cover).

Cybus Corporation Official Website. http://www.cybuscorporation.com/main.html. Accessed July 2006.

"Dalek." *Doctor Who: The Complete First Series*. DVD. BBC Video, 2006.

"The Daleks." *Doctor Who: The Beginning*. DVD. BBC Video, 2006.

"The Daleks' Master Plan." *Doctor Who: Lost in Time*. DVD. BBC Video, 2004.

"David Bowie Straight." *Rolling Stone Magazine*. Cover Story. May 12, 1983.

Davies, Russell T. *Doctor Who: The Shooting Scripts*. London: BBC Books, 2005.

Death Race 2000. DVD. Image Entertainment, 1998.

DeLillo, Don. *The Names*. New York: Knopf, 1982.

_____. *Underworld*. New York: Simon and Schuster, 1997.

Dicks, Terrance. *Doctor Who and the Sunmakers*. London: Target Books, 1982.

"The Doctor Dances." *Doctor Who: The Complete First Series*. DVD. BBC Warner, 2006.

Doctor Who: Attack of the Cybermen. VHS. BBC Warner, 2002.

Doctor Who: Battlefield. VHS. 20th Century Fox, 1998.

Doctor Who: Carnival of Monsters. DVD. BBC Video, 2002.

Doctor Who: City of Death. DVD. BBC Video, 2005.

Doctor Who: Colony in Space. VHS. BBC Warner, 2003.

Doctor Who: Day of the Daleks. VHS. 20th Century Fox, 1995.

Doctor Who: Death to the Daleks. VHS. BBC Warner, 2000.

Doctor Who: Destiny of the Daleks. VHS. 20th Century Fox, 1997.

Doctor Who: Dragonfire. VHS. BBC Warner, 2000.

Doctor Who: Earthshock. DVD. BBC Video, 2003.

Doctor Who: Enlightenment. VHS. 20th Century Fox, 1994.

Doctor Who: Full Circle. VHS. BBC Warner 2000.

Doctor Who: Genesis of the Daleks. DVD. BBC Video, 2006.

Doctor Who: Ghost Light. DVD. BBC Warner, 2005.

Doctor Who: Kinda. VHS. BBC Warner, 2000.

Doctor Who: Lost in Time. DVD. BBC Video, 2004.

Doctor Who: Mawdryn Undead. VHS. BBC Warner, 2000.

Doctor Who: Meglos. VHS. BBC Warner, 2004.

Doctor Who: New Beginnings. DVD. BBC Video, 2006.

Doctor Who: Paradise Towers. VHS. 20th Century Fox, 1997.

Doctor Who: Planet of the Spiders. VHS. 20th Century Fox, 1994.

Doctor Who: Pyramids of Mars. DVD. BBC Video, 2004.

Doctor Who: Remembrance of the Daleks. DVD. BBC Video, 2001.

Doctor Who: Resurrection of the Daleks. DVD. BBC Video, 2002.

Doctor Who: Revelation of the Daleks. DVD. BBC Video, 2005.

Doctor Who: Revenge of the Cybermen. VHS. 20th Century Fox, 1994.

Doctor Who: Robot. VHS. 20th Century Fox, 1994.

Doctor Who: Shada. VHS. 20th Century Fox, 1994.

Doctor Who: Silver Nemesis. VHS. BBC Warner, 1994.

Doctor Who: Snakedance. VHS. BBC Warner, 2000.

Doctor Who: Spare Parts. CD. Big Finish Audio, 2002.

Doctor Who: Spearhead from Space. DVD. BBC Video, 2001.

Doctor Who: State of Decay. VHS. BBC Warner 2000.

Doctor Who: Survival. DVD. BBC Video, 2007.

Doctor Who: Terminus. VHS. 20th Century Fox, 1994.

Doctor Who: Terror of the Autons. VHS. 20th Century Fox, 1995.

Doctor Who: Terror of the Zygons. VHS. 20th Century Fox, 2000.

Doctor Who: The Ark in Space. DVD. BBC Video, 2002.

Doctor Who: The Armageddon Factor. DVD. BBC Video, 2002.

Doctor Who: The Audio Scripts, Volume Three. Maidenhead: Big Finish, 2003.

Doctor Who: The Aztecs. DVD. BBC Video, 2002.

Doctor Who: The Beginning. DVD. BBC Video, 2006.

Doctor Who: The Brain of Morbius. VHS. 20th Century Fox, 1995.

Doctor Who: The Caves of Androzani. DVD. BBC Video, 2002.

Doctor Who: The Claws of Axos. DVD. BBC Video, 2005.

Doctor Who: The Complete First Series. DVD. BBC Warner, 2006.

Doctor Who: The Complete Second Series. DVD. BBC Warner, 2006.

Doctor Who: The Curse of Fenric. DVD. BBC Warner, 2005.

Doctor Who: The Curse of Peladon. VHS. BBC Warner, 2000.

Doctor Who: The Deadly Assassin. VHS. 20th Century Fox, 1995.

Doctor Who: The Face of Evil. VHS. BBC Warner, 2000.

Doctor Who: The Five Doctors. DVD. BBC Video, 1999.

Doctor Who: The Greatest Show in the Galaxy. VHS. BBC Video, 1999.

Doctor Who: The Green Death. DVD. BBC Video, 2004.

Doctor Who: The Hand of Fear. DVD. BBC Video, 2006.

Doctor Who: The Happiness Patrol. VHS. BBC Warner, 2000.

Doctor Who: The Horns of Nimon. VHS. BBC Warner, 2003.

Doctor Who: The Invasion. DVD. BBC Video, 2006.

Doctor Who: The Invasion of Time. VHS. BBC Warner, 2000.

Doctor Who: The Invisible Enemy. VHS. BBC Warner, 2003.

Doctor Who: The Leisure Hive. DVD. BBC Video, 2004.

Doctor Who: The Mark of the Rani. DVD. BBC Warner, 2006.

Doctor Who: The Mind Robber. DVD. BBC Video, 2005.

Doctor Who: The Movie. DVD. BBC Video, 2001.

Doctor Who: The Pirate Planet. DVD. BBC Video, 2002.

Doctor Who: The Robots of Death. DVD. BBC Video, 2000.

Doctor Who: The Sea Devils. VHS. BBC Warner, 2000.

Doctor Who: The Sun Makers. VHS. BBC Warner, 2003.

Doctor Who: The Talons of Weng Chiang. DVD. BBC Video, 2003.

Doctor Who: The Three Doctors. DVD. BBC Video, 2003.

Doctor Who: The Tomb of the Cybermen. DVD. BBC Video, 2002.

Doctor Who: The Trial of a Time Lord. VHS. 20th Century Fox, 1995.

Doctor Who: The Twin Dilemma. VHS. BBC Warner, 2000.

Doctor Who: The Two Doctors. DVD. BBC Video, 2003.

Doctor Who: The Visitation. DVD. BBC Video, 2004.

Doctor Who: The War Games. VHS. BBC Warner, 2000.

Doctor Who: Time and the Rani. VHS. BBC Warner, 2000.

Doctor Who: Time-Flight. VHS. BBC Warner, 2001.

Doctor Who: Underworld. VHS. BBC Warner, 2003.

Doctor Who: Vengeance on Varos. DVD. BBC Video, 2001.

Doctor Who: Warrior's Gate. VHS. BBC Video, 2000.

Doctor Who: Warriors of the Deep. VHS. BBC Warner, 2000.

Doctor Who and the Silurians. VHS. 20th Century Fox, 1995.

Doctor Who Magazine. 240. July, 1996.

Doctor Who Magazine. 242. September, 1996.

Donnie Brasco. DVD. Sony Pictures, 2000.

"Doomsday." *Doctor Who: The Complete Second Series.* DVD. BBC Warner, 2006.

Dunn, Peter. "Beware of Hell's Grannies." *New Statesman,* 134:4720. January, 2005.

"The Empty Child." *Doctor Who: The Complete First Series.* DVD. BBC Video, 2006.

"The End of the World." *Doctor Who: The Complete First Series.* DVD. BBC Warner, 2006.

Enron: The Smartest Guys in the Room. DVD. Magnolia, 2006.

"The Evil of the Daleks." *Doctor Who: Lost in Time.* BBC Video, 2004.

"Father's Day." *Doctor Who: The Complete First Series.* DVD. BBC Warner, 2006.

"Fear Her." *Doctor Who: The Complete Second Series.* DVD. BBC Warner, 2006.

Fiedler, Leslie. *Freaks: Myths and Images of the Secret Self.* New York: Simon and Schuster, 1978.

Foucault, Michel. *The History of Sexuality: Volume I: An Introduction.* New York: Vintage Books, 1990.

Franken, Al. *Lies and the Lying Liars Who Tell Them.* New York, Dutton: 2003.

Freaks. DVD. Warner Home Video, 2004.

"Gay." *Absolutely Fabulous.* BBC Video, 2002.

Gerbner, George. "Reclaiming Our Cultural Mythology." *Ecology of Justice*, Spring 1994.

"The Girl in the Fireplace." *Doctor Who: The Complete Second Series*. DVD. BBC Warner, 2006.

Gladwell, Malcolm. *Blink: The Power of Thinking Without Thinking*. New York: Little, Brown and Company, 2005.

Godfather DVD Collection. DVD. Paramount, 2001.

Good, Bill. "Out of Control." *BC Business*, 33:7. July, 2005.

Goodfellas (Two Disc Special Edition). DVD. Warner Home Video, 2004.

The Graduate. DVD. MGM, 2005.

Greenspan, Stanley I. and Stuart G. Shanker, D. Phil. . *The First Idea: How Symbols, Language, and Intelligence Evolved From Our Primate Ancestors to Modern Humans*. New York: Da Capo Press, 2004.

Hayakawa, S.I. and Alan R. Hayakawa. *Language in Thought and Action*. New York: Harcourt, Inc., 1990.

Howarth, Chris and Steve Lyons. *The Completely Useless Encyclopedia*. London: Doctor Who Books, 1996.

Howe, David J. and Stephen James Walker. *The Television Companion: The Unofficial and Unauthorized Guide to* Doctor Who. Surrey: Telos, 1998.

I ♥ Huckabees! DVD. 20th Century Fox Video, 2005.

"The Idiot's Lantern." *Doctor Who: The Complete Second Series*. DVD. BBC Warner, 2006.

"The Impossible Planet." *Doctor Who: The Complete Second Series*. DVD. BBC Warner, 2006.

Juvenal. *Satires*. Cambridge: Cambridge UP, 1996.

Katz, Jack. *How Emotions Work*. Chicago: University of Chicago Press, 2001.

Klein, Naomi. *No Logo*. New York: Picador, 2002.

Lebo, Harlan. *The Godfather Legacy*. New York: Fireside Books, 1997.

Lee, Laura. *The Pocket Encyclopedia of Aggravation*. New York: Black Dog & Leventhal Publishers, Inc., 2001.

Lofficier, Jean-Marc. *The Doctor Who Program Guide*. London: Target, 1981.

"Logopolis." *Doctor Who: New Beginnings*. DVD. BBC Video, 2006.

Long, A.A. and D.N. Sedley. *The Hellenistic Philosophers*. Cambridge: Cambridge UP, 1987.

"The Long Game." *Doctor Who: The Complete First Series*. DVD. BBC Video, 2006.

"Love and Monsters." *Doctor Who: The Complete Second Series*. DVD. BBC Warner, 2006.

Malory, Sir Thomas. *Le Morte D'Arthur*. New York: Hyperion, 2004.

Miles, Lawrence and Tat Wood. *About Time*. (Vol. 1–5). Illinois: Mad Norwegian Press, 2005.

Miller, J. Hillis. "Narrative." *Critical Terms for Literary Study*. Ed. Frank Lentricchia and Thomas McLaughlin. Chicago: The University of Chicago Press, 1990.

"The Moonbase." *Doctor Who: Lost in Time*. DVD. BBC Video, 2004.

Moore, Steve. "Throwback: The Soul of a Cyberman." *Doctor Who Weekly 5–7* (14–28 November, 1979).

Morrison, Grant. "Pop Magic." *Book of Lies* (Richard Metzger, ed.). New York: The Disinformation Company, Ltd., 2003.

_____. *Seven Soldiers: Shining Knight*. Issue 3. New York: DC Comics, 2006.

The Mutations. DVD. Subversive Cinema Inc., 2005.

Newman, Kim. *Doctor Who: A Critical Reading of the Series*. London: British Film Institute, 2005.

"New Earth." *Doctor Who: The Complete Second Series*. DVD. BBC Warner, 2006.

The Office. DVD. BBC Video, 2003.

Orwell, George. "Shooting an Elephant." *Shooting an Elephant and Other Essays*. New York: Harcourt, 1984.

Palahniuk, Chuck. *Choke*. New York: Anchor Books, 2001.

Parkin, Lance. *A History of the Universe: From Before the Dawn of Time and Beyond the End of Eternity*. London: Doctor Who Books, 1996.

Parsons, Paul. *The Science of Doctor Who*. London: Icon Books, 2006.

"The Parting of the Ways." *Doctor Who: The Complete First Series*. DVD. BBC Warner, 2006.

Perry, Kathryn. "Unpicking the Seam: Talking Animals and Reader Pleasure in Early Modern Satire." *Renaissance Beasts: Of Animals, Humans, and Other Wonderful Creatures*. Ed. Erica Fudge. Illinois: University of Illinois Press, 2004.

Platt, Marc. *Lungbarrow*. London: Virgin Publishing, 1997.

Postman, Neil, *Amusing Ourselves to Death: Public Discourse in the Age of Show Business.* New York: Penguin, 1985.

Pound, Ezra. "Portrait d'une Femme." *Poems and Translations.* New York: Library of America, 2003.

Raiders of the Lost Ark. DVD. Paramount Home Video, 2003.

Richards, Justin. *Doctor Who: The Legend Continues.* London: BBC Books, 2005.

"Rise of the Cybermen." *Doctor Who: The Complete Second Series.* DVD. BBC Video, 2006.

"Rose." *Doctor Who: The Complete First Series.* DVD. BBC Warner, 2006.

"The Runaway Bride." Television Broadcast. BBC, 2006.

"The Satan Pit." *Doctor Who: The Complete Second Series.* DVD. BBC Video, 2006.

Saussure, Ferdinand de. "Nature of the Linguistic Sign." *The Critical Tradition.* Ed. David H. Richter. Boston: Bedford, 1998.

Scheuer, Jeffrey, *The Sound Bite Society: Television and the American Mind.* New York: Four Walls Eight Windows, 1999.

"School Reunion." *Doctor Who: The Complete Second Series.* DVD. BBC Warner, 2006.

The Seventh Seal: Criterion Collection, The. DVD. Criterion, 1999.

Shakespeare, William. *Hamlet.* New York: Folger Shakespeare Library, 1994.

Shelley, Mary. *Frankenstein.* New York: Penguin Classics, 2003.

Snakes on a Plane. DVD. New Line Home Video, 2006.

The Sopranos: Complete First Season. HBO Home Video, 2000.

Spaceballs. DVD. MGM, 2000.

Sssssss. DVD. Universal, 2004.

Stand by Me. DVD. Sony Pictures, 1997.

Star Trek: The Motion Picture. DVD. Paramount, 2001.

Star Trek II: The Wrath of Kahn. DVD. Paramount, 2002.

Star Trek III: The Search for Spock. DVD. Paramount, 2002.

Star Trek IV: The Voyage Home. DVD. Paramount, 2003.

Tegler, Eric. "Loaded for Bear." *AutoWeek,* 55:19. May, 2005.

"Tooth and Claw." *Doctor Who: The Complete Second Series.* DVD. BBC Warner, 2006.

"An Unearthly Child." *Doctor Who: The Beginning.* DVD. BBC Video, 2006.

White, Michael. *A Teaspoon and an Open Mind.* London: Allen Lane, 2005.

White, T.H. *The Once and Future King.* New York: Putnam, 1958.

Williams, Wendy Ide. "Complex Trauma: Approaches to Theory and Treatment." *Journal of Loss and Trauma* 11 (2006): 321–355.

Wordsworth, William. "The Tables Turned." *Selected Poems and Prefaces.* Ed. Jack Stillinger. Boston: Houghton Mifflin Company, 1965.

"World War III." *Doctor Who: The Complete First Series.* DVD. BBC Video, 2006.

Wood, Samuel S. & Ellen Green Wood. *The Essential World of Psychology.* Boston: Allyn and Bacon, 2000.

Zizek, Slavoj. *The Sublime Object of Ideology.* New York: Verso, 1989.

Index

Cassandra *see* O'Brien, Lady Cassandra
"Castrovalva" 1, 48
"The Caves of Androzani" 119, 166–168, 171, 184
Chapman, James 5
Cheetah People 23, 24
Chesterton, Ian 53, 67, 137–139, 147, 152
chicken-brained biological disaster *see* Condo
Cho-Je 93
Choke 53
"The Christmas Invasion" 68, 124
chronic hysterisis 33–34
"City of Death" 57, 59, 139, 166
"The Claws of Axos" 166, 176
Coke 150, 151
"Colony in Space" 88
The Company 129–132
Condo 170
The Consumer Society 122
Cook, Captain 28–30
The Corporation 127–128
Couch, Steve 5
culture jam movement 9, 120
"The Curse of Fenric" 62, 66
"The Curse of Peladon" 98
Cusick, Raymond 100–101
Cybermen 8–9, 30, 33, 36–38, 44, 60, 69, 74, 80, 89, 94, 96–97, 111–117, 118, 120, 125–126, 157, 159, 163, 178, 182
Cybus Industries 114–116, 119, 125, 127, 132

Daily Download 116
"Dalek" 72, 105, 119, 124
Daleks 8–9, 23, 30, 33, 36–38, 44, 49, 51, 73, 74, 76–79, 80, 83, 89, 94, 96–98, 100–111, 117, 118, 119, 120, 124, 134, 157, 159, 163, 178, 179, 182, 185, 193
"The Daleks' Master Plan" 70, 166
Darth Vader 136
Dastari, Joinson 82
Davies, Russell T. 56, 63, 65, 71, 111, 118, 182
Davison, Peter 59, 60, 168
Davros 37, 100, 102, 103, 105, 107, 117, 119
Day, Martin vii
"Day of the Daleks" 40, 55
DC Comics 86
"The Deadly Assassin" 48, 53, 83–86, 90, 92, 190
Death Race 103
Death Race 2000 102
"Death to the Daleks" 42
The Death Zone 42–44, 92

DeLillo, Don 103, 158–159
Dent, Arthur 136
DePompadour, Madame Reinette 56, 64, 99, 159, 186
"Destiny of the Daleks" 58–59, 100
Deva Loka 148
dialectic 161, 173
Dicks, Terrance 88
The Discontinuity Guide vii
Dissociative Identity Disorder *see* Multiple Personality Disorder
The Doctor: first incarnation 40–44, 48, 49, 54, 56, 66, 67, 76, 96, 166; second incarnation 9, 32, 34, 40–46, 48, 54, 66, 67–68, 76, 79, 82, 93, 118, 132, 140; third incarnation 24, 32, 34, 37, 40–44, 48, 54, 55, 56, 57, 68, 76, 79, 87, 88–90, 93, 118, 120, 128, 132, 159, 160, 166, 182; fourth incarnation 9, 14, 25, 26, 34, 39, 45–46, 48, 50, 57, 58, 64, 68, 69, 76, 79, 90, 93, 96, 119, 120, 129, 136, 159, 169, 174, 176, 177; fifth incarnation 16, 24, 25, 39, 41–44, 48, 55, 59–60, 69, 93, 94, 112, 115–119, 162, 166, 168, 171, 176; sixth incarnation 18, 20, 44–45, 47, 48, 60–61, 81, 91, 100, 113, 119, 168, 178, 187; seventh incarnation 10, 25, 28, 36, 46, 47, 49, 54, 61–62, 66, 80, 101, 106, 119, 134, 149, 168, 180; eighth incarnation 49, 55, 62–63, 180–182; ninth incarnation 10, 14, 21, 27, 49, 50, 51, 55, 56, 63, 72–74, 83, 99, 100, 105, 107, 118, 120, 122, 136, 185; tenth incarnation 14, 23, 24, 26, 37, 44, 52, 56, 64, 66, 68, 73–74, 94, 114–115, 123–124, 129, 154, 160, 187, 190
"The Doctor Dances" 64, 73, 186
Doctor Who: A Critical Reading of the Series 5
Doctor Who and the Pescatons 180
"Doctor Who and the Silurians" 24, 68
Doctor Who Magazine, vii, 88, 133, 178, 181
Doctor Who: The Early Years 101
Doctor Who: The Legend Continues vii
Doctor Who: The Movie 33, 46, 49, 53, 62–63, 94, 133, 169, 178–181, 182
Doctor Who: The Shooting Scripts 111, 182
Doctor Who: The Unfolding Text 5, 124
"Doomsday" 36–38, 52, 65, 74, 94, 157, 187
"Dragonfire" 61, 119, 134
Dunn, Peter 104

Earpods 116, 125